ROSA LUXEMBURG

HER LIFE AND WORK

by

PAUL FRÖLICH

Translated by

EDWARD FITZGERALD

LONDON
VICTOR GOLLANCZ LTD
1940

PRINTED IN GREAT BRITAIN BY RICHARD CLAY AND COMPANY, LTD. (T.U.)
BUNGAY, SUFFOLK.

CONTENTS

CONTENTS

CHAPTER EIGHT

CAPITALISM INEVITABLY DOOMED?

CHAPTER NINE

THE STRUGGLE AGAINST IMPERIALISM

CHAPTER TEN

THE CONSUMING FLAME

CHAPTER ELEVEN

THE WORLD WAR

CHAPTER TWELVE

THE RUSSIAN REVOLUTION

CHAPTER THIRTEEN

THE GERMAN REVOLUTION

CHAPTER FOURTEEN

THE LAMP LIES SHATTERED

TRANSLATOR'S PREFACE

THE following book represents the first serious attempt to give a full-length biography of the most remarkable woman the international socialist movement has ever produced, and at the same time an account of her ideas and an indication of her permanent contribution to socialist thought.

The author, Paul Frölich, is well known in Germany as a writer on political and historical matters, and he was well equipped to perform his task, difficult though it was. He was born in Leipzig in 1884, the child of a working-class family. Both his parents were staunch social democrats, who continued to work actively for the Social Democratic Party even under Bismarck's anti-socialist laws. Frölich therefore grew up in an atmosphere of socialist ideas and activities, and he entered the working-class movement at an early age. From 1901 down to the present day he has taken an active part in political life. From the very beginning he was deeply influenced by Rosa Luxemburg, Franz Mehring, and their followers. In 1907 he began to work as a journalist on the social-democratic *Leipziger Volkszeitung*, and from this time dates his close co-operation with the famous pamphleteer Karl Radek, which lasted down to the outbreak of the World War. By 1910 Frölich had become an editor of the social-democratic *Hamburger Echo*, and when war broke out in 1914 he was an editor of the social-democratic *Bürgerzeitung* in Bremen.

During the war he was a prominent member of the small band of men and women who remained steadfastly loyal to the cause of international Socialism. He became one of the leaders of the Left-Wing Radicals, who had their headquarters in Bremen, and he co-operated closely with Rosa Luxemburg and her followers in their opposition to the pro-imperialist and pro-war policy of the official Social Democratic Party. He was present as the representative of the Left-Wing Radicals at the famous international socialist conference in Kienthal

(Switzerland) in April 1916, which marked the beginning of the mass-revolutionary movement against imperialist war and culminated in the collapse of the Central Powers. He was an active member of the Left Wing of the revolutionary Marxists, the " Lenin Group ", and co-founder of the revolutionary-socialist *Arbeiter-Politik* in Bremen, to which he continued to contribute regularly when already in uniform at the front.

When the Spartakists and the Left-Wing Radicals joined forces to form the Communist Party of Germany, Frölich became a member of the Central Committee of the new party, together with Rosa Luxemburg. He retained this position until 1924. He also represented the Communist Party in the Reichstag from 1921 to 1924 and from 1928 to 1930. As a result of the onslaught on the Right Wing of the Communist Party in 1928 and the subsequent years, he was expelled from the party, together with Brandler, Thalheimer, and others. For some time he was a leader of the Communist Opposition, and then, with a large section of that movement, he joined the Socialist Workers Party (S.A.P.), which had in the meantime been formed as a radical break-away from the official Social Democratic Party, and which is roughly analogous to our Independent Labour Party. Frölich was a member of the Central Committee of this party when he was arrested in March 1933 under the national-socialist régime. He was held in prison for four months, and for a subsequent five months in Lichtenberg concentration camp. After his release he succeeded in escaping from Germany, and he has since lived in Paris as a political fugitive.

Paul Frölich is the author of a number of important historical and political works, including " Ten Years of War and Civil War ", and the translator of several well-known socialist classics, including Lissagaray's famous " History of the Paris Commune ". For many years he had worked closely with Rosa Luxemburg, and subsequently he made a special study of her ideas, so that when arrangements were made for the publication of her collected works, her executors and an international committee, consisting of Clara Zetkin, Nikolai Bucharin, Julian Karski, and Adolf Varski, unanimously chose him as chief editor of the venture.

Three volumes of the collected edition of Rosa Luxemburg's

works had appeared when Hitler's accession to power in 1933 put a stop to the undertaking—for the moment, at least. Vol. I, " The Accumulation of Capital ", appeared in 1923; Vol. II, " Against Reformism ", in 1925; and Vol. III, " The Trade-Union Struggle and the Mass Strike ", in 1928. Vol. IV, " Imperialism and the Danger of War ", was held up for a long time owing to political differences between Paul Frölich and the publishers (the publishing house of the German Communist Party), but an arrangement was finally reached, and the book was actually in print when Hitler came to power. The proofs were seized and destroyed together with all other communist and socialist material on which the fascist authorities could lay their hands, and the type was broken up.

Unfortunately, too, very valuable material collected by Frölich in many years of study devoted to Rosa Luxemburg's life and ideas was also lost, but, once in France, Frölich resumed work. He has succeeded in repairing very much of the damage, and the sum total of his studies is now incorporated in this biography. He can be congratulated on having performed an extremely difficult task with great distinction.

EDWARD FITZGERALD.

CHAPTER ONE : YOUTH

1. AT HOME

ZAMOSC IS a little Polish town in the Lublin district, not far from the Russo-Polish frontier. It is a poverty-stricken place, and the cultural level of its populace is low. Even after the great agrarian reform introduced by Tsarism (after the failure of the insurrection led by the Polish nobles in in 1869) in order to play off the peasants against the Junkers, the dependence, sufferings. and difficulties of the lower strata of the population from the days of serfdom still lingered on. The introduction of the monetary system brought this district, far removed as it was from the industrial centres, only the hardships attendant on the destruction of the old order of society, and not the advantages of the new.

And fate laid a particularly heavy hand on the big Jewish population. They shared the common sufferings and miseries of their fellows, the severities of Russian Absolutism, the burdens of foreign domination, and the general impoverishment of the country. And, in addition, theirs was the misery of an outcast and despised race. In a society in which each was the slave of his immediate social superior, the Jew was the despised slave of all, and the kicks and cuffs distributed at all stages in the social scale finally descended with interest to him. Dogged at every turn, intimidated and maltreated by a hateful system of anti-Semitism, his liberty of movement hindered by exceptional laws, the Jew strove to earn a bare subsistence by tenacious and relentless haggling, and to save himself from the hostility of his surroundings by withdrawing behind the ghetto walls of his religion.

In this gloom, lit only by the feeble flickering of Sabbath candles, a narrow fanaticism flourished, fed by pride in a far-away past and by Messianic faith in a better future, and imposing absurd practices on the faithful. It was an out-of-the-way, backward world of resignation and greed, obscurantism, dirt, and poverty.

It was in this Zamosc that Rosa Luxemburg was born on March 5th, 1871, but it was not in this rotting morass that her character formed and her spirit developed. The house of the Luxemburg family was one of the few oases in the town and in the Jewish community where the culture of Western Europe was at home. Rosa's grandfather had succeeded in raising his family to a certain well-being. The timber trade in which he was engaged not only brought him in touch with the Polish Junkers, but took him to Germany, and that lifted him out of the narrowness of Zamosc. He gave his children a modern education, and sent his sons to the commercial high schools in Berlin and Bromberg. From Germany Rosa's father brought back Liberal ideas and an active interest in world affairs and in Western European literature. He emancipated himself from the strictness of the ghetto and from Jewish orthodoxy, but he served his people in his own way by furthering their cultural aspirations.

Hostility to Tsarism, democratic convictions, and a love of Polish literature gave him all his father lacked to complete his Polish assimilation. He was sympathetic towards the national-revolutionary movements amongst the Poles, but he was not politically active himself, and he devoted his attention to cultural questions, and in particular to the Polish school system. He was a man of considerable energy, and material well-being and education had given him confidence, and he felt himself called upon to work for the commonweal beyond the horizon of his family and his profession. He belonged, in fact, to that type which has produced the Jewish intellectual and found its highest development in world-famous Jewish artists, men of science, and social pioneers.

There is very little material available concerning Rosa Luxemburg's childhood. She was reticent in all personal matters, and she spoke very little about her youth. Only whilst she was in prison, when memories crowded in on her, and she sought to break the leaden stillness by writing letters, did she sometimes mention her young days. There are then often passages of deep feeling, but the incidents they relate are usually too insignificant to give us any satisfactory picture of the outward circumstances of her childhood, and, in addition, it is often difficult to distinguish what has its origin in the ideas and emotions of the child, and what belongs to the literary art of the mature writer. Such an episode occurs in a letter written to Louise Kautsky in the autumn of 1904 whilst Rosa Luxemburg was in Zwickau Prison.

She described how as a child she crept to the window very early one morning and, looking out, watched the big yard come to life, and the servant, " Old Antoni ", begin his work, after loud yawning and half-sleepy ruminations :

> " And I firmly believed then that ' life ', ' real life ', was somewhere far away, over the roofs. And since then I have been travelling after it. But it is still hidden away behind roofs somewhere. . . . Life is still playing hide and seek with me. It always seems that it is not in me, not here where I am, but somewhere far away. . . . And perhaps in the end it was all a cruel game with me, and life, real life, stayed there in the yard."

Who can tell whether the belief of the child that real life was somewhere beyond the roofs was anything more than the interest in the unknown outside world which moves every child, or whether it contained the seed of that unrest, that longing and that urge which drove the mature Rosa Luxemburg beyond the humdrum pettiness of the daily round, and was always an incentive to action ? There are many such observations in her letters, and they offer fascinating material to the psychologist, tempting him to undertake adventurous excursions, though they might not always end happily. However, we are almost completely restricted to the material provided by her brothers and sisters.

On the whole, her youth was a happy one. Her parents experienced straitened circumstances occasionally, and once Rosa lit the lamp with a piece of paper which afterwards turned out to be the only money left in the house. But apart from such times life in the home of her parents was a secure and comfortable one, marked by that intense intimacy which is characteristic of Jewish families.

Rosa was the youngest of five children. Hip disease in early life kept her in bed for a whole year. It was wrongly diagnosed as tuberculosis of the bone, and the subsequent treatment caused irreparable damage. Small wonder that she was treated with especial consideration and love by her family. Her disposition was happy, and she was a lively and active youngster who quickly won the sympathy of everyone with whom she came in contact. At five she could read and write. At first her language was Polish, and that was the domestic tongue, but German was often spoken too, and, though very seldom, Yiddish, but it seems that Rosa never spoke it. Copying the letter-writing of her elders, she began to write letters to her parents and to her brothers and sisters about everything which occupied her mind, and she insisted on receiving answers which showed that her efforts were being taken seriously. Whilst still a child she began to translate both poetry and prose into Polish. Her first literary attempts were sent to a children's magazine. Her gift for teaching showed itself early too: hardly had she learnt to read when the servants in the house had to be her pupils.

The mother exercised considerable influence on the intellectual development of the children, and particularly on Rosa's. Her own education and interests were far above those of the average Jewish woman. She was an eager reader not only of the Bible, but also of German and Polish classical literature, and there was almost a cult of Schiller in the house, though Rosa seems to have turned away from him very early and to have learned to appreciate him only very much later in life, under the influence of Franz Mehring. This early rejection of Schiller has been interpreted, according to the Freudian theory, as an unconscious protest against her mother; but the truth is that Schiller's sententiousness has frequently produced the same result amongst young people of intelligence. It was obviously Schiller's idealistic, but pathetic and very cloudy worship of freedom which touched related cords in the Luxemburg family, but at the same time the ambiguity and pathos were likely to revolt Rosa Luxemburg, whose political ideas ripened very early.

On the other hand, her devotion to the classical Polish authors, and in particular to Mickiewicz, whom at one time she placed even above Goethe, remained unshaken. We do not know when she found her way to Russian literature, but later we hear her speaking of it with great enthusiasm. The atmosphere of the home in which she was brought up was created by Polish and German culture and a love of their literatures. Rosa avidly devoured the great works of classical literature. The magic of rhyme and verse seized her when she was still a child, and she began to produce poems of her own. Her early intellectual development was naturally the pride of her parents, and they were unable to resist the temptation to show off her talents to visitors. However, an instinctive aversion to pose and affectation guarded her against the danger of such experiments, and she would often react with a certain obstinacy, and, to the embarrassment of her parents, utilise her natural gift for satire to make fun of those before whom she was expected to shine.

When she was three years old her family left for Warsaw, her father being anxious to give his children a better education than Zamosc could afford.

2. THE STRUGGLE BEGINS

In the ordinary way, school would have presented no difficulties to a lively and confident girl like Rosa, who found it easy to learn, but there is no doubt that her experiences under the school régime of oppressed Poland contributed to turning her life towards its final fulfilment. Russianisation was carried through with particular ruthlessness in the schools. The leading High School in Warsaw was reserved almost exclusively for Russians, both for boys and girls. The pupils were the children of Russian officers and officials, and only very few Polish children of Russianised families were permitted to attend. Jews, of course, were completely barred. And even at the next best school—the one which Rosa attended—there was a strict *numerus clausus* for Jews. The use of the Polish tongue, even amongst the pupils themselves, was strictly forbidden, and many of the Russian teachers even descended to spying on their pupils in order to enforce the prohibition.

Such narrow-minded repression naturally did not fail to awaken the spirit of resistance amongst the pupils, whose relation to their teachers was one of open hostility, occasionally expressing itself in rebellious demonstrations, which usually coincided with some political clash in the world outside the school. The High Schools were hotbeds of political conspiracy, though the conspiracies were usually of a youthful and romantic character, but occasionally they were linked up with the political movement outside. Polish national

resistance to forcible Russianisation in the schools easily led
its supporters into the socialist revolutionary movement, and
in those days most of its recruits came from the ranks of the
intellectual youth.

The Liberal spirit and the Polish nationalist feelings of
her family, her own hatred of Absolutism, and her defiant
independence quickly drove young Rosa into this school
opposition. In fact, she soon began to play a leading part in
it, and this is vouched for by the fact that the gold medal to
which her attainments would have entitled her on leaving the
school was withheld expressly " on account of her rebellious
attitude towards the authorities ". We may also regard this
very severe punishment as an indication that, in the last few
years of her school life at least, her oppositional activities were
of a serious nature and probably brought her into touch with
the revolutionary movement outside. Although we do not
know for certain that her opposition was consciously socialist
or connected in any way with the illegal organisations outside,
it is quite certain that very soon after leaving school in 1887
she was a member of the revolutionary socialist party
" Proletariat ", and that she co-operated closely with the
leader of the Warsaw group of the party, the workman Martin
Kasprzak.

Rosa Luxemburg joined the political struggle at a time when
the revolutionary movement in Russia and in Poland was
going through a severe crisis in a period of great depression.
She has described the then-prevailing conditions in her
" Accumulation of Capital " :

" The seventies and eighties in Russia represent a
transitional period, a period of internal crisis with all its
difficulties. Large-scale industry was just celebrating its
advent thanks to a period of strict protectionism. . . .
' Primitive accumulation ' of capital was flourishing in
Russia, favoured by State subsidies, guarantees, premiums,
and orders, and reaping profits such as already belonged
to the realm of fable in the West. At the same time the
internal conditions of Russia presented a far from attractive
or hopeful picture. In the rural areas the decline and
degeneration of peasant economy under the combined
pressure of fiscal exploitation and money economy resulted

in horrifying conditions: periodic famines and periodic peasant revolts. On the other hand, the factory proletariat in the towns had not yet developed socially and intellectually into a modern working class. . . . Primitive forms of exploitation provoked primitive methods of defence. At the beginning of the eighties spontaneous factory outbreaks and the destruction of machinery were necessary to give an impetus to the introduction of the first forms of factory legislation under Tsarism. Thus in the economic field Russia manifested at every turn all the shocking disharmonies of a transitional period, and this was supplemented by a crisis in the intellectual life of the country. The Narodniki,[1] Russia's native socialists, who based their theories on the peculiarities of Russia's agrarian constitution, were politically bankrupt following on the fiasco suffered by their extremist elements, organised in the terrorist party *Narodnaya Volya* (People's Freedom Party), after the successful attempt on the life of Alexander II in 1881. The writings of Georg Plechanov, which were intended to introduce Marxist ideas into Russia, were not published until 1883 and 1885, and even then they appeared for about a decade to have very little influence. During the eighties and even into the nineties, the intellectual life of Russia, and in particular that of the oppositional, socialist intelligentzia, was dominated by a peculiar mixture of ' native ' remnants of Narodniki ideas and snapped-up elementary trifles of Marxism, a mixture whose chief characteristic was a disbelief in the possibility of capitalist development in Russia. . . . ''

The frame of mind of the Russian intelligentzia of that day has been described by Rosa Luxemburg in her introduction to Vladimir Korolenko's " History of a Contemporary ":

" In the eighties, after the assassination of Alexander II, a period of numb hopelessness descended on Russia. The Liberal reforms of the sixties with regard to the judiciary

[1] The Narodniki were socialists who rejected Marxism and held that a peasant revolution would usher in a utopian form of agrarian socialism. In this way they hoped to spare Russia the trial of first experiencing a period of capitalism. The Narodniki were the forerunners of the social revolutionaries of a later date.

and local self-government were thoroughly revised, and under the leaden sway of Alexander III's government the silence of the graveyard prevailed. Russia, equally discouraged by the collapse of all hopes of peaceable reform and by the apparent impotence of the revolutionary movement, was passing through a period of depression. In this atmosphere of apathy and despondency, metaphysical and mystical tendencies began to make headway amongst the Russian intelligentzia. . . . The influence of Nietzsche could be clearly felt, and *belles-lettres* were dominated by the hopeless and pessimistic tone of Garshin's novels and Nadson's poetry. The spirit of the day was perhaps best exemplified in Dostoevsky's mysticism as expressed particularly by the ' Brothers Karamazov ', and in Tolstoi's ascetism. The propaganda of ' non-resistance to evil ', the condemnation of all violence in the struggle against the dominant reaction (which was to be opposed only by ' the inner purification ' of the individual), and the general theory of social passivity developed in the atmosphere of the eighties into a serious danger for the Russian intelligentzia, particularly as they were supported by such powerful allies as the pen and moral authority of Leo Tolstoi."

Poland was economically more highly developed than Russia, and her intellectual attitude was nearer to that of Western Europe, but the leaden heaviness of general depression weighed her down too. The national-revolutionary movement led by the Polish Junkers was dead. The new *bourgeoisie* worshipped the Golden Calf, rejected all ideas which could not be turned into immediate profits, and submitted with calculated slavishness to the sway of Absolutism. The party " Proletariat ", the hopeful forerunner of the modern socialist movement in Poland, had been involved in the defeat of the *Narodnaya Volya* and almost put out of action by the incarceration of its leaders in the Schlüsselburg Fortress and by mass arrests amongst its members, and intellectually, too, it was on the downgrade. After its first great strikes, the Polish working class had again subsided into apathy. The young intelligentzia was intimidated, and for some years the stream of new blood into the revolutionary movement from this source had been reduced to a trickle.

When Rosa Luxemburg entered the revolutionary movement the stream was beginning to flow again, bringing gradual regeneration with it, a regeneration which was to show itself clearly five years later. The way from rebellious opposition at school to revolutionary Socialism was predestined for Rosa. She felt the yoke of Russian Absolutism threefold: as a subject of the Russian State, as a member of a subject people, and as a member of the outcast Jewish race. Throughout her life she showed great readiness to take up the cause of the suffering and the oppressed, and she felt doubly every blow that fell on others. Sympathy with the lowly and the humiliated was the prime motive of her life, and it expressed itself in every word she uttered, and went with her even to the highest peaks of theoretical abstraction. But this sympathy could not exhaust itself or find satisfaction in individual assistance or in palliative measures. Her powerful emotions were always bridled by a keen intellect, and from the beginning she recognised what she wrote in a letter to her friend Hans Diefenbach after the outbreak of the World War—that when the dimensions of a misfortune turn it into a world historic drama, then only an objective and historical judgement can hope for validity, and all other considerations must give way before it.

For Rosa Luxemburg an objective and historical judgement meant the search for the common origin of all individual phenomena, the search to lay bare the motive-forces of development and find the synthesis in which the conflict would resolve.

Her membership of the party " Proletariat " undoubtedly greatly encouraged a natural aptitude for such inquiries, because, although the party was small, it represented an *élite* of enlightened workers who jealously guarded its theoretical heritage. In this way she made the acquaintance of the underground literature, which must have included the writings of Karl Marx and Friedrich Engels, which were later to become the basis of her ideas. Towards the end of her stay in Warsaw the working-class movement began to develop rapidly. New circles were formed in the factories, and she probably took part in the founding of a new organisation, the Polish Workers' League. In any case, she co-operated with it closely from the moment of its formation in 1889.

It was in this year that she had to leave Poland. Her activity in revolutionary circles was discovered by the police, and the threat of imprisonment, and perhaps banishment to Siberia, hung over her. She was at all times prepared to accept the consequences of her actions without shrinking, but her comrades decided that it would be better for her to go abroad rather than to graduate in the "University of Revolutionaries" —i.e., Siberia. Whilst abroad she could study and still serve the movement. Martin Kasprzak organised her flight. She was to be smuggled over the German frontier, but in the frontier village difficulties arose. Kasprzak then had recourse to a stratagem: he visited the Catholic priest of the village and informed him that a Jewish girl wished to become a Christian, but, owing to the violent opposition of her family, she could do so only abroad. Rosa Luxemburg played her part in the pious deception so adroitly that the priest willingly gave his assistance, and, hidden under straw in a peasant's cart, she crossed the frontier into freedom.

CHAPTER TWO: THE FATE OF POLAND

1. ZURICH

FROM WARSAW to Zurich, that is the path from a strong-hold of Absolutism into the freest country in Europe, from the dank and misty lowlands to the free and windswept heights. Zurich was the most important centre of Polish and Russian emigration, and its University was the Alma Mater of innumerable revolutionaries. For the most part they were young people who had already made acquaintance with the serious side of life. Many of them had suffered imprisonment or banishment to Siberia. And all of them had been torn away from their families and out of the social sphere in which they belonged. They lived apart from the ordinary middle-class students, whose only aim was a career. The young emigrants worked resolutely at their chosen studies, but they thought less of their bread and butter in the future than of the future of humanity. In their colony men and women were equal. Free thought prevailed amongst them, but at the same time a strict and almost ascetic morality. Poverty was general, and with it went a natural and unsentimental solidarity.

Unlike many of the other students, they were seldom to be found in the traditional drinking-haunts. Their discussions were tireless and never-ending, and the subjects innumerable: philosophy, Darwinism, the emancipation of women, Marx, Tolstoi, the fate of the *Obshtchina*,[1] the last remnant of Russian Agrarian Communism, the prospects and the historical importance of capitalist development in Russia, the upshot of Nihilist terrorism, Bakunin, Blanqui, the methods of the revolutionary struggle, the demoralisation of the western *bourgeoisie*, Bismarck's fall, the victorious struggle of German Social Democracy against the Anti-Socialist Laws, the emancipation of Poland, the teachings of Lavrov and Tchernishevski, the " treachery " of Turgeniev committed in his novel " Fathers and Sons ", Emile Zola, and a thousand other " questions "; but always the same theme : Revolution.

Little bread and much tea, cold attics full of cigarette smoke, shining eyes and excited gestures, exuberance and romanticism. Many of these young men and women were destined to die for their ideals in the prisons of Tsarism or Siberian banishment, whilst others quietly turned their backs on the exaltation of their youth and returned to Russia to become respectable factory-owners, lawyers, doctors, teachers, and journalists, to live and die unnoticed in out-of-the-way places. Only very few of them were privileged to live through the revolutionary storms for which they all longed.

Rosa Luxemburg touched only the fringe of this emigrant *Bohème*, and its endless debates, leading nowhere, provoked her ironic amusement. She took up her quarters in the family of the German social democrat and political emigrant Lübeck, a bed-ridden invalid who made a penurious living from his pen. He assisted her in her study of the German working-

---

[1] The Russian peasant system of common land ownership by local communities, with periodical redistribution. The peasant community was collectively responsible for all taxes and other obligations arising out of the emancipation of the serfs. In 1900 there were still 122 million hectares of land owned in this fashion. The system was finally destroyed by the agrarian legislation of Stolypin in 1917.

class movement, and she helped him with his literary work, occasionally writing an article herself for him. It was not long before the reins of the neglected household were in her hands.

At the University of Zurich she put her name down for Natural Science. What she felt for the world of plants and animals was more than interest, it was almost a passion, and to the end of her life it remained a refuge from the intensity of her political life. However, her real destiny was political, and it was therefore not long before she turned her attention to the political sciences. The official curriculum of the University probably offered her very little. The political sciences are too closely connected with class interests to permit them to be a field of objective and unprejudiced inquiry to the same extent that other sciences can be. And German political economy, born into the world only after the decay of classical theories, was a cripple from birth, and the fear of the social consequences likely to result from fearless scientific investigation kept its luminaries always within the bounds of humdrum popularisation.

Julius Wolf occupied the chair of political economy at the University of Zurich. He was a typical representative of that class of German professors who work through vast masses of detailed material with relentless industry, but always remain eclectics, and never succeed in achieving any complete and logical picture of society and its system. Rosa Luxemburg's whole urge, however, was to obtain this synthesis, this ultimate goal of all scientific inquiry. She studied the economic classics, Adam Smith, Ricardo, and Marx, and as a preliminary result she developed an overwhelming contempt for the typical German professorial luminary:

" the plodding bureaucrat who cuts the living material of social reality into the finest slices, classifies and lists them according to his own rigid pre-conceived notions, and having killed it stone dead passes on the result as scientific material for the administrative and legislative activity of our Elder Statesmen."

She was unable to resist letting her worthy professor feel her quickly-won superiority. Her friend and fellow-student,

Julian Marchlevski, describes in his memoirs—which, unfortunately, are not yet published—how the students made Professor
Wolf's life difficult. One of their number would innocently
ask a carefully prepared question, and when the unfortunate
professor had hopelessly entangled himself, Rosa Luxemburg
would get up and blandly expose his incompetence point by
point. To his credit, it would seem that Julius Wolf took the
malicious game in a good-humoured fashion, and in an autobio-
graphical sketch he has paid high tribute to his most brilliant
pupil.

Side by side with her studies Rosa Luxemburg took part
in the Zurich working-class movement and in the intense
intellectual life of the leaders of the political emigration.
In this way she came into touch with leading Russian Marxists:
Paul Axelrod, the Nestor of Russian Social Democracy,
though at that time it was no more than an idea; Vera
Sassulitch and Georg Plechanov, the most brilliant Marxist
of his day. She greatly admired Plechanov's attainments,
but even towards him she never abandoned her own personality and ideas. She also made the acquaintance of Parvus-
Helphand, who was studying in Basle, and his lively imagina-
tion, practical grasp of political affairs, and great energy
appealed to her deeply. She was still more closely connected
with one or two fellow-students, who had already won their
spurs in the Polish socialist movement, and who were to prove
her staunch supporters, including Julian Marchlevski and
Adolf Varshavski-Varski.

2. LEO JOGICHES

The friendship of Leo Jogiches, who came to Zurich in
1890, was to prove of the greatest importance for her intellectually, politically, and personally. The life of this
unusual man, who played a prominent part in the Polish
and Russian working-class movements, and who was finally
to lose his life at the head of the Spartakus League in Germany,
was hidden in the gloom of conspiratorial activity even to
those few who worked closely with him. He was extremely
reserved, and never spoke of his past. Nothing is known of his
youth, and what little is known about him has been collected
by J. Reyzin, who made exhaustive inquiries amongst those

who had known Jogiches when he first entered the political movement.

Leo Jogiches was born in 1867 in Vilna, of a rich Jewish family. His grandfather was a well-known Talmud scholar, but his father had already become Russianised, and Yiddish was seldom spoken in the family. Whilst still at high school, Leo began to conduct revolutionary propaganda amongst his school-fellows, and he left school prematurely in order to devote himself entirely to political work. In or around the year 1885 he founded the first revolutionary circle in Vilna, and A. Gordon, the well-known leader of the Jewish Workers' League (which was founded in 1896), regards him as the first leader and real founder of the working-class movement in Lithuania. The groups he founded remained weak because the urban proletariat was weak, whilst the decline of the *Narodnaya Volya* had discouraged oppositional tendencies amongst the intellectual youth. However, many well-known socialist leaders developed out of these little Vilna groups, including Charles Rappaport, who has since made a name for himself as a theoretician in the French Socialist Party.

Jogiches enjoyed a tremendous reputation amongst his followers. One of them has informed us: " Jogiches was a clever and forceful debater, and his presence was that of a man of importance. He was utterly devoted to his work as a socialist, and his followers idolised him." He sternly disciplined himself, and did everything he felt necessary or desirable in the interests of the revolutionary movement. For instance, he once worked as a mechanic at the bench, not with the deliberate self-abasement of the previous generation of revolutionaries who " went amongst the people ", but in order, as a worker himself, to understand the workers better and to be able to influence them more effectively. At the same time he sought to get into touch with the army, and he actually succeeded in organising a circle of Russian officers. Very early he developed that ability for the strictest conspiratorial activity which was to govern his whole subsequent life. In pursuance of his aims he also learnt engraving and printing. Not only did he impose the rigidest discipline on himself, but he also demanded that all his followers should strictly observe the rules of conspiratorial activity. He obtained very considerable knowledge by hard study, and he became the teacher of his comrades, and demanded from them that they should study too. Karl Radek tells an anecdote about how, at the height of the confusion caused by the 1905 Revolution, Leo Jogiches compelled him to wade through the works of a number of old authors whose names had been almost forgotten.

Naturally, it was not long before his activities came to the attention of the police. He was arrested for the first time in 1888, and incarcerated in the Vilna Citadel. After his release he was again arrested in May 1889, and remained in prison until the following September. On his release this time he was placed under police surveillance. His term of military service then came due. He considered the situation carefully, but reached the conclusion that, as a political suspect, he would be given little chance of working politically amongst his fellows. In addition, he feared that his own temperament would betray him in such circumstances, so he decided to make his escape. He did so under circumstances analogous to those of Rosa Luxemburg's escape, though in his case the straw was replaced by far less agreeable clay. In the winter of 1890 he arrived in Switzerland.

He was in possession of very considerable means, and he used them in the cause of socialist propaganda. He proposed to Plechanov that they should found a theoretical organ for the movement, and Plechanov readily agreed, hoping that the journal might prove a valuable instrument for building up a real social democratic movement in Russia, and hoping, too, that it would release him from the slavery of earning his own living by addressing letters, and permit him to devote his great talents as a theoretician and a propagandist to the socialist cause. The two did actually draft an agreement, but then the project collapsed on the question of who was to be the political director of the venture. Plechanov had his own share of *amour propre*, and, in any case, how could he agree to place such an important weapon in the hands of a rich youngster who had still to prove his mettle? But Leo Jogiches knew his value, and he was unwilling to give his own creation even into the hands of Plechanov. He was unwilling to subordinate himself to Plechanov, and his nature was dominating to the point of tyranny. He therefore left the Russian movement entirely and plunged into the Polish movement, in which he immediately became the unchallenged leader and organiser, and a personality recognised as the equal of the great Russian working-class leaders.

It was at this time that he first met Rosa Luxemburg, and a political alliance soon developed into an alliance for life. At first sight such a match must seem strange: Rosa with her happy disposition and impetuous temperament, her great talents, and her readiness to spend them liberally on all sides; and Leo, whose character was hard and sternly disciplined, who lived only for duty—duty to the point of pedantry—and demanded the same of others, who was prepared cold-bloodedly to sacrifice himself and others, and who seldom, and then only for fleeting moments, showed the depths of feeling of which he was capable. In fact, for each of them this deep contrast in character and temperament proved a source of strength, and it is an indication of the strength of character of both of them that their union was a lasting one, that the temperamental differences between them did not exhaust and hamper them, but rather increased their capacities. Clara Zetkin, who knew them both intimately, declares that Leo Jogiches was always the incorruptible critic of Rosa Luxemburg's actions and writings, and her practical and theoretical conscience. At times he saw further and was the one to take the initiative, whilst Rosa retained the keener and more embracing vision. And it is deeply true when Clara Zetkin says of Leo Jogiches: " He was one of those rare men who can tolerate a great personality in the woman by his side, working with him in loyal and happy comradeship, without feeling her growth and development as a limitation on his own personality." And later on, at a time when the emotional feelings of the two for each other had subsided, this deep comradeship lost nothing of its lasting strength.

3. THE PARTY " PROLETARIAT "

There is much of the very best Leo Jogiches had to offer incorporated in Rosa Luxemburg's life-work, and it is impossible to mark off the limits of this contribution. We do not know which of the two made the decisive moves and gave the impetus to the political system which she created and to which she devoted her life. Leo Jogiches remained deliberately in the background and attached no value to any public recognition of the part he played, but Rosa's supreme confidence in scientific and theoretical questions indicates that in this field at least she was the stronger and gave the most.

It was just at this time that a revision of socialist ideas became necessary. International Socialism was on the brink of a new phase of development. The foundation of the new International in 1889 in Paris was the outward expression of the internal consolidation of the socialist movement. In France the period of uncertainty and confusion which followed on the defeat of the Commune was at an end, though half-a-dozen different tendencies still wrestled with each other. In Great Britain the New Unionism was rising side by side with the old hide-bound unions. The New Unionism organised the unskilled workers, abandoned the Liberalist traditions of class collaboration, and restored the ideas of the class struggle. New leaders like Tom Mann, John Burns, and Ben Tillett were coming to the fore, and it seemed almost as though organisations like the Social Democratic Federation and the Socialist League were about to develop beyond the narrow limits of little sects, whilst in 1893 Keir Hardie and Tom Mann founded the Independent Labour Party. In Germany the working-class movement was once again above ground, and the legal hindrances to its organisational growth were removed. Two extremist tendencies immediately began to attack traditional policy vigorously: the radical " youth ", with their semi-anarchist leanings, on the Left, and the reformists on the Right. At the same time the trade-union movement grew and strengthened, raising new questions and new tasks.

The socialist movement in Poland had entered into a period of crisis. It had originated in 1877, at a time when Polish capitalism, deliberately favoured and encouraged by Tsarism, was experiencing a wild boom. Profits of 100% were nothing out of the ordinary, and the average rate of profit was between 40 and 50%. This orgy of " primitive accumulation " took place at the expense of a proletariat harnessed for fourteen and fifteen hours a day to the treadmill, enjoying no State protection of any sort against even the most reckless exploitation, and having no means of defending even its most elementary human rights.

In this situation the banner of Socialism was raised by young students, led by Ludwig Varynski, a man of considerable courage, political far-sightedness, and organisational ability, ably supported by Kasimir Dluski, Stanislaus Mendelssohn, and Simon Dickstein. They went amongst the factory-workers, formed little circles, founded defence funds as the nucleus of illegal trade unions, organised the first strikes, and spread socialist ideas amongst the advance guard of the workers. The difficulties they had to face were enormous. The little circles were broken up again and again, and waves of arrests were followed by mass trials. During the first four years of their activity 120 members of the movement were sent to prison or banishment, and this represented a very serious weakening for an illegal organisation compelled to work under the conditions of Russian Absolutism.

However, the movement grew nevertheless, and in 1882 the various circles and workers' committees were formed into the socialist revolutionary party " Proletariat ". In 1883 the new party was the life and soul of a tremendous mass movement occasioned by an insolent ukase issued by the Warsaw police chief, placing women who worked in factories on the same footing as common prostitutes, and ordering them to subject themselves to humiliating examinations. A passionate appeal issued by the party " Proletariat " brought the workers into movement, and 6,000 in the Zryardov mill came out on strike. The strike was bloodily suppressed by armed force, but it attained its end, and the shameful ukase was withdrawn. The workers therefore resumed work with the consciousness that they had won their first important success against the absolutist régime. Varynski then took up relations with the *Narodnaya Volya* in Petersburg, and in the following year a formal alliance was concluded between the two parties. However, before this occurred Varynski himself was arrested, and that was the beginning of a whole series of arrests which broke the back of the party. In December 1885 the leaders were court-martialled. Varynski defended and justified the actions of the party in a passionate and courageous speech. Four of the accused were sentenced to death, and twenty-three to long terms of hard labour, whilst about 200 others were banished. On January 28th, 1886, the first martyrs of the Polish socialist movement, Bardovski Kunitzki, Ossovski, and Petrusinski, were hanged. Varynski himself escaped the gallows, but he was sentenced to sixteen years hard labour, and he died a slow death in the Schlüssel-burg Fortress. The party he had founded fell to pieces, and when Rosa Luxemburg entered the movement about a year after the great trial, only remnants of the organisation remained.

However, from the very beginning the party " Proletariat " was a step ahead of the revolutionary movement in Russia, both in its principles and its programme. It was founded in the great days of the *Narodnaya Volya*, in days when its triumphant progress awakened fantastic hopes, so that even Karl Marx expected that it would overthrow Tsarism. But the *Narodnaya Volya* was not a party of the proletariat either in its political actions or its ideology. The Russian revolutionary movement was still engaged in the bitter dispute as to whether Russia would have to tread the same path to Socialism via capitalism as the " degenerate and corrupt " western countries of Europe, or whether the old Russian peasant community, already in decline though it was, would offer a native basis for a socialist organisation of Russian society.

As Rosa Luxemburg put it, " the very physical existence of the Russian working class had first of all to be proved from the arid columns of official industrial statistics; the existence of each mathematical proletarian, so to speak, had to be fought for in passionate polemics ". And the *Narodnaya Volya* was exclusively a movement of intellectuals, without any basis amongst the masses of the people, without any conception of the social process, and without even a clear programme concerning the future development of Russian society. It was a little group of idealists who appeared in the lists against Absolutism and thought to win freedom for a hundred million souls with nothing but their own heroic audacity and a few bombs and revolvers. All that humanity can offer in its grandest moments of idealism, devotion, self-sacrifice, and courage was concentrated in a brilliant galaxy of men and women like Sheliabov, Kibalshitch, Sophie Perovskaya, Vera Figner, and their followers. On

March 1st, 1881, they succeeded in destroying Alexander II, but just as Kibalshitch blew himself to pieces in killing the Tsar, so the greatest triumph of the *Narodnaya Volya* proved its own undoing. The political methods of the movement were seen to be false. The greatest heights of heroism attainable by the individual are insufficient to win what only the efforts of the whole people can obtain—liberty.

In its recognition of social reality and the conditions neces sary for the successful prosecution of the struggle for liberty, the party " Proletariat " was as much ahead of the *Narodnaya Volya* as the social development of Poland was ahead of that of Tsarist Russia. It recognised the development of capitalism as a fact, and it declared itself unambiguously in its name and in its programme to be a party of the working class. It stressed its international character, broke with the old tradi- tions of the Polish revolutionary movement, and abandoned the independence of Poland as a political aim, declaring: " We want neither a Poland of the Junkers nor a Poland of Democracy. And not only that, but we are convinced that either would be an absurdity." The leaders of the party " Proletariat " took up this uncompromising attitude towards the question of Polish independence because they were convinced that indulgence in Polish patriotism would in- evitably turn the Polish proletariat into a hanger-on of other classes, whereas the primary need of the moment was to sever it from other classes and to awaken the consciousness of its own political mission. The natural ally of the Polish working class was to be found in the revolutionary movement in Russia, and not anywhere in Poland. The Polish national question would be solved within the framework of the inter- national socialist revolution. This revolution would over- throw not only Tsarism but also capitalism, and give power to the proletariat, which would then proceed to build up Socialism. Thus, the party " Proletariat " did not regard a *bourgeois* revolution in Russia as an essential step on the way to Socialism, and only its most talented thinker, Varynski, hesitatingly approached the problem of fighting for demo- cratic liberties in order that the working class might develop more freely both culturally and organisationally.

The party " Proletariat " was active in Poland for about five years. It formed educational circles and workers' committees in various parts of that country. It organised strikes, including the big textile workers' strike of 1883, and it laid the foundations for a trade-union movement, but it did not succeed in developing a real and lasting mass movement. The Polish workers were already capable of making isolated spasmodic efforts, but they were still too backward for mass organisations, and the party " Proletariat " was able to control only a small *élite*. And then came the heavy blows delivered by the police. These blows not only disorganised the party, but caused it to lose its course. The alliance with the *Narodnaya Volya* proved to be a fatal error. The fundamental opinions of the party " Proletariat " were in irreconcilable contradiction with the terrorist tactics of the *Narodnaya Volya*. But if the alliance was to be anything but a mere formality, the Polish party would have to accept the terrorist methods and the Blanquist ideology of the *Narodnaya Volya*, which believed that the revolution would be achieved as the result of a conspiracy, and not as the result of mass action on the part of the working class. The party " Proletariat " degenerated, in fact, into an organisation of conspirators co-operating with the *Narodnaya Volya* in the planning of terrorist deeds, though it never actually took part in any. And when the *Narodnaya Volya* broke up, the party " Proletariat " was involved in the catastrophe. All that was saved from the wreck were the small circles in which Rosa Luxemburg spent her political minority.

4. THE FIGHT AGAINST BLANQUISM

In 1888 the working-class movement in Poland again began to make progress. The party " Proletariat " was reorganised, and it once more turned its attention to the masses. Defence funds for factory-workers were founded as a new start towards the formation of trade unions, and as a result of these efforts the Polish Workers' League was formed. This organisation limited its activities almost exclusively to furthering the economic interests of the working class, and it even went so far on occasions as to reject political action altogether. It was analogous to the " Economistic " movement which sprang up in the young socialist movement of Russia a decade later. The party " Proletariat " and the Workers'

League co-operated in various actions—for instance, in the organisation of the May-day celebrations of 1892, when 8,000 workers struck in Warsaw and as many as 60,000 in Lodz. In Lodz Cossacks carried out a massacre of striking workers, and forty-six were killed and over 200 wounded. The subsequent persecutions affected both parties, and in the end a programmatic *rapprochement* led to the fusion of the party " Proletariat ", the Polish Workers' League, and one or two smaller organisations into the Polish Socialist Party. The organ of the new party was the *Sprava Robotnicza* (" The Cause of the Workers "), founded by Leo Jogiches, edited by Adolf Varski, and brilliantly inspired by Rosa Luxemburg.

The formation of the new party urgently demanded a thorough review of the ideological equipment taken over from its predecessors. Whilst still in Zurich, and with the passionate thoroughness which marked all she did, Rosa Luxemburg had studied the history of Poland and of its national-revolutionary and socialist movements, as well as the theoretical basis of the international working-class movement, and the results of her studies she incorporated in the first important document we have from her pen, an exhaustive report on the Polish situation, presented by the Polish Socialist Party to the International Congress of 1893 in Zurich.

The first aim of this document was to establish the necessity for a social-democratic—i.e., a Marxist—policy for the Polish working-class movement. To this end Rosa Luxemburg had to wage war on two fronts: against Blanquism and against reformism, against both the traditions of the party " Proletariat " and the " Economistic " tendencies which had shown themselves. She opposed the Blanquist idea that the overthrow of Tsarism was identical with the social revolution, and she was against a tactic which sought to undermine Absolutism by a mere conspiracy, a conspiracy which might, if need be, appeal to the masses, but which in practice would replace them by the initiative of an *élite*. The masses themselves must lead the fight; but how could they be won?

" At last it was realised," wrote Rosa Luxemburg, obviously generalising too widely from her own perceptions, " that the rôle of Social Democracy was the deliberate assumption of leadership in the mass struggle against the existing order of society, a struggle which must take into consideration the actual conditions of that social order. At last it was realised that the economic struggle for the daily interests of the working class, and the struggle for a democratic form of government, was a school through which the proletariat must necessarily go before it would be able to overthrow the existing social order."

She pointed out how, in its struggle for better wages, against unconscionably long working hours, and against the shameful punishment system in the factories, the working class inevitably came up against the absolutist régime, and how it could be led into the struggle for democratic liberty. At the same time she sternly rejected all illusions about the real condition of the working class. When Polish social democrats declared that it was not possible to form trade unions in Prussian Poland, but only a political party of Poles, she wrote on September 27th, 1893, to her Russian friend Kritchevski : " And that's in a country where the masses are completely indifferent and apathetic, a country where they could be brought into movement only by an appeal to their immediate interests—by wage struggles ! " And she complained that even Bebel was giving way to such ideas. She refused to accept wishes as reality. She was always ready to utilise the smallest matters in the interests of the movement, but she was anxious that the party should not lose itself in the daily struggle and forget the path of development laid down for it by history, but that it should be guided by its final objective in every practical step it took. She regarded the *bourgeois* revolution as an objectively indispensable phase in the development of Russia, and the democratic rights to be won in the revolution and the struggle for those rights as means to raise the working class morally, intellectually, and organisationally and prepare it for the final struggle for power.

To-day such ideas seem very much a matter of course, but in those days they were nothing of the sort. Even many years later Rosa Luxemburg's opponents in the Polish movement (whom she dubbed social patriots) considered the idea of an organised trade-union struggle in Poland to be Utopian, and that any attempt to begin such a struggle would break any party. Instead they spent their time chasing after wills-of-the-wisp. The significance of Rosa Luxemburg's ideas in those days can be judged from the fact that even in our own times violent disputes have raged round them. In the nineties her ideas were nothing more nor less than a theoretical programme of socialist strategy. Such a theory might have been built up with some difficulty from various more or less incidental hints dropped by Marx and Engels, but in fact the whole trade-union and parliamentary activity of Social Democracy in Western Europe was purely empirical in its nature, and the dangers of this were soon to make themselves visible in the revisionist movement. Rosa Luxemburg's achievement is astounding for a young woman of twenty-three. Despite her own fiery and revolutionary temperament, and despite the fact that she had to work in the conditions created by Absolutism (conditions in which romantic revolutionary ideas and schemes flourished like weeds), she was able to think soberly and realistically. That achievement was the fruit of serious study of revolutionary theories and revolutionary history, and at the same time the first expression of a keen and reliable political instinct.

5. The National Question as a Strategic Problem

A second task faced her: some solution of the national question had to be found for the working class. The party " Proletariat " had rejected the independence of Poland as an immediate aim of the socialist struggle, but in the crisis experienced by the Polish working-class movement in those years the old comrades of Varynski—Mendelssohn, Yanovska, Dashinski, and others—once again raised the banner of Polish independence. There was no doubt that the party " Proletariat " had not sufficiently explained its attitude, and its ideas rested more on cosmopolitanism than on Marxist internationalism. Rosa Luxemburg rejected the idea that the national problem was about to be solved for Poland as a matter of course in an approaching socialist revolution. She believed the *bourgeois* revolution to be an unavoidable intermediate stage, and she therefore had to decide whether the Polish socialist movement should reject the idea of Polish national independence as a strategic aim within *bourgeois* society. If it did, then that meant a break with the policy of Marx and Engels, the founders of scientific Socialism, a

policy which they had upheld to the last, and which Friedrich
Engels was still upholding, and which had, in fact, become
a dogma for Western European Socialism.

The report to the Zurich Congress previously mentioned
set out her general ideas on the Polish national problem,
but she returned to the problem again and again, examining
new aspects of the relation between the proletarian struggle
and the struggle for national freedom. She defended her
ideas in innumerable polemical articles, and at the same time
she studied the problem deeply. For decades she worked
on a history of Poland, and she probably completed it in
prison during the World War. Unfortunately the manuscript
was lost with many other important works during the German Revolution. Perhaps it was destroyed by marauding
soldiery. Only a skeleton of it is extant. Franz Mehring
used Rosa Luxemburg's manuscript for the explanatory
notes to his edition of the Literary Remains of Marx and
Engels from the years 1848 to 1849,[1] and it is not difficult
to distinguish the intellectual influence of Rosa Luxemburg
in his work. There is also a study by her on capitalism in
Poland,[2] and it has since become the basis of all subsequent
investigations into Polish economic history. These historical
studies enabled Rosa Luxemburg to develop her own standpoint in the Polish national question.

Since the Polish insurrection of 1830–31 it had become a
matter of course for Western European Democracy to support
the struggle of the Poles for national independence—so long
that is, as there was a real, progressive, and vigorous Democracy in Western Europe. Until Rosa Luxemburg came on
the scene the restoration of Polish independence had been a
dogma for the social democratic movement, and the attitude
of Varynski had been incomprehensible heresy. This dogma
was based on the policy pursued steadfastly by Marx and
Engels since the forties. For them the national-revolutionary
movement of Poland had been a barrier against the chief
force of European reaction, Tsarist Russia. Tsarism had
been the nucleus of the Holy Alliance which for decades

[1] " *Aus dem literarischen Nachlass von Karl Marx, Friedrich Engels und Ferdinand
Lassalle*," Vol. III. Dietz, Stuttgart, 1902.
[2] Rosa Luxemburg, " *Die industrielle Entwicklung Polens* " (" The
Industrial Development of Poland "), Doctoral Dissertation, Leipzig,
1898.

had stifled every continental movement for freedom. It was
the bulwark of every feudal Power in Central Europe. The
waves of the 1848 revolution broke against the frontiers of
Tsarist Russia. The Tsar was the power behind the King
of Prussia in all his counter-revolutionary actions. Russian
troops finally liquidated the revolution when they defeated
the Hungarian people's army in 1849. And in the following
year the Tsar intervened openly in Germany's domestic
affairs and under threats compelled Frederick William IV
to sign the shameful Treaty of Olmütz and to abandon all
efforts to unify Germany. Any big democratic reform
measure seemed impossible in Western Europe so long as
this sinister power existed in the East, with its Cossack hordes
ready to be loosed on Europe.

For this reason both Marx and Engels regarded the defeat
and weakening of Russia as the preliminary condition for
any real political progress in the West, and after the defeat
of the revolution in 1848 the restoration of Poland appeared
to them as the prime demand of any democratic and proletarian policy. In a memorandum to the First Congress of
the International in 1866 in Geneva, Marx explained why
the workers of Europe should occupy themselves with the
Polish question:

" In the first instance because middle-class writers and
agitators conspire to suppress it, although they patronise
all sorts of other nationalities, even Ireland. Whence this
reticence? Because both aristocrats and *bourgeois* look
upon the dark Asiatic power in the background as a last
resource against the advancing tide of working-class
ascendancy. That power can effectually be put down only
by the restoration of Poland upon a democratic basis. In
the present changed state of Central Europe, and especially
Germany, it is more than ever necessary to have a democratic Poland. Without it Germany will become the
outwork of the Holy Alliance, with it a co-operator with
republican France. The working-class movement will
continually be interrupted, checked, and retarded until
this great European question is set at rest." [1]

[1] Quoted by N. Riazanov, " Karl Marx and Friedrich Engels on the
Polish Question ", *Archiv für die Geschichte des Sozialismus und der Arbeiterbewegung*, 1915.

Marx was certainly of the opinion that no country could really be free itself so long as it continued to oppress other countries, but it was not general national ideas which caused him to adopt his attitude on the Polish question. Like Engels he was sceptical about the right of self-determination, and his support of an independent, democratic Poland was determined by the exigencies of political strategy.

Rosa Luxemburg approached the problem from the same angle. She rejected the foreign-political postulate of Marx and Engels as no longer applicable, although all other Marxists now accepted the whole idea as a political dogma, without troubling to examine its hypotheses at all. However, European regroupings and social processes had fundamentally altered the hypotheses. Just at the time when Rosa Luxemburg was mastering this question the French Republic was preparing to ally itself with Russian Absolutism. This in itself was sufficient to indicate that republican France was no longer the sacred vessel preserving the holy fire of the revolution, and that Russia was no longer the stronghold of European reaction in its former sense. It was true that all the reactionary forces in Europe still sought support from Russia, but it was no longer the direct threat of Russian bayonets which propped up their power, but diplomacy, and no buffer State could do anything about that; only the overthrow of Tsarism itself could bring about a change. The Russian rouble no longer rolled in Europe; on the contrary, francs and marks rolled in the opposite direction, to finance Tsarist Russia's armaments. The old bulwark of European reaction now had itself to be supported on all sides. At a time when Tsarism was seriously threatened at home by the *Narodnaya Volya*, Bismarck concluded the agreement which gave Russian diplomacy valuable backing in continental politics. In fact, Tsarism refreshed itself at French and German springs for its struggle with the threatening revolution at home.

The strongest reason for Marx's policy was the apparent vigour of Absolutism in Russia, where social relations had remained static for centuries. Tsarism was based primarily on the primitive agricultural economy of Russia and the serfdom connected with it. As long as this primitive agricultural economy remained unchanged all the great peasant revolts must fail. However, in furthering its own interests Tsarism was compelled to encourage capitalist development in Russia. Russian society began to break up, and the result was the peasant emancipation of 1861. The peasant was forced into commodity production, and at the same time he was ruined by oppressive taxation. When American competition began to make itself felt on the European grain market, causing the first agrarian crisis, the Russian large-scale landed property system, already very shaky, began to collapse. The terrible famine of 1891–93 and the outbreak of pestilence revealed the process of decay which had been going on within the absolutist régime. The stronghold of European reaction was crumbling. At the same time a new class was developing in Russia, the proletariat, a class which had not yet come forward independently, but which would in the end, as Rosa Luxemburg and all Marxists recognised, destroy Absolutism. Whilst there were no longer any democratic Powers in Europe anxious to cast off the yoke of Russian Absolutism, in Russia itself forces were arising which would give the sinister colossus the *coup de grâce*. For these reasons revolutionary political strategy needed alteration.

The objective of Marx's strategy no longer existed, and the means with which he hoped to attain it—the national-revolutionary movement in Poland—were no longer to hand. The standard-bearer of all Polish national insurrections was the Polish aristocracy, and in particular the minor aris-tocracy, which had been deeply influenced by the demo-cratic ideas of Western Europe, and whose best elements fought as brilliant officers in all revolutionary struggles in Europe throughout the nineteenth century up to the days of the Paris Commune. However, the class itself is not identical with its individual representatives, and it cannot advance beyond its own inherent limitations. As has so often been the case with aristocracies, its aim lay in the past, and not in the future. As a class it was anti-capitalist, but the real reason was that it wished to restore the old feudalist rule of the aristocracy, and, for this reason alone, all its insurrections failed. They could have been successful only if they had received the enthusiastic support of the peasantry, but only the prospect of an agrarian revolution could have won that. The democratic leaders of the aristo-cratic party proclaimed the principle of agrarian reform from 1846 onwards, but nothing was ever done about it, and in the end it was Tsarism itself which put it into execution after the insurrection of 1863 and abolished the final vestiges of serfdom in Poland. With this the former primitive agri-cultural system vanished in Poland too, and the aristocracy was deposed from its privileged social position. Capitalism began to flourish and the new *bourgeoisie* took over the social leadership of Poland. It also took over the national pro-gramme as a heritage, in order first to emasculate it and then to bury it, because the *bourgeoisie* owed its very existence to the fact that Tsarism encouraged the development of capitalism as far as it could, and in Tsarist Russia the Polish *bourgeoisie* found the big market it needed. Under such circumstances any restoration of Polish independence would have meant separation from Russia and the loss of the Russian market. Thus the Polish *bourgeoisie* was not at all anxious for national unity and national independence. It wished to use Absolutism for its own ends, and it therefore subordinated itself willingly. It is true that thousands of individual Polish *bourgeois* were opponents of the Russianisa-tion of Poland, but the *bourgeoisie* as a class was not. And the higher its profits rose and the more resentful the Polish working class became, the more the Polish *bourgeoisie* stressed its loyalty to the oppressors of Poland. Only one stratum of the population cherished the old idea of national inde-pendence: the Polish intelligentzia. However, the intelli-gentzia represented no real social force; it could provide good officers, but no troops, and in the end its own impotence drove it into romantic adventurism.

And the Polish working class? How was it possible for the Polish workers to uphold the national heritage? They regarded "the leader of the nation", the *bourgeoisie*, as their deadliest enemy, and they had to fight bitterly for even the most elementary rights. And how could the Polish workers possibly create a *bourgeois* Polish national State against the vital economic interests of the *bourgeoisie* itself—particularly as Poland was carved up into three parts, each under the oppressive rule of a different foreign Power? As Rosa Luxem-burg put it:

B 2

" In order to win independence for Poland the Polish proletariat would have to break the power of the three strongest governments in Europe, and at the same time violate the material conditions of existence of its own *bourgeoisie*. In other words, despite its own social position as an oppressed class it would have to take the position of a ruling class and use its rule to create a new class State which would at the same time be the instrument of its further oppression."

If the Polish proletariat had sufficient strength to perform this herculean task, then it would certainly have sufficient strength to accomplish the social revolution itself, and only the social revolution offered the hope of a solution of the Polish national problem acceptable to the working class.

From all this Rosa Luxemburg concluded that the national independence of Poland could not be accepted as an immediate aim of the Polish proletariat, because the proletariat must follow aims which arise out of the objective course of social development, and which offer the material conditions for their attainment, and not aims which have nothing to recommend them but their theoretical desirability. In other words, the working class must not chase after wills-of-the-wisp, but pursue a sternly realistic policy; not " practical politics " in the traditional, conservative, *petit-bourgeois* sense, but a realistic policy arising out of given conditions, and always striving ceaselessly towards the final revolutionary objective.

When Rosa Luxemburg first put forward these ideas she met with the combined resistance of all nationalist elements amongst the Poles and of all those elements in the Polish working-class movement which held fast to what was regarded as the Marxist tradition. Karl Kautsky was considered the greatest Marxist authority of the day, but although he agreed with Rosa Luxemburg on the most important points, he disagreed with her conclusions. In particular he insisted that the anti-national tendencies of the Polish *bourgeoisie* pointed out by her were a temporary phenomenon only: in the nineties a struggle had broken out between Polish and Russian industry, and the Tsarist State was vigorously intervening in the interests of Russian industry and against the

Poles. This struggle, Kautsky contended, would bring the Polish *bourgeoisie* back to the ideal of national independence and it would then rally the urban middle classes, the intelligentzia, and the peasants around the national standard:

> " From the grave of the old feudal struggle for the restoration of Poland a new national Polish movement will rise up after a time, a movement born of modern development, a vital and promising movement."

Rosa Luxemburg subjected this hope to a thorough examination in her doctoral dissertation, and she exposed it as an illusion. She pointed out that Russian and Polish capitalism were bound to each other by powerful common interests; that they depended on each other and profited from each other. Naturally, the traditional " war of all against all " prevailed everywhere in capitalist society, and the dispute between the textile barons of Lodz and those of Moscow was a part of this general war. Naturally, too, " the trivial subject of their dispute was hung around with an ideological cloak of nationalism ". The measures taken by Tsarism, allegedly against the interests of Polish industry, aimed in reality at causing Polish industry to take Russian, in preference to foreign, raw materials. And, finally, the Tsarist policy of imperialist expansion was even more in the interests of Polish industry than of Russian, because Polish industry was better equipped to take advantage of it. With this the last hope of any regeneration of the Polish national idea through the instrumentation of the Polish *bourgeoisie* must disappear.

However, there was certainly one thing which might be able to turn (and actually did in the upshot) the idea of the restoration of Poland from a Utopia into a political reality—and that was war. However, this means could naturally play no rôle in the drawing up of Rosa Luxemburg's political programme, though it was not pacifism which caused her to exclude the factor of war from her political calculations, because she was well aware that historical progress often realises itself in wars and revolutions, and will continue to do so as long as human society is disrupted by national and class antagonisms. She declared that for the moment the alignment of powers in a war could not be determined with any certainty, and therefore, although during the war itself reasonable expectations might properly determine the tactics to be adopted, they could not be permitted to shape a programme intended for the daily struggle of the working class in peace-time. Later on, at a time when imperialist antagonisms were being rapidly aggravated, she regarded speculation on war as dangerous political adventurism which would end in turning the Polish proletariat into a mercenary troop in the hands of one or other of the imperialist groups.

In her opinion the next great aim of the Polish working class in its struggle must be the overthrow of Absolutism, and not the political restoration of an independent Poland; and this was to apply to the attitude of the Polish proletariat in foreign affairs as well. The alliance of the Polish *bourgeoisie* with Tsarism must be answered by an alliance of the Polish proletariat with the Russian proletariat. In a Russian democratic republic arising as a result of a revolution Poland would win autonomy in all cultural matters. In course of time this strategic aim was accepted by all prominent Marxist theoreticians.

In the nineties Rosa Luxemburg undertook a further revision of the accepted Marxist tradition, and as a result she appeared in the eyes of many to be an even more fanatical enemy of the Polish people and their " national interests " than before. When the insurrection of the Greeks on the island of Crete in 1896 raised the Turkish problem once again in Europe, she came out vigorously in favour of national emancipation for all the peoples oppressed by Turkey: for Greeks, Serbians, Bulgarians, Armenians, and others. Her attitude seemed in crying contradiction to her beliefs in the Polish question.

It was the reversal of the contradiction which was evident in the policy of Marx and Engels, a contradiction which found its solution then, as now, in a uniform political strategy. In the Balkans and on the frontiers of Tsarist Russia in Asia Minor the desirability of creating or maintaining a bulwark against Tsarist Absolutism was fundamental for Marx's policy towards national questions. Turkey held guard against Russia in the south-east of Europe and in the Near East. Her own vital interests compelled her to oppose

Russian expansion, and therefore, in Marx's view, the general interests of European democracy demanded the preservation of the Ottoman Empire, particularly as the nationalist elements in the Balkans had been poisoned by the reactionary ideas of Pan-Slavism, and the existing Statelets were nothing but outworks and passive instruments of Tsarism. Thus, during the Crimean War, Marx vigorously supported Turkey against Russia and equally vigorously denounced the weak and vacillating conduct of the war by Great Britain and France. And in 1878 he again defended the territorial integrity of Turkey [1] " because a Russian defeat would greatly accelerate the social transformation, whose elements are now present everywhere in Russia, and thereby also accelerate the transformation throughout Europe ".

In the opinion of Rosa Luxemburg, however, there was no further need for foreign Powers to act as midwives to the Russian Revolution. She relied on the inherent revolutionary forces of Russia, though these needed time in which to develop. Turkey, on the other hand, was increasingly becoming the storm-centre of Europe. By her existence as an oppressor Power she maintained the old corrupt and rotten Austro-Hungarian Empire. Turkish domination crippled the development of the culturally and economically more advanced peoples of the Balkans, and the *bourgeoisie* of these peoples now represented a real national desire for independence. As far as the danger of Russian influence in the Balkans was concerned, Rosa Luxemburg was quite certain that the throwing off of the Turkish yoke would not further it; on the contrary, she declared that Russian influence would remain strong only so long as the Balkan peoples were oppressed by the Turks; as soon as they had won their national freedom and founded independent national States their own interests would inevitably bring them together in a united front against Russia.

Thus Rosa Luxemburg was not guided by any political dogma in the matter of national independence, and she accepted no generally applicable formula for the solution of all national problems: " National States and Nationalism are empty vessels into which each epoch and the class relations in each particular country pour their particular material content ". In her opinion all national movements in the

[1] In a letter of advice sent to Liebknecht on February 4th, 1878.—TR.

period of *bourgeois* revolutions, whether in Germany or Italy, Poland, the Balkans, Ireland or India, should be carefully examined and analysed each on its own merits. Such movements could be historically progressive or reactionary, according to existing social relations and international conditions, and according to the character and interests of the class or classes which took the lead in them. As a result, therefore, the attitude of the socialist parties to national tendencies might well change, and under all circumstances the primary consideration must remain the interests of the proletarian revolution. As a result of all these considerations she refused to accept the right of self-determination as a real principle applicable to all peoples and under all circumstances.

At a later date she clashed violently with Lenin over this question of self-determination, and the conflict prevented the realisation of one of her hopes in the struggle against Tsarism : the organisational affiliation of the Polish party to Russian Social Democracy. The real reason for their disagreement lay in the fact that objective conditions had placed the two great working-class leaders in different positions. Rosa Luxemburg represented the working class of an oppressed nation, and she had to guard against the proletarian class struggle being falsified and overlaid by nationalist tendencies, so that her insistence was always on the necessity of a fighting alliance between the Polish and Russian working classes. Lenin, on the other hand, worked under Pan-Slav conditions as a member of a nation which " oppressed a hundred other nations ", and in order to unite the revolutionary forces of all these peoples against Absolutism, he had to recognise without cavil the national interests of the peoples oppressed by the Pan-Slavs, and grant them the right of self-determination, including, if need be, the right of separation from Russia, so that he insisted always on the right of self-determination for all peoples, a right which Marx and Engels never recognised, and which Rosa Luxemburg showed with cogent arguments to be inapplicable to the given situation, though it was to develop into an important psychological factor for Russian Social Democracy. Rosa Luxemburg failed to recognise the psychological aspect of this question. In her anxiety to preserve intact the general line of proletarian strategy in Poland, she under-estimated the rôle the national question could play in certain big movements—for instance, in Ukrainia and in the Caucasus.

How far Lenin agreed with Rosa Luxemburg in her solution of the strategic problem for Poland can be seen from the big discussion which took place in 1916 between him and a number of opponents of the right of self-determination (Karl Radek, Hermann Gorter, Henriette Roland-Holst). Referring to the Polish question he wrote:

" To favour a European war purely and simply in order to obtain the restoration of Poland would be nationalism of the worst sort; it would place the interests of a few Poles above the interests of the hundreds of millions of people who would suffer in such a war. The supporters of the right wing of the Polish Socialist Party (P.P.S.) are such nationalists and they are socialists only in words. Polish Social Democracy is absolutely right in its attitude towards these people. To put forward the slogan of Polish independence now, in the present relations which exist between Poland's great imperialist neighbours, would be to chase after a will-of-the-wisp, to get lost in the pettiest form of nationalism, and to forget the interest of the European Revolution—even the interests of the Russian and German Revolutions. . . .

" It is not a paradox, but a simple fact that the Polish proletariat can serve the cause of Socialism and liberty, including Polish socialism and Polish liberty, only if it is prepared to join hands with the proletariat of the neighbouring countries and fight against the Polish nationalists. We must not deny the great historical services rendered by the Polish social democrats in the struggle against these people. . . .

" The situation is undoubtedly very confused, but there is a solution which would permit all of us involved to remain good internationalists, and that is if the Russian and German Social Democracies demand the unconditional ' right of separation ' for Poland, and the Polish social democrats fight for proletarian unity both in the small and big countries, whilst refraining from putting forward the demand for Polish independence in the given epoch." [1]

[1] N. Lenin and G. Zinoviev, "*Gegen den Strom*" ("Against the Stream"), German Edition, 1921, pp. 407–9.

Despite various reservations which might be made with regard to certain of the arguments put forward by Lenin in the discussion on the right of self-determination, he was on the whole correct when he declared that the nationalist opponents of Rosa Luxemburg in Poland repeated the words of Marx like parrots without understanding their spirit, and that she was quite correct in her Polish policy, but tended to generalise its application excessively outside Poland—for instance, this caused her to under-estimate the importance of the national aspirations of the Ukrainians.

Was her solution of the Polish problem correct, after all, however? Has not history disproved her theories? She declared that Polish national independence under capitalist conditions was impossible, but an independent Poland was founded. Nevertheless, she was right; it was the idea of the restoration of Poland by revolutionary means which appeared to her impossible and fatal for the Polish working class. It was hardly possible for her to visualise what new territorial relations might spring from a war which brought about the political collapse of half Europe, and, in any case, she rejected such a solution on principle, and all the means to bring it about. She was right when she declared that the nationalist group in the Polish socialist movement would be demoralised by its political attitude. That was demonstrated in the Russian Revolution of 1905, and it revealed itself again in the reactionary dictatorship of Pilsudski and his " Colonels " after 1921. And she was also right when she declared that international revolutionary strategy must adopt no aim which would turn Poland into a bulwark of capitalist Europe against revolution in the East. She was " refuted " by history, much as were the Radical Democrats of 1848 when they strove for the establishment of a Greater-German Republic including Austria, and saw the establishment of Bismarck's semi-absolutist Greater-Prussian Germany, which held up historical progress in Central Europe for half a century and finally plunged the whole of Europe into war.

With her solution of the Polish national problem and of the national problem of the peoples oppressed by Turkey Rosa Luxemburg abandoned the postulates of Marx's foreign policy, but in doing so she proved herself a real pupil of Marx, for the capacity to act independently on the principles of the master distinguishes the creative pupils from the mere parrots, who solemnly continue to mumble the formulas of the master irrespective of whether the conditions which led him to them have fundamentally changed in the meantime or not. The creative pupil grasps the spirit of the master, always maintains his own critical faculties, and is capable of applying the fundamental principles of the master to changed conditions—i.e., the creative pupil is a master himself. The essential conditions in the case of Rosa Luxemburg were a stern rejection of mere hopes and wishes, an understanding of the objective historical process, and the guiding of the working class to contribute to its development in the same way as the physical scientist seeks to master Nature: by studying her laws and subordinating himself to them.

This first great political achievement of Rosa Luxemburg was all the more admirable because she hated Russian Absolutism wholeheartedly and was herself closely bound up with the culture and the fate of the Polish people. She was an internationalist in the best sense, but she never ceased to be a Polish patriot—once again in the best sense, and never in the sense of narrow-minded *petit-bourgeois* nationalism. Her revision of Marxist tactics in the Polish question was therefore the triumph of an incorruptible critical faculty over strong personal emotions.

6. THE FOUNDING OF POLISH SOCIAL DEMOCRACY

Rosa Luxemburg was well aware of her intellectual strength, and her letters at the beginning of the nineties reveal that great confidence which later on was to arouse and aggravate political enmities. However, the supreme confidence which caused unwillingness to make concessions in matters of principle was absolutely necessary for her in the violent disputes in which she was immediately involved after her first public appearance on the political field.

The unification of all Polish socialists in the Polish Socialist Party (P.P.S.) did not last long. In the autumn of 1892 an " Association of Polish Socialist Abroad " was formed in Paris by the old leaders of the party " Proletariat ", and they now adopted the slogan of Polish restoration, which they had formerly rejected. They did not succeed in persuading any considerable group in Poland itself to adopt their new views, and the contradiction in political outlook and in the tactical attitude it involved was so great that common membership of the same party quickly proved impossible.

Unfortunately the dispute was not settled by any objective discussion of the points at issue. Even after the differences had led to the complete organisational separation of the social-democratic group of Rosa Luxemburg from the social patriots, there was no thorough objective discussion. On the one hand the nationalists were not agreed amongst themselves, and their ideas were not based on logical thought, but almost exclusively on emotion. In the beginning they contented themselves with repeating the old arguments of Marx and Engels, but in the long run such mere repetitions proved to have little effect either on the advanced workers in Poland or on the International, and then, in their search for a more tenable theoretical position, some of them represented the restoration of Poland as a slogan to be realised by the socialist revolution. In this they approached a long way towards Rosa Luxemburg's own position, but the slogan completely lost its character as the central axis of the day-to-day struggle in Poland. Others declared that the weakness of the Russian working-class movement made any hope of winning political liberty under Russian rule illusory, and therefore Rosa Luxemburg's principle of an alliance with Russian Social Democracy was worthless: the Polish proletariat could become powerful only on a purely national basis. Others adopted completely confused theories and tactics, and almost all of them looked down with nationalist arrogance on the Russians and on the other oppressed peoples of Russia. With such very feeble arguments it was difficult to enter the arena against a trenchant fighter like Rosa Luxemburg.

The struggle against the young social-democratic group was therefore waged along the lines of intrigue, insinuations, and slander. It began with a fierce campaign against Kasprzak, the first mentor of Rosa Luxemburg. For years Kasprzak had wandered from one prison to the next, both German and Russian, and in consequence his health had been completely ruined, but this did not prevent his being publicly accused as an agent of the Ochrana [1] by the Galician leader

---

[1] Ochrana: the Russian Imperialist Secret Police.—Tr.

Dashinski and his followers. For two decades he was harried by this foul calumny, and the fact that he was declared innocent on a number of occasions by committees of investigation appointed by the International did not put an end to it until finally his absolute loyalty to the revolutionary socialist movement was placed beyond all doubt by his death on the gallows.

This method of fighting reached its culmination at the Zurich Congress of the International in 1893. The Association of Polish Socialist Abroad—i.e., a body composed exclusively of fugitives, emigrants, students, etc.—was represented by ten delegates, including Mendelssohn, Yanovska, Perl, and Dashinski—i.e., men who already had some reputation internationally and who were personally acquainted with the leaders of the International. The members of the social-democratic delegation all belonged to the new generation, they were almost unknown in international socialist circles, and Karski's mandate was rejected, although it was the only one put forward by the real organisation in Russian Poland. Rosa Luxemburg was a delegate from the *Sprava Robotnicza*, under the name of Kruszynska. Her opponents began to spread suspicion against her, and in particular against the editor of the *Sprava Robotnicza*, Varski (Michalkovski), and a disagreeable atmosphere of lies and intrigues was created.

When Rosa Luxemburg took the floor she showed no trace of self-consciousness at being in the presence of the illustrious heads of the international socialist movement. On the contrary, the unknown young woman defended her cause by launching a vigorous attack upon its opponents. With a wave of the hand she dismissed all the petty intriguing on the question of mandates, and went straight to the heart of the political differences, winning a signal moral success. Vandervelde has given us his impression of her first appearance :

" Rosa, 23 years old at the time, was quite unknown outside one or two socialist groups in Germany and Poland. . . . Her opponents had all they could do to hold their ground against her. I can see her now : how she rose from amongst the delegates and stood on a chair to make herself better heard. Small and looking very frail in a summer dress which cleverly concealed her physical defects, she represented her cause with such magnetism and such compelling words that she won the majority of the congress at once and they raised their hands in favour of the acceptance of her mandate."

The general impression Vandervelde gives here from memory after forty years is probably correct, but in one point he is wrong: it was not the members of the Congress who decided on her mandate, but a commission which afterwards rejected her mandate by nine votes to seven.

The intolerance of the old Polish leaders at the Congress, and in particular the cassation of Karski's mandate, caused the disruption of the Polish Socialist Party. The whole organisation in Poland broke away from the P.P.S. and founded the Social Democratic Party of the Kingdom of Poland—i.e., Congress Poland—which thereafter was under the leadership of Rosa Luxemburg and Leo Jogiches. However, this complete disavowal did not bring the leaders of the P.P.S. (which had now become a social patriotic party pure and simple) to reason. It only increased their blind fury, and at the London Congress they again tried to secure the cassation of their opponents' mandates, and by the same methods. In the meantime the accusations against Varski had been dismissed as groundless by a committee of investigation under the chairmanship of the old Russian revolutionary Peter Lavrov, but this did not prevent his enemies from raising them again, and at the same time a rumour was spread that Rosa Luxemburg was in special favour with the Warsaw Police Chief, Markgrafski. It was Dashinski who thundered against the leaders of the new party at the Congress:

"We cannot tolerate our movement being compromised by such knaves as Rosa Luxemburg, Urbach, and others. We are determined to fight against this scandal with all possible means. We are determined to unmask all those who are besmirching our movement with ink. We must clear the ranks of our international army from a band of publicistic brigands who are out to destroy our fight for liberty."

However, on this occasion not even such round abuse proved effective, and Rosa Luxemburg had the satisfaction of seeing a resolution put forward by the leaders of the P.P.S. on the restoration of Poland rejected by the Congress, and another resolution on self-determination adopted—a resolution which was so formulated that the Polish social democrats were able to accept it. But her enemies did not give up, and in 1900, at the Paris Congress of the International, a new attempt was made to secure her exclusion from the Congress, though this time the attempt was pitiful, because she held mandates from Posen and Upper Silesia, and a third mandate from the workers of Warsaw, to which 218 signatures were appended, including the signatures of twenty-seven political prisoners, and at the same time she had been entrusted by the Congress committee with the drawing up of the very important report on militarism.

Rosa Luxemburg's Polish policy was met by her opponents not with objective arguments, but with contemptible and utterly baseless accusations and innuendos, and with a spate of vulgar abuse. Touched on the raw, and only too conscious of their intellectual inferiority, her social-patriotic enemies could only howl that she was an " ambitious intriguer " and " a hysterical spinster ". And when she published a series of articles on the Oriental question, even Wilhelm Liebknecht attacked her fiercely with as much invective as her Polish enemies, and although he made no attempt to refute her arguments, he launched a scarcely veiled accusation against her of being a mercenary of the Russian Ochrana. Even her final martyrdom did not silence her enemies, and after her terrible death Dashinski could not refrain from referring to her as " that pedantic and quarrelsome person with her mechanistic interpretation of Marxism ". But abuse had no effect on her. In political argument she could be extraordinarily trenchant, and her irony was often biting, but she remained objective always. The mud thrown at her was so ineffective that she never bothered to answer it or defend herself in her writings. In that respect she obviously agreed with Goethe:

> " Wirbelwind und trocken Kot
> Lass sie drehen und stäuben! " [1]

Her feelings were sensitive enough towards her friends, but where enemies were concerned her only aim was to fight them to the best of her ability, and never to lower her point for an instant.

[1] Approximately: " Gusts of wind and dried up dung; let them swirl and bluster! "—TR.

She had sufficient troubles without bothering about personal abuse. The Polish working-class movement, at whose head she stood, developed quite favourably in the beginning, but it soon had to suffer all the usual inflictions which befall an illegal party. Arrests followed each other so rapidly, and were so numerous, that by 1896 only remnants of the organisation were left, and even the party organ *Sprava Robotnicza* had to stop publication. It was 1899 before a new phase of progress began, a phase in which young Djerjinski [1] showed great energy and organisational capacities. He succeeded in winning the support of Lithuanian Social Democracy for Rosa Luxemburg's ideas, and in amalgamating the two parties into the Social Democratic Party of Lithuania and the Kingdom of Poland.

Rosa Luxemburg made use of the difficult years in which the Polish movement was almost at a standstill to continue her studies and complete her doctoral dissertation on " The Industrial Development of Poland ". At the same time she was active in the Swiss working-class movement. In 1896–97 she lived for some time in France, where she was closely connected with Russian political fugitives, and in particular Peter Lavrov, and also with such prominent French socialist leaders as Jules Guesde, Allemane, and Vaillant, and she became particularly friendly with Vaillant, the old Communard, who had studied in Germany and who brought the French Blanquist movement into the Marxist camp.

Chapter Three: IN DEFENCE OF MARXISM

1. In the Ranks of German Social Democracy

Rosa Luxemburg's apprentice years were at an end. She had founded a party and given it a fixed course. She had overthrown obsolete Marxist traditions, and completed her own first scientific and theoretical work. She now felt an urge

[1] Felix Djerjinski, later a prominent leader of the Russian Revolution and head of the Tcheka.—Tr.

to take an active part in the political struggle, and the laborious minor tasks in the Polish movement (which was still in its infancy and hampered at every turn by illegality) no longer satisfied her. The Kingdom of Poland was too small a field of activities for her. She was drawn irresistibly to the centre of the international working-class movement—to Germany, where there was a lively interest in all questions of political theory and tactics. A formal marriage with Gustav Lübeck, the son of her old friend, gave her German nationality and protected her from the attentions of the German police, who were invariably willing and even anxious to do Tsarism a good service by persecuting such Russian revolutionary fugitives as sought sanctuary in Germany.

It was not long before she had won an acknowledged position in the front rank of German Social Democracy. The young woman from Poland conducted herself in the ranks of the illustrious greybeards of the party as though she had stood shoulder to shoulder with them throughout the difficult years of Bismarck's Anti-Socialist Laws, and it was very difficult for anyone to play a prominent rôle who had not shown his mettle in the testing years. She was already in touch, through her literary work, with Karl Kautsky, the Pope of Marxism, as he was called, but now she made his personal acquaintance and it developed into a long friendship. She was soon at home in the circle of August Bebel, Paul Singer, and Franz Mehring, and in Clara Zetkin she found a lifelong friend who loyally supported her in all situations. However, a certain amount of bad blood remained between her and Wilhelm Liebknecht almost up to the latter's death. Parvus, as editor of the *Sächsische Arbeiterzeitung* [1] in Dresden, opened the way for her into the daily press of the German party. Common intellectual interests and a similarity of temperament brought her into close touch with Bruno Schönlank, the founder of the *Leipziger Volkszeitung*, who had raised the social-democratic Press from the level of a mere party mouthpiece and given it real cultural value. Well read both economically and historically, vigorously active, and sensitive to all the phenomena of social life, Schönlank was a born journalist. Rosa Luxemburg, on the other hand, was theoretically better founded and had a surer hand in tactical matters; she saw

[1] The Saxon organ of the Social Democratic Party of Germany.—Tr.

beyond the events of the day to their relation with the whole
and with the general tendencies of development. Schönlank
was not slow to recognise her worth, and he sought to win
her for his paper.

With a lively temperament, a sharp tongue, and new ideas
which stirred up the dust of routine ages, Rosa Luxemburg
inspired mistrust rather than confidence in the " Fathers of
the Party ", but it was not long before they were compelled
to recognise that she was no mere shooting star crossing the
horizon in a shower of sparks, but a personality of real
moment, devoted to the cause of the working class with all
her heart and imbued with an earnest sense of responsibility.
Before long, too, her influence on most of the party leaders was
indisputable. In her co-operation with others she gave more
than she received, and she quickly earned recognition and
admiration. Bruno Schönlank was only voicing the general
opinion of all who came into close contact with her when he
declared that, young though she was, she showed an accuracy
of political judgement and a capacity to see through the tricks
and deceptions of the enemy usually only the result of long
years of political experience. This was all the more extraordinary because up to that time she had hardly ventured
beyond the circle of Russian and Polish political emigrants;
she was not familiar with the workings of a great party, with
all its internal struggles and disputes, and she was taking part
in practical politics for the first time. Her political acumen
was instinctive rather than acquired.

For the first time, too, she was able to speak to masses of
people. More than one local organiser pulled a long face
(to her secret amusement) when he fetched his speaker from
the railway station and found the frail little woman was the
expected guest. But her meetings were triumphs. Not that
she was an agitator in the usual sense. She avoided pathos,
and appealed to the reason of her audience rather than to
their feelings. But she roused them out of their usual little
circle of ideas, opened up wider horizons, and carried them
along with the fire of her delivery and the force of her personality. She returned from every speaking tour with new laurels
and triumphs, and she wrote delightedly to Leo Jogiches about
her successes. His reaction was disappointing; he feared to
lose her.

That was not the only bitter drop in the cup of her success. A few years later, after a disagreeable experience as a result of petty intrigues, she wrote to Bebel complaining that from the very beginning she had been given " a strange reception " in the German social-democratic camp—and not only by those who opposed her ideas. She attributed it to the fact that she was a foreigner, *pas de la maison*, but the real reason was probably even pettier: she, a woman, had dared to interfere in politics, an almost exclusively male affair. Not only that, but she had not contented herself with modestly asking the opinions of the " practical politicians ", who were years her senior, but had put forward her own ideas, and, what was worse, supported them with such brilliant arguments that the greybeards were forced to capitulate, and they bore her a grudge for it. It was not long before this pettiness of spirit was to bring about her first defeat, and she had to contend with it for the rest of her life.

In September 1898 Parvus and Marchlevski were expelled from Saxony, and they made their further co-operation in the production of the *Sächsische Arbeiterzeitung* conditional on Rosa Luxemburg's being given the editorship. She tightened the slack reins, introduced new departures, interested herself actively in the work of the various departments, and sought to give the paper a uniform policy. This caused resentment on the editorial staff, whose members were used to going their own way just as they pleased, and matters came to a head when she published a trenchant answer to a clumsy polemical article by Georg Gradnauer in the *Vorwärts*.[1] Gradnauer happened to be the Reichstag's deputy for Dresden, and therefore, of course, taboo in the organ of the Saxon party, and the affair was a convenient cloak for an inner-editorial rebellion. The local party leaders, who controlled the paper, intervened on the side of the staff, and sought to limit Rosa Luxemburg's editorial rights even to the point of forbidding her to reply under her own name to attacks made on her. It is recorded that they were astonished when she promptly resigned.

She then moved to Berlin, and contributed chiefly to the socialist theoretical organ *Die Neue Zeit* and to the *Leipziger Volkszeitung*, around which Bruno Schönlank had gathered a

[1] The central organ of the Social Democratic Party published in Berlin.—TR.

brilliant body of contributors. However, it was she who gave the paper its Marxist basis and enhanced its reputation amongst socialist newspapers.

2. THE ADVANCE OF REFORMISM

When Rosa Luxemburg first began to work in the Polish working-class movement, international Socialism was experiencing a new phase of activity, and this had impelled her to make her first independent inquiries. At the same time a change was taking place in the structure and policy of the big capitalist States and the characteristic features of this change were already clearly visible towards the end of the nineties. Later on, in the *Juniusbroschüre*, Rosa Luxemburg described the situation as follows:

" The flourishing period which began for capitalism in a newly-constructed Europe after the wars of the sixties and seventies (and in particular the period following the long depression which set in after the fever of the founder years had abated, and after the great crash of 1873, and rose to an unexampled height in the prosperity of the nineties) opened up a new and vigorous phase for the capitalist States of Europe : a phase of highly competitive expansion to non-capitalist countries and zones throughout the world. Since the eighties a new and particularly forceful movement towards colonial conquest was making itself felt. Great Britain obtained control of Egypt and created herself a new powerful empire in South Africa. France seized Tunis in North Africa and Tonkin in the Far East. Italy sought a foothold in Abyssinia. Russia concluded her conquests in Central Asia and pressed forward into Manchuria. Germany obtained her first colonial possessions in Africa and in the South Seas. And finally the U.S.A. entered the ring and acquired ' interests ' in Eastern Asia by her seizure of the Philippine Islands. This period of African and Asiatic dismemberment ushered in a ceaseless chain of bloody wars, beginning with the Sino-Japanese War of 1895, culminating in joint imperialist action against China, and ending with the Russo-Japanese War in 1904.

" These rapidly moving events created a great variety of

new imperialist antagonisms outside Europe: between Italy and France in North Africa, between France and Great Britain in Egypt, between Great Britain and Russia in Central Asia, between Russia and Japan in Eastern Asia, between Japan and Great Britain in China, and between Japan and the U.S.A. in the Pacific. It was a troubled sea of antagonisms, temporary alliances, sudden tensions and subsequent reliefs. And every few years the storm threatened to break in war between the European Powers, but the danger was circumvented again and again. . . . "

And she pointed out that the tremendous development of commerce and industry in Germany had produced the strongest industrial cartellisation and the biggest banking concentration in the world. The two (developed into finance capital) canalised all their tremendous and ruthless energies into imperialism. She prophesied that this young, powerful, and reckless movement would bring about tremendous international upheavals.

The phenomena described by Rosa Luxemburg, the naval armament race, the Spanish-American War, the Boer War, and the joint action of the European Powers against China demanded a review of the whole social and political situation, and they were examined and their underlying forces analysed with very considerable accuracy in the works of Kautsky, the investigations of Parvus, the political writings of Wilhelm Liebknecht, and in numerous speeches of Clara Zetkin, all of which proclaimed that the capitalist world had entered into a new period of foreign and domestic catastrophes, and that a world war was approaching.

There were others, however, who were unwilling to see the approaching storm-clouds. They basked in the sun that was still shining, and painted an idyllic picture of future social development. According to them, capitalism had left its brutal youthful escapades behind it; it had become tame and reasonable in its maturity. For over two decades no big crisis had taken place: there had been no more than minor disturbances and rumblings, instead of the regular ten-year crises which Marx had prophesied would shake society to its foundations. A growing period of prosperity was in full swing.

Since 1870–71 no wars had taken place in Europe, except in
the Balkans. The working-class movement was no longer
persecuted, and the young Kaiser Wilhelm II had promised
his people a social monarchy of labour legislation and labour
protection. Democracy was making progress everywhere, and
German Social Democracy was winning increasing successes
at the polls. The trade unions were growing in strength, and
wages were rising. Workers' co-operative societies were
developing rapidly as " socialist oases in the capitalist desert ".
All these phenomena combined to produce a new tendency
inside the working-class movement: reformism developed
into a conscious theoretical conception.

In the German working-class movement, as everywhere
else in the capitalist world, radical and reformist views
existed side by side, but German Social Democracy was
different in many respects from working-class organisations
in other parts of the world. It originated a decade and a
half after the semi-revolution of 1848, and it was therefore
without any revolutionary experience. Its whole activity
was directed to obtaining those *bourgeois* reforms which had
been abandoned by the *bourgeois* opposition, and this fact
determined its real character even more than its formal avowal
of Socialism. At the same time, however, it had to work in
a semi-absolutist State which was merely cloaked with
democratic forms and still considered the working-class
movement something to be dealt with by energetic police
action. Naturally, Social Democracy was in irreconcilable
antagonism to this State, but its enmity was directed
more against feudal Junkerdom than against the modern
capitalist *bourgeoisie*. And, finally, numerous radical-
bourgeois elements streamed into the social-democratic
ranks because the ordinary *bourgeois* parties offered them
no scope for their democratic activities, and inside the
Social Democratic Party they naturally strengthened the
reformist wing. This contradictory situation was responsible
for the character of the party: although it was radical enough
in its political activities, it was essentially reformist in principle.
Its outward radicalism became more decided than ever.
The Anti-Socialist Laws of Bismarck intensified the antagonism
between the party and the semi-feudalist State, and Marxist
notions became popular as far as the general situation

allowed, i.e., they became popular without any grasp of their revolutionary implications. As there was no possibility of any understanding with the police State of Prussian Junkerdom, Social Democracy preserved the character of a radical opposition party. It watched zealously to ensure that it was not compromised by any acceptance of reformist principles, and when the once-radical Vollmar broke a lance in favour of reformism in 1891, his sally was repulsed without difficulty.

In 1895 Friedrich Engels died, the man who had been the lifelong friend and collaborator of Marx, and after Marx's death the adviser of international Socialism and the jealous guardian of Marxist ideas. His death removed a great obstacle to the advance of opportunism in the working-class movement, and it was not long before " the mature and enlightened Engels " was being quoted as the chief witness in favour of reformism. His last work was an introduction to Marx's book on the French Revolution of 1848, " Class Struggles in France ", and it represents one of the most important documents of Marxist strategy. " The General ", as Engels was nicknamed, on account of his wide military knowledge, pointed out in this introduction that the old revolutionary barricade tactics based on a defensive strategy of attrition had been rendered inoperable by the development of military technique and modern town-planning, and that future insurrections would have to take on a very different character, and be carried out by masses of the people in a powerful offensive against the military forces of the enemy. This would demand more elaborate preparations and a far more thorough organisation of the working class than had, up to then, been achieved. As long as these preliminary preparations had not been carried out, any toying with the idea of insurrection must be condemned. For a long time international Social Democracy would have to confine itself to utilising all its legal possibilities; it should follow the example of German Social Democracy, which had made the franchise into an instrument of emancipation.

The Central Committee of the German Social Democratic Party feared that, as it stood, the revolutionary trenchancy of this document might offer the reaction in Germany an excuse for further repressive measures (a Bill against " revolutionary machinations " was before the Reichstag at the time), and it therefore cut out all reference to the possibility of future armed struggles. At first Engels protested against this emasculation of his introduction, but then he submitted to the tactical considerations of the moment with a good grace, and the result was that his bowdlerised introduction went into history as " the testament of Friedrich Engels ", a condemnation, as it seemed, of all forms of violence and of all future revolutionary movements, and a glorification of legality, under whose beneficent sway working-class parties would grow strong and vigorous. It was not until 1924 that Riazanov brought Engels' own manuscript to light and published the original text.

Books have their own history, and they make history. Engels' " Testament " in the form in which it was published by the German Social Democratic Party quite plainly demanded a revision of the Marxist conception of history, and as the leaders of the party obstinately remained silent about their bowdlerisation of the original text, the " Introduction " became a powerful weapon in the hands of the reformists. Even the radicals were given pause. Kautsky knew from Engels that something was wrong with the text, but he did not know what. Even Parvus adopted the " Testament ", with its condemnation of all forms of violence, as the basis for his attempts to radicalise the policy of the German Social Democratic Party. Rosa Luxemburg was alone in her refusal to accept the conclusions of the " Testament ", and she steadfastly refused to regard it as representing Engels' real opinions.

A member of Engels' immediate circle, Eduard Bernstein, was instrumental in carrying out the " Revision of Marxism ". He was the editor of the *Sozialdemokrat*, which was founded in Zurich during the Bismarck persecutions and then transferred to London, from whence copies were smuggled into Germany. Under Engels' influence he had developed from an ethical *petit-bourgeois* socialist into a radical socialist. However, he had been greatly impressed by conditions prevailing in England; by the existence of liberal democracy; by the policy of economic co-operation pursued by the powerful British trade unions; and by the social-reformist ideas of the Fabians. A study of the French Revolution of 1848 shocked his fundamentally *petit-bourgeois* instincts, and he recognised with horror that the policy of the Radical Clubs (Auguste Blanqui) was identical in essential points with that of Marx. From 1896 to 1898 he wrote a series of articles in *Die Neue Zeit* on " The Problems of Socialism ", attacking the fundamental principles of Marxism more and more openly. At first the import of his articles was not realised, and no opposition arose until Hyndman's friend, Belfort Bax, counter-attacked, declaring: " Bernstein has completely abandoned the final aim of the socialist movement in favour of the ideas of present-day *bourgeois* Liberalism and Radicalism." Similar opinions began to be voiced in Germany, but Bernstein was still defended by Wilhelm Liebknecht, Karl Kautsky, and Bruno Schönlank. However, when he came out into the open with the now famous words: " The final aim of Socialism, whatever it may be, does not matter to me; it is the movement itself which matters ", Parvus took up the cudgels in the *Sächsische Arbeiterzeitung*, and the great Bernstein discussion opened. It was just at this time that Rosa Luxemburg began her activity in the German party.

The Bernstein discussion led to the longest and most difficult crisis in the history of pre-war international Social Democracy. Marxist theoreticians and practical socialist politicians in all countries entered the lists: Parvus, Kautsky, Mehring, Bebel, and Clara Zetkin in Germany; Plechanov in Russia (who defended the theory of historical materialism on the philosophic field); Antonio Labriola in Italy; and Jules Guesde and even Jean Jaurès in France. The lively temperament of Jaurès, nourished by the traditions of the Great French Revolution, caused him to reject the plodding and pedantic ideas of Bernstein, although fundamentally they were closely related to his own.

3. DEVELOPMENT OF AN IDEOLOGY

Rosa Luxemburg was in the forefront of this intellectual strife. Though she was the youngest of all, she outdid all the others in *élan*, in the depth of her ideas, and in her polemical brilliance. Almost instantaneously she became a leading figure in the international working-class movement, and she even put Kautsky into the shade, though since the death of Engels he had been regarded as the leading exponent of

Marxist theory. Even those who suffered signal defeat at her hands were compelled to express their admiration. Poor Schippel came in for a terrible drubbing in economic and military questions, and was compelled to beat a retreat in utter confusion, but he was big enough to praise his vanquisher for her " lively polemical abilities, her unimpeachable convictions, and her stimulating dialectics ", and to declare that he observed " the rapidity with which she developed her ideas to their logical conclusion with admiration and astonishment ". It is indeed true that her great strength lay in the fact that she thought out all the problems of the day to their logical end and was never afraid to accept the final consequences. The trump card she played out again and again was that facts have their own logic, even if individuals lack it; and she regarded it as her main task to lay bare the logic of facts rather than to develop any formal system of political logic.

Her method in all theoretical and political discussions was typical: she never proceeded from formal premises for which she then sought proofs, and she seldom appealed to the patristic authorities of Socialism, for it was in contradiction to her whole intellectual character to develop her ideas dogmatically from strings of quotations. Her highest aim was to lay bare the tendencies of development from the facts of social life, and to use the resources of the working-class movement to the greatest possible effect in conjunction with this process.

At the same time she was a decided opponent of all empiricism, both in political ideas and political action. Her policy and, as far as she could make it so, the policy of her party were based on objective scientific thought. Her instrument was the Marxist method of investigation. Like Marx, she regarded history as a process in which class-forces struggled with each other for their own interests as they developed out of objectively given economic conditions. For her Marxism was not a theoretical system solving all questions once and for all, but a method of examining the process of economic change at each new stage of its development, with all its effects on the interests, ideas, aims, and political activities of each group in society. Marxism was a weapon enabling her to maintain intellectual mastery of the social process as

a whole, and to make suitable political decisions for
situation that arose. In her opinion the moral and
attitude of the working class in each individual situation
depended largely on this total process. She was firmly convinced that Marxism proved beyond all cavil the inevitability
and the historical necessity of Socialism, and that it was possible
to speak of scientific Socialism precisely because Marx had
demonstrated the inevitability of the collapse of capitalism
as the result of natural social laws.

Certain critics of Rosa Luxemburg have sought to convict
her of objectivism in this connection, of a conception of
historical development in which objective forces must act
with fatalistic accuracy to certain predestined ends, leaving
no room for the human will or the will of social classes to
operate. This accusation is totally false. On the contrary,
in this respect she was far in advance of the routine Marxist
conceptions prevalent in her day. Slavish pupils of Marx
and Engels had raised " economic conditions " into an almost
mystical and supernatural power, which ploughed its mechanical way onward irrespective of human will-power or human
destinies, and they quite forgot that economic conditions are
nothing but the result of the relations into which men enter
in the process of production, and that they are therefore the
result of human activities and human struggles. They interpreted Marx's ideas mechanically: " Men make their own
history, but they do not make it completely of their own free
will and not under conditions chosen by themselves, but
under pre-established conditions which have come down to
them from the past." [1] Rosa Luxemburg preferred to
paraphrase the idea:

" Men do not make history of their own free will, but
they do make their own history. The proletariat is dependent in its action on the given degree of maturity in
social development existing at the time, but social development does not proceed independent of and apart from
the proletariat, and the proletariat is as much its cause
and mainspring as it is its product and consequence. The
action of the proletariat is a determining factor in history.

[1] Karl Marx, " The Eighteenth Brumaire of Louis Bonaparte ", Martin
Lawrence, Ltd., London 1935.

C

And although we can no more jump over the stages of historical development than a man can jump over his own shadow, still, we can accelerate or retard that development. . . . The victory of the socialist proletariat will be the result of iron historical laws, and it will depend on a thousand steps in a previous, laborious and all-too-slow development. However, it will never be fulfilled unless the material conditions brought together slowly by the historical process are vitalised with the life-giving spark of conscious will-power generated in the great masses of the people." [1]

Marx formulated his passage against the excessive systematisers in politics, whilst Rosa Luxemburg formulated hers in order to stress once again the fact that men do make their own history, and thereby to oppose the indolent, complacent, and baseless optimism which relied on mechanical development to bring victory, and also in order to remind the working class and its party of their responsibilities before history for their own fate. Her motto was: in the beginning was the deed! And the deed must be performed with the fullest possible knowledge of the historical process. In writing of Marx in the following lines, she was incidentally sketching her own ideas, her own vital principle, and her own character:

" Just as in Marx himself the keen historical analyst was indissolubly bound up with the daring revolutionary, the man of action with the man of ideas, supporting and complementing each other, so for the first time in the history of the modern working-class movement Marxism allied theoretical knowledge with the revolutionary *élan* of the proletariat, the one illuminated and fructified the other. Both aspects belong equally to the inner core of Marxism; if they are separated Marxism becomes a pitiful caricature of itself." [2]

She was completely free of that blatant, arrogant vulgarisation of Marxism which impudently pretends to interpret the richly varied social life of a people from a column of economic statistics, and draws the wildest conclusions from it con-

cerning future social development. She was well aware
that "apart from purely economic factors, political and
historical factors have such a great influence on the rate of
bourgeois development that they must falsify any mechanically
worked-out theories about the duration of the capitalist order
of society ".[1]

She displayed an almost visionary ability to grasp as a
whole the great historical process, in which technique, the
organisation of production and distribution, historical tradition, scientific achievement, juridical conceptions and laws,
and scores of other factors interact to accelerate or retard the
cyclopean battle of the classes, but in which, in the long run,
economic factors are the determining force shaping the
organisation of society. From her wider standpoint she was
never prepared to accept the surface phenomena of every-
day social life uncritically, and she always investigated below
the surface, seeking the motive power of development, and
often arriving at conclusions which seemed nothing but wild
speculations to her contemporaries, but which were afterwards brilliantly justified by history.

4. REFORM AND REVOLUTION

This method of looking at history is demonstrated with
particular clarity in her book " Social Reform or Revolution ".[2] It appeared in two series of articles in the *Leipziger
Volkszeitung*, the first in September 1898 as an answer to
Bernstein's articles in *Die Neue Zeit*, and the second in April
1899 in answer to his book " The Pre-Conditions of Socialism
and the Tasks of Social Democracy ".[3]

The Bernstein discussion revolved around the fundamental
character of the socialist working-class movement. Disputes
on the point have existed since the very beginning of the movement, and finally they ended in its disruption into two parts.
Bernstein's book culminated in the advice to Social Democracy
to summon up sufficient courage " to emancipate itself from
outworn phraseology, and to come out in its true colours as a

[1] Rosa Luxemburg, " Collected Works " (German), Vol. III., p. 269.
[2] Rosa Luxemburg, " *Sozialreform oder Revolution* " (" Social Reform or
Revolution "), Leipzig, 1900, 2nd ed. 1908.
[3] Eduard Bernstein, " *Die Voraussetzungen des Sozialismus und die Aufgaben
der Sozialdemokratie*", Stuttgart, 1899.

democratic socialist reform party ". That raised the question : reform or revolution? Or rather, the question of the exact relation between the two. That was the theme of the little book with which Rosa Luxemburg entered the arena of German socialist polemics, and it was the theme of all her important writings for half a decade of intellectual struggle. The Reformists praised their policy of achieving more and more reforms by legal means as good practical politics, and as the slow but certain method of leading society to the goal of Socialism. They regarded revolution as a policy which, although it might have had some justification under absolutist rule, was now, under democratic rule, exclusively the obsession of dangerous fanatics. Rosa Luxemburg rejected both extreme positions, and declared herself for both reform and revolution. Her analysis of this fundamental problem of the working-class movement brilliantly demonstrates her dialectical and polemical abilities :

" Legal reform and revolution are not different methods of obtaining social progress, like hot and cold dishes at the buffet of history to be chosen according to taste; they are different factors in the development of class society, factors which condition and supplement each other, but at the same time are antithetic to each other, like the North Pole and the South Pole, or like the *bourgeoisie* and the proletariat.

" Further, the existing social constitution is nothing but the product of revolution. Revolution is the political act of creation in class society, whilst subsequent constitutional legislation is the monotonous political continuation of that creation. The work for legal reform has no motive power in itself and independent of revolution. In every phase of history it develops along the lines laid down by the previous revolution, and it does so only as long as the impetus lent to it by that revolution is still operative, or, to put it more practically, it can develop only within the framework of the social form created by the last revolution. That is the core of the whole question.

" It is fundamentally false and completely unhistorical to regard the work for legal reform as nothing but the revolution spread out over a longer period of time, or to regard the revolution as reform concentrated into a short period of time. Social revolution and legal reform are different not only in point of time; they are fundamentally different factors. The whole secret of historical revolutions brought about by the use of political power lies precisely in the transition from merely quantitative changes to qualitative changes, or, to put it more concretely, in the transition from one phase of history, from one social order, to the next.

" Therefore whoever choses the path of legal reform as a substitute for, and in contradiction to, the conquest of political power is not choosing a more peaceful and slower path to the same aim, but is choosing a different aim altogether. . . .

" Democracy is indispensable, not because it renders the conquest of political power by the proletariat superfluous, but, on the contrary, because it makes this seizure of power both necessary and inevitable. When Engels revised the tactics of the working-class movement in his introduction to Marx's ' Class Struggles in France ', and put forward the legal struggle against the barricade struggle, he was not, as every word of it demonstrates abundantly, dealing with the question of the final conquest of political power, but with the contemporary daily struggle, not with the attitude of the proletariat towards the capitalist State at the moment of its seizure of power, but with its attitude within the framework of the capitalist State. In other words, Engels was giving guidance to the oppressed proletariat and not to the victorious proletariat. . . .

" The necessity of the seizure of power by the proletariat was never at any time in doubt in the mind of either Marx or Engels, and it was Bernstein's privilege to proclaim *bourgeois* parliamentarism the organ predestined to accomplish the greatest of all world revolutions: the guidance of human society from capitalist into socialist forms." [1]

Rosa Luxemburg was thus by no means an opponent of reforms. She regarded the struggle for reforms (for the improvement of living standards, for labour protection, and for the extension of democratic rights within the framework of the *bourgeois* State, etc.) as a means of preparing the working

[1] Rosa Luxemburg, " Collected Works " (German), Vol. III., pp. 85–90.

class for its coming revolutionary tasks, as a means of training and organising it, and of showing it in practical experience that the capitalist State must be overthrown if the proletariat is ever to be freed from the shackles of wage slavery:

> " Only in the broad current of contemporary political life, in the daily struggle with the contemporary State, and adapting itself to the variety of situations which arise in life, can the proletariat be guided in a social-democratic direction. In fact, everyday life will urge it in this direction with compelling force." [1]

However, she did not believe that the working class would necessarily and under all circumstances become socialist as a result of its daily struggle for reforms. She was in complete agreement with the attitude taken up by Lenin at that time against " Economism " in Russia, against the idea of " spontaneity "—i.e., of a direct and instinctive struggle on the part of the workers against the effects of capitalism, a struggle uninfluenced by social theories. She condemned the policy of the trade unions in Great Britain, not only because it lacked any conscious and logical striving for Socialism, but because in her opinion it led away from the real aim of the working class to *petit-bourgeois* aimlessness. And this was her attitude to reformism in general—i.e., to the attempt to make revolution unnecessary by an endless chain of reforms. The struggle of the trade unions for improved conditions of life, and the parliamentary struggle for social reform and democratic liberties, received a fundamental and socialist character only if their final aim was Socialism.

As early as 1893, in her report to the Zurich Congress of the International, she gave a theoretical basis to the relation between the daily struggle of the working class and its final aim, and at the same time she defended the necessity of daily activity for minor aims against the Blanquist elements in the Polish socialist movement. She then formulated her old ideas still more definitely, and set up the strategic thesis that the proletarian daily struggle must be organically connected with its final aim. Even the minor questions of the day must be so dealt with that their solution lead the working class onwards,

[1] Rosa Luxemburg, *ibid.*, p. 281.

if ever so slightly, to its final aim, and never away from that
aim.

> " And by final aim I do not mean this or that conception
> of some future State, but that which must necessarily pre-
> cede the establishment of any future socialist society, i.e.,
> the conquest of political power by the proletariat." [1]

. Rosa Luxemburg put forward this fundamental thesis again
and again, and it became the controlling principle of her own
tactical decisions.   It was a sure shield against any temptation
to pursue momentary advantages which might result in the last
resort in a strengthening of the enemy, which might sacrifice
the interests of the working class as a whole to the interests of
individual working-class groups, or which might lead to an
alliance with national capital at the expense of international
working-class solidarity, and which, under such circumstances, must emasculate the party intellectually and rob it of
its revolutionary socialist character.   This strategic principle
has been confirmed again and again by the course of events.
It is the unfailing, the acid test of revolutionary as distinct
from reformist politics.

The question of reform or revolution must have appeared as
a purely theoretical and academic one at the end of the
nineties, for there was not the faintest prospect of revolution
in Western Europe, but Rosa Luxemburg's analysis of the
relation between reform and revolution led to one practical
conclusion which has proved of decisive importance for the
content and character of the proletarian daily struggle: it
saved it from the confusion of empirical trials and experiments,
and gave it a direction and an aim.

5. Capitalism Tamed?

Bernstein had attacked Marxism as a whole, and, in particular, he had declared that the idea of the inevitable collapse
of capitalism had been refuted by experience.   Capitalism
had proved itself very adaptable, and the recurrent economic
crises had already been reduced to minor vacillations in the
general trend of prosperity.   The anarchic nature of the

[1] Rosa Luxemburg, *ibid.*, p. 127.

capitalist mode of production was being overcome progressively by the credit system, the industrial cartels, and trusts. The introduction of the limited liability share was bringing about a more democratic distribution of capital ownership, as exemplified in particular in the small share system prevalent in Great Britain.

One of Bernstein's followers, Konrad Schmidt, himself a prominent socialist economist, finally crowned Bernstein's theories with the contention that, owing to the activity of the trade unions and to various social reforms, the owners of capital were being reduced more and more to the standing of mere administrators: in the end the capitalists would be so reduced in power by this process that the management of the factories, etc., could be taken out of their hands altogether.

Such opinions collided full on with the convictions of Rosa Luxemburg. If the inherent contradictions of the capitalist system were not intensifying, as Marxists believed, and capitalism was in reality " progressively adapting itself to its own conditions of existence ", then Socialism ceased to be objectively necessary. Further, it could no longer be supported by scientific arguments, but only by ethical appeals, and the working class would no longer have that vital interest which Marxists contend it has in the overthrow of the capitalist social order. In short, Socialism would revert to what it was before Marx developed his ideas—Utopianism.

In her investigations Rosa Luxemburg found that Bernstein judged all economic phenomena from the standpoint of what is known as vulgar political economy—i.e., from the standpoint of the individual capitalist. It was quite true that credit might under certain circumstances assist the individual capitalist to overcome pressing difficulties, but the general effects of the credit system for capitalism as a whole were different. Capitalist economic crises developed from the contradiction between production's permanent tendency to extend and the limited consumption capacity of the capitalist market. Credit had the effect of still further extending production, and it was therefore a factor ceaselessly urging production beyond the limits of the capitalist market. However, at the first sign of crisis, credit immediately took fright, and proved itself ineffective and useless when it was most needed: it called in its commitments, and thus intensified the crisis.

Far from assisting in the adaptation of capitalism, it intensified the internal contradiction of capitalism by furthering the concentration of capital in the form of joint-stock companies and commercial credit, weakening the vitality of the smaller undertakings in the competitive struggle, thus helping to destroy them, separating production from property, and merely stressing still further the contradiction between the social character of production and the capitalist nature of private property:

> " The first step of capitalism to adapt itself to its conditions of existence ought to be the abolition of credit therefore. As credit exists to-day in the capitalist system it is not a means of adaptation, but a means of destruction, and its effect is highly revolutionary."

With regard to cartels and trusts, Rosa Luxemburg admitted that their nature had been insufficiently examined, and it was only towards the end of last century that they began to make their triumphant way in industry. However, one thing was already quite clear—namely that if they were to bring about any diminution of capitalist anarchy they would have to become the general capitalist productive form. As it was, their function consisted in forcing up the rate of profit in one branch of industry at the expense of others by limiting competition, and even in this they were successful only on the domestic market, whereas on the world market competition and anarchy were being intensified. In addition, cartels and trusts brought about an increase in the rate of their profits only by a desperate expedient—namely, by letting a part of the accumulated capital lie fallow, a phenomenon usually restricted to times of economic crisis. As Rosa Luxemburg pointed out, " such a cure closely resembles the disease ". Her whole argument culminated in an idea which she dealt with later in greater detail in her chief work, " The Accumulation of Capital ":

> " If the capitalist market begins to shrink as the result of the utmost development and exhaustion of the world market by the competing capitalist countries (and it obviously cannot be denied that such a situation must arise sooner or later), then the artificial and partial withdrawal of capital

C 2

from use must naturally take on such an extent that the cure develops into the disease itself, and the capital already highly-socialised in this fashion reverts to a private capitalist character. The cartels and trusts intensify the contradiction between the international character of the capitalist economic system and the national character of the capitalist State because they are accompanied by general tariff warfare which necessarily intensifies the antagonisms existing between individual capitalist States." [1]

She then analysed the history of economic crises, and came to the conclusion that all the economic crises which had taken place up to 1873 were the effects of sudden extensions of production and of the world market, and that they did not represent the type of economic crisis Marx had in mind when elaborating his theories:

" As a whole this formula fits rather to a fully developed capitalist economic system in which the world market is presupposed as something already existing. Only under such circumstances can crises develop recurrently as a result of the inner movement of the process of production and distribution in the mechanical fashion laid down by Marx, and without the necessity of any outward cause such as a sudden upheaval in productive and market relations. When we examine the economic situation as it exists to-day, we are compelled to admit that we are not yet in that phase of full capitalist maturity which is postulated in the Marxist theory of periodically recurring crises. The world market is still being developed. . . . Although therefore we have on the one hand the sudden and rapid opening up of new areas to the capitalist economic system, such as took place periodically up to the seventies and resulted in the previously experienced crises (crises of growth, so to speak), we have not yet reached that stage of development and exhaustion of the world market which would automatically produce periodical and inevitable collisions between the productive forces and the limits of the capitalist market—i.e., crises no longer of growth but to decline. . . .

" However, it follows logically from the same conditions

[1] Rosa Luxemburg, *ibid.*, pp. 45–46.

which caused a temporary absence (1873–1900) of the crises that we are now steadily and inevitably approaching the beginning of the end for capitalism, the beginning of the period of capitalism's final crises. When once the world market is more or less fully developed and can no longer be suddenly extended and enlarged, and assuming that the productivity of labour-power continues to increase, then sooner or later the periodic collisions between productive forces and market barriers must set in, and they will then become more and more violent by virtue of their ceaseless repetition. Now if there is one factor above all others which is calculated to bring us into this phase more rapidly, to develop the world market more quickly, and to exhaust it equally quickly, then it is precisely the phenomenon to which Bernstein looks to bring about an ' adaptation ' of capitalism—namely, the credit system and the cartels and trusts." [1]

Those words were written in 1898. Two years later a crisis broke out whose effects were particularly severe in precisely those industries in which the credit system and the cartels were most highly developed. Bernstein was refuted. But it was thirty years later before the first of those terrible " crises of decline " occurred and led to the breaking up of the world market, permanent national tariff warfare, general efforts towards economic " self-sufficiency ", and the feverish armament race towards a further redistribution of world markets and raw-material resources. Another brilliant prophecy of Rosa Luxemburg had been justified in the event.

6. The Labour of Sisyphus

With the refutation of Bernstein's " adaptation " theory, all hope was destroyed of any steady decline of class antagonisms, but in the meantime events have confuted any such ideas so thoroughly and so conclusively that it is no longer necessary to deal in any detail with the arguments of Rosa Luxemburg against Bernstein and his followers on this point. Their hope that capitalist exploitation would be progressively overcome in the trade-union struggle seemed to have a rather better basis.

[1] Rosa Luxemburg, *ibid.*, pp. 48–49.

All over the world, and particularly in Germany, the nineties saw a great strengthening of the trade-union movement. In one wave of big strikes after the other the German workers made up for the time lost in the period of Bismarck's Anti-Socialist Laws, when there were no legal possibilities of resistance. In these struggles the German trade unions (better suited to the needs of the workers than were the English unions) became a real social power. Parvus, a theoretician much despised by the " practical politicians ", had stressed the great importance of the trade unions for the socialist class war, and raised his voice warningly against the under-estimation of their value by certain party leaders. There is no doubt that Rosa Luxemburg was in complete agreement with Parvus, who was then one of her closest collaborators, but at the same time it was necessary to oppose certain illusions which were developing in connection with the rapid progress of the unions. In his book Bernstein had declared that the struggle between the rate of profit and the rate of wages would result in the rate of profit being progressively depressed until in the end no surplus value would remain, and capitalist exploitation would cease, and it was therefore necessary to show clearly the limits of trade-union possibilities.

Rosa Luxemburg pointed out that the trade unions were essentially defensive organisations of the working class against capitalist exploitation, and not weapons of offence. They fought against the tendency to progressive pauperisation always present under capitalism, if not always able to make its full effects felt. They were instruments for giving free vent to the capitalist law of wages—i.e., the sale of labour-power at its prevailing market price—rather than instruments for the abrogation of that law. The workers should not let themselves be deceived by temporary successes:

" If long stretches of social development are reviewed, it becomes impossible to close our eyes to the fact that on the whole we are approaching times of increasing difficulty for the trade-union movement rather than times of triumph. When the development of industry has reached its culminating point the period of decline will set in, and then the trade-union struggle will become doubly difficult: first of all, the objective market conditions for the sale of labour-power will deteriorate as a result of the fact that demand will slow down whilst supply will increase more rapidly than is the case at the moment, and secondly, in an effort to recoup itself in part at least for its losses on the world market, capital will encroach more and more ruthlessly on that part of the product which should fall to the share of labour-power, because, after all, the reduction of wages is one of the most important ways of retarding a fall in the rate of profit." [1]

As a matter of fact, the difficulties Rosa Luxemburg prophesied arose long before the period of economic decline set in. Even before the World War the advance of the trade unions in the most important branches of industry (the heavy industries, shipyards, etc.) was held up by trustification and by the formation of powerful employers' associations, and only the sustained demand for qualified labour-power in that period of vigorous industrial progress prevented a rapid decrease in wages. However, she was not content merely to point out the general tendency of development, and her analytical abilities caused her to define the limits of the trade-union struggle:

" Thanks to objective processes at work in capitalist society the trade-union struggle develops into a labour of Sisyphus. However, this labour is indispensable if the worker is to obtain the wage rate due to him in each phase of the labour market; if the capitalist law of wages is to operate freely; and if the depressive tendency of economic development is to be countered, or rather ameliorated. However, to regard the trade unions as an instrument for diminishing profits gradually in the interests of wages means to presuppose first of all the suspension of the proletarisation of the middle classes and of the growth of the working class, and secondly a suspension of the growth in the productivity of labour-power, i.e., in both cases a reversion to conditions existing prior to the advent of large-scale capital."

The labour of Sisyphus! The expression caused a burst of indignation from the trade-union leaders. They did not examine her meaning or follow her arguments (which would

[1] Rosa Luxemburg, *ibid.*, p. 53.

have demanded some knowledge of Marxist theories), and they assumed that the expression meant that all trade-union effort was utterly useless. They were quite unable to appreciate that she was rating the trade unions very highly when she gave them the task of protecting working-class standards against the immanent tendency of the capitalist social order to depress them progressively, the task of erecting a barrier against a complete slide into the abyss. For them Rosa Luxemburg was now " an enemy of the trade unions ".

According to the trade-union leaders and other reformists, the trade unions were gradually to obtain power in the factories. Taking over the management of affairs, first of all in co-operation with the employers, and later on alone. In this way they would prepare the way for Socialism. These ideas were put to the practical test after the World War in the policy of class collaboration, industrial democracy so called, and industrial truce, and they suffered complete eclipse. Rosa Luxemburg knew that they would, and she prophesied it. In her opinion the struggle for power in the factories was possible at all only in the epoch of immediate revolution, and as part of the general working-class struggle for power.

For her the trade unions were economic organisations of the working class for the struggle with the employers to secure the unhindered operation of the capitalist law of wages. Beyond that their rôle was to school the workers for their tasks in the final struggle.

CHAPTER FOUR: THE PROBLEM OF POLITICAL POWER

1. THE LIMITATIONS OF PARLIAMENTARISM

THE HOPES of the reformists that the trade unions would be able to take over the management of industry stage by stage gradually dwindled, but another hope remained, and it was their strongest card: Democracy and parliamentarism. Democracy was on the march everywhere; it had become the very law of modern history; Junkerdom and Absolutism were being compelled to retreat step by step before it; and the workers of all capitalist countries were utilising parliament more and more successfully. The path for fundamental socialist reforms would lie open once Social Democracy obtained a parliamentary majority and could command the legislative machinery. So ran the argument, and Progress and Democracy became almost supernatural powers; the ballot-paper was invested with a mystical force against which the bayonets of Absolutism would shiver and the power of capital collapse; the fate of the world depended on the satisfactory arrangement of parliamentary coalitions behind the scenes, and on the more or less dexterous formulation of legal enactments.

Rosa Luxemburg approached the institution of democracy as she approached all the other phenomena of social and political life: as a product of great historical processes. She came to the conclusion that to regard democracy as " the great fundamental law of historical development " was an absurdity, and nothing but an ignorant and superficial generalisation of one comparatively short stage in the political development of mankind. She also asserted that there was no inevitable relation between capitalist development and democracy, that the particular form of government prevailing under capitalism would always be determined by the whole sum of internal and external political factors, and that, subject to that proviso, it could range readily from the most absolutist monarchy to the most democratic republicanism.

And as for parliamentarism, whilst its zealous supporters could see nothing but roses, roses all the way, Rosa Luxemburg could already descry clear signs of its approaching decrepitude, and she pointed out that both the class struggle of the pro-letariat and the world politics of the *bourgeoisie* were contributing to this inevitable decline:

" *Bourgeois* world politics plunge the whole economic and social life of capitalist countries into a whirl-pool of incalculable and uncontrollable international happenings, conflicts, and upheavals in the midst of which *bourgeois* parliaments are tossed about impotently like flotsam in a mill-race."

And again:

" Parliamentarism is very far removed from being the absolute law of democratic development, the absolute law of human progress, or any other such noble thing: it is nothing but the particular historical form resulting from the class rule of the *bourgeoisie* and its struggle against feudalism. *Bourgeois* parliamentarism remains a vital thing only so long as the struggle between the *bourgeoisie* and feudalism is still proceeding. Once the fire of this struggle has died down parliamentarism loses its historical *raison d'être* from the standpoint of the *bourgeoisie*. For a quarter of a century now the general trend of political development in all capitalist countries has been towards a compromise with feudalism. The effacing of any real difference between the Whigs and the Tories in England, and between the Republicans and the clerical-monarchist aristocrats in France, was the result of this tendency to compromise. In Germany the same compromise stood Godfather to the class emancipation of the *bourgeoisie*." [1]

The real political struggles of the *bourgeoisie* have given way to squabbles of party cliques. As a result, the general level of parliamentarism has declined, and the great personalities and great orators of former days are no longer to be found. This inevitable decline of *bourgeois* parliamentarism was clear enough even at that time to anyone accustomed to judge on the basis of historical development as a whole rather than on the superficial phenomena of everyday life. After the World War there was a certain revival of parliamentarism, but that was the result of revolutionary ferment in the European working class, and it was used in order to deflect the advancing working class away from its real aim. It was a last bright tongue of flame, and it was then extinguished altogether by Fascism in some countries and by the proletarian dictatorship in Russia, whilst in the rest of the world it died away to a mere flicker.

Despite her conclusions, Rosa Luxemburg did not propose that the working class should boycott parliament, and she regarded parliamentary elections as a good opportunity for socialist propaganda and as an indication of how far the idea of Socialism had extended its influence over the masses. Parlia-

[1] Rosa Luxemburg, *ibid.*, p. 391.

ment itself she regarded as an excellent tribunal from which to arouse the masses of the people. But her interest in parliamentarism went much farther than mere propaganda, and she believed that the socialist parliamentarian should take part in the work of practical legislation in the interests of the working class, though, unlike most social-democratic leaders, she recognised clearly that this would become increasingly difficult witn the growth of socialist strength in parliament. The parliamentary fraction of the working class could perform its tasks satisfactorily only if it remembered always that it was an oppositional party, whilst at the same time seeking for the golden mean between sectarian negation and mere *bourgeois* parliamentarism. It must be conscious always that its real strength lay outside parliament. And above all, of course, it must never under any circumstances harbour the dangerous illusion that a socialist working-class party could ever bring about Socialism by a majority vote in parliament.

2. The First Practical Experiment

At a time when the dispute about the merits of parliamentarism had reached fever pitch in Germany, the first practical experiment in the conquest of political power through parliament was launched in France. In June 1899 Alexandre Millerand entered the Radical Ministry of Waldeck-Rousseau in company with General Galliffet, slaughterman-in-chief to the French *bourgeoisie* at the time of the Paris Commune, and his action was acclaimed as a turning-point in world history. Jaurès extolled the courage of the French Socialists in sending a representative " into the fortress of *bourgeois* government ", and his attempt to justify their action by formulating a new theory was joyfully accepted by the reformists in the International : a transitional stage had been reached in the development of capitalist society, a stage at which political power was being wielded jointly by the *bourgeoisie* and the proletariat, and the participation of a socialist in the government was the political expression of this situation.

Rosa Luxemburg followed the experiment with close attention, and she criticised it in painstakingly-thorough investigations which revealed an astonishing knowledge both of French political history and French conditions. She

judged far more coolly and far more accurately concerning
the general significance of the great political crisis which was
shaking France than any of the party leaders directly involved ;
and even in those rare instances where her judgement was seen
to go beyond the mark, it transpired that she had only antici-
pated future developments.

Immediately after Millerand's entry into the Government
she dealt (in the *Leipziger Volkszeitung*) with the whole question
of government and parliamentary power on the basis of
general Marxist principles. Analysing the experiment down
to the smallest detail, she drew tactical conclusions for the
working class which went far beyond the importance of the
Millerand affair. Since then the results of the coalition
policy of post-war German Social Democracy, of MacDonald's
policy in Great Britain, and finally of the French *Front Populaire*
have justified her conclusions as a prophecy of extraordinary
accuracy.

She laid it down as a fundamental principle that Social
Democracy should occupy only such positions as would permit
it to continue the class struggle. This it could do as a parliamentary opposition, but if it entered a capitalist government
its experiment would fail immediately it acted according to
its nature as a staunch opponent of the existing system. In
the alternative, it must carry on the daily functions necessary
to the continued existence of the *bourgeois* machinery of
government, but thereby it would cease to be socialist. A
social democrat striving as a member of a *bourgeois* government
to obtain social reforms whilst at the same time supporting
the continued existence of the *bourgeois* State was, in the best
case, reducing his Socialism to the level of ordinary *bourgeois*
democracy :

> " The representatives of the working class can enter into
> a *bourgeois* government without renouncing their class rôle
> on one condition only, namely that they enter it with the
> intention of seizing the reins of government and turning
> the government into the organ of a victorious working
> class. . . .
>
> " The character of Social Democracy in *bourgeois* society
> is essentially oppositional : it may come forward as a
> governmental party only on the ruins of the *bourgeois* State." [1]

[1] Rosa Luxemburg, *ibid.*, p. 273.

She pointed out that this fundamental principle did not forbid all co-operation with *bourgeois* democracy. Thanks to its social position between the *bourgeoisie* and the working class, the *petit-bourgeoisie* had certain aims in common with the working class, and alliances with the *petit-bourgeoisie* were therefore unavoidable, but in such circumstances the working class must always establish its own hegemony:

" In the present period of development the proletariat is called upon to be the leading, dominating element, and the *petit-bourgeoisie* must play the rôle of incidental factor, and not the other way round. In other words, where the path of a socialist party coincides for a stretch with that of *bourgeois* democracy it must not confine its own struggle to the narrower field it has in common with the *petit-bourgeoisie*, but must, on the contrary, systematically seek to exceed and intensify the efforts of the *petit-bourgeois* parties." [1]

In a *bourgeois* government, however, the *bourgeois* members, under the pressure of capitalist powers, dictate the policy of the socialist members, and therefore of the socialist party as well. This was seen to be the case in the Waldeck–Rousseau Government, and in all subsequent governments in which socialists took part. After the first fine proclamations even the appearance of concessions to the socialists was abandoned, and more and more openly reactionary measures were adopted. Under pressure from their Radical allies, who threatened to break up the Government and leave the field to the reaction, the French Socialist Party adopted a " lesser-evil " policy, a policy which always leads to more and more concessions, and finally to the compromising of the socialist party and of the working class itself.

The social policy pursued by Millerand was at first praised to the skies, but it rapidly developed into an attempt to gloss over class antagonisms in the interests of the *bourgeoisie*, and it culminated in a massacre of striking workers. The bringing of the Dreyfus criminals to justice, which was the chief task of the Cabinet, ended in the granting of a general amnesty for the criminals and their victims. The foreign policy of the Cabinet was characterised by French participation in the

[1] Rosa Luxemburg, *ibid.*, p. 336.

expedition of the European Powers against China, by an expedition against Turkey, and finally by the whipping up of a wave of hysterical enthusiasm when Tsar Nicholas of Russia visited France, the socialist Minister taking his fair share in the reception ceremonies.

Rosa Luxemburg concluded from the French experiment that " practical politics " were, in fact, the most unpractical the working class could possibly pursue, because it was bound hand and foot by the participation of its party in the Government, and therefore unable to make its own power felt. On the other hand, " arid opposition ", as its opponents termed it, proved to be the only practical policy, because, " far from rendering real, immediate, and tangible reforms of a progressive character impossible, an oppositional policy is the only way in which minority parties in general and socialist minority parties in particular can obtain practical successes ". Whereas socialist participation in the Government led to the disruption and crippling of the working-class movement, causing great numbers of workers to turn their backs on politics and parliamentarism altogether, and to seek salvation in the illusions of ultra-radical syndicalism.

Rosa Luxemburg's examination of the Millerand experiment represents one of the most important writings in the whole of socialist literature. Her political logic, hammered out on the anvil of hard facts, closed every loophole of escape, and her final judgement has a universal validity against all attempts to serve the cause of Socialism with the methods of capitalist State power. As we know, her judgement did not prevent the experiment being repeated, but what began in France as a sorry farce ended in Germany, under more critical conditions, in a bloody tragedy. As early as 1901 Rosa Luxemburg was far-sighted enough to realise that such a course created the social basis for political Caesarism, and with extraordinary intuition she declared:

" Jaurès, the tireless defender of the republic, is preparing the way for Caesarism. It sounds like a bad joke, but the course of history is strewn with such jokes."

Thirty-two years later the final fruits of the policy of Millerand and Jaurès were harvested on German soil, and Hitler entered the Reichskanzlei.

3. ULTIMA RATIO

In her polemics against Berstein and Jaurès, Rosa Luxemburg exposed the inadequacy and the Utopian character of reformist ideas and reformist policy, and showed the dangers such ideas and such a policy involved for the working class. And when, as a final despairing argument, the reformists declared that she left the working class nothing for the realisation of Socialism and the conquest of political power apart from violence, she immediately agreed with them. Every fundamental examination of working-class tactics finally arrives at the problem of violence, and this problem arose at every turn throughout the whole course of the discussion with the reformists. Following on the Belgian general strike in 1902, Rosa Luxemburg dealt with the problem exhaustively in a polemic against Emile Vandervelde.

As far as German Social Democracy was concerned, the condemnation of the use of force in the political struggle had become practically a dogma. Wilhelm Liebknecht once declared that force always served reactionary ends, and the remark was repeated with gusto on every possible occasion. The introduction written by Engels to Marx's " Class Struggles in France ", to whose history we have already referred, was appealed to as confirming Liebknecht's attitude, and Bernstein proclaimed that what he called the over-estimation of violence in the reconstruction of society was a Blanquist remnant in Marxist theories. In France Jaurès employed all his great eloquence to convince the working class that legal action was the only possible way to win political power. Stronger even than the exhortations of all these prominent socialists was the effect of daily experience, working-class organisation, elections, and parliamentary action, which for many years had been the only activity of international Social Democracy. In a polemic with Rosa Luxemburg, Vollmar even declared that the workers of Paris would have been much wiser if they had gone home to bed instead of taking up arms and defending the Commune.

First of all Rosa Luxemburg exposed the narrow and ignorant misconception which lay at the root of the legalist theories, and the woman who was ceaselessly decried as a dreamer and a visionary once again proved her unshakable realism. At grips with Vandervelde she wrote:

" What is actually the whole function of *bourgeois* legality? If one ' free citizen ' is taken by another against his will and confined in close and uncomfortable quarters for a while, everyone realises immediately that an act of violence has been committed. However, as soon as the process takes place in accordance with the book known as the penal code, and the quarters in question are in prison, then the whole affair immediately becomes peaceable and legal. If one man is compelled by another to kill his fellow men, then that is obviously an act of violence. However, as soon as the process is called ' military service ', the good citizen is consoled with the idea that everything is perfectly legal and in order. If one citizen is deprived against his will by another of some part of his property or earnings it is obvious that an act of violence has been committed, but immediately the process is called ' indirect taxation ', then everything is quite all right.

" In other words, what presents itself to us in the cloak of *bourgeois* legality is nothing but the expression of class violence raised to an obligatory norm by the ruling class. Once the individual act of violence has been raised in this way to an obligatory norm the process is reflected in the mind of the *bourgeois* lawyer (and no less in the mind of the socialist opportunist) not as it really is, but upside down: the legal process appears as an independent creation of abstract ' Justice ', and State compulsion appears as a consequence, as a mere ' sanctioning ' of the law. In reality the truth is exactly the opposite: *bourgeois* legality (and parliamentarism as the legislature in process of development) is nothing but the particular social form in which the political violence of the *bourgeoisie*, developing its given economic basis, expresses itself." [1]

Looked at in this way, we observe that " legality " has not dethroned violence at all; it is nothing but the form in which violence is perpetuated and sanctified. The idea of over-coming the ruling powers through their own legal forms is

[1] Rosa Luxemburg, *ibid.*, pp. 361–62.

therefore absurd. It is fantastic to imagine that the legality which makes the class violence of the *bourgeoisie* the prevailing social code can be turned into a weapon to destroy the *bourgeoisie*. As Rosa Luxemburg pointed out, behind this insistence on legalism at all costs was the idea of revolution as a deliberate and chosen solution of social problems in preference to other means of arriving at the same end, the idea that revolutions can be made or renounced according to whether they appear useful, superfluous, or perhaps deleterious. However, the idea that violent mass upheavals were brought about at the deliberate decision of political leaders or political parties was one fit only for the minds of policemen and other simpletons. Revolution was a matter of historical development. German Social Democracy could certainly claim that it had liquidated the idea of violent revolution as the only means of waging the class struggle, but that did not abolish the problem of violence, or even discredit the use of violence under certain circumstances as a means of working-class action. The daily struggle for parliamentary power in parliament could be successful only if it was backed outside parliament by the latent force of the working class:

" The use of violence will always remain the *ultima ratio* for the working class, the supreme law of the class struggle, always present, sometimes in a latent, sometimes in an active form. And when we try to revolutionise minds by parliamentary and other activity, it is only in order that at need the revolution may move not only the mind but also the hand."

In this point also Rosa Luxemburg developed the ideas of the reformists to their final and logical conclusion, and, like a modern Cassandra, she warned the working class of the terrible consequences which would result if the advice of the opportunists were taken:

" If Social Democracy were to accept the opportunist standpoint, renounce the use of violence, and pledge the working class never to diverge from the path of *bourgeois* legalism, then its whole parliamentary and other activity would sooner or later collapse miserably and leave the field to the untrammelled dominance of reactionary violence." [1]

The fascist dictatorship in Germany is the realisation of her prophecy.

4. THE FIGHT AGAINST REFORMISM

It is in these polemics with the reformists that Rosa Luxemburg gives us her own ideas of the historical development of capitalist society, the proletarian class struggle, and its tactical requirements, and we can only regret that she never did so in a lasting and concise form in the shape of a book. However, she was never professorial, and she had no desire to manufacture compendiums for industrious students. She was, above all, a fighter; for her polemics were both a weapon and a means of expressing her own ideas, and her brain never worked more brilliantly than when she had her opponent at the point of her rapier. She loved intellectual combat, and when she was urging on Karl Kautsky from her prison cell she wrote: " You must do it with a will, and with heart and soul, not merely as a troublesome intermezzo. The general public becomes infected with the spirit of the combatants, and the joy of battle lends all arguments a higher tone and a greater moral pitch." This joy of battle expresses itself in all her passages at arms, and in particular in her pamphlet " Social Reform or Revolution ".

The work was certainly strongly influenced by the " Communist Manifesto " in the daring flow of its ideas, the wide horizons it opened up, and the brilliance of its style. However, as is invariably the case with all great artists who have learned from their predecessors, such influences were sublimated. This was characteristic of Rosa Luxemburg's attitude towards Marxism. She had assimilated Marxist principles so thoroughly that she had become a creative Marxist in her political activity and had no need to appeal constantly to the works of Marx and Engels for her justification. The other opponents of Bernstein contented themselves with defending Marxist traditions, but Rosa Luxemburg's writings show a fine mastery of the historical process,

[1] Rosa Luxemburg, *ibid.*, p. 366.

an awareness of coming great upheavals, and, above all, an impetuous will to revolutionary action. There is nothing surprising in this. Something more than the genius of its originators was necessary for the development of the Marxist conception of history—namely, the given historical situation, the approach of the German revolution which demanded the solution of theoretical problems from a new and revolutionary standpoint. The West-European successors of Marx and Engels lived in a period of slow development, a period in which the revolutionary pulse was weak. Rosa Luxemburg, on the other hand, was a Russian-Polish revolutionary, and the conditions under which she developed were similar to those which prevailed in Germany prior to the March Revolution of 1848: the revolution was approaching; it was already determining the practical politics of the day and raising problems which could not be solved along the old mechanical lines. This situation enabled her to appreciate the revolutionary principle in Marxism, and to see the West-European situation from an angle completely beyond the scope of the indigenous bureaucrats. It was this historical situation which explains why in the nineties it was the Russians who began to come more and more to the forefront in matters of Marxist theory, until finally they assumed undisputed leadership.

When Rosa Luxemburg took up the struggle against the reformists she was almost thirty. It is an age at which, generally speaking, an individual has developed his main characteristics and formed his own picture of the world around him. Rosa Luxemburg's writings in this period are marked by maturity and strength, and at the same time by youthful vigour, and by a confident acceptance of all the logical conclusions of an argument.

" Anyone can stand by principles; no knowledge is necessary for that," observed Vollmar during the discussion, and he expressed the contempt of the practical man for the narrow, hidebound, and unrealistic theoretician with his warningly raised forefinger. Vollmar was wrong; practical experience was demonstrating even then how much theoretical knowledge and practical wisdom were necessary to guide the working-class movement, and how necessary theory was in order to prevent its being stranded. Rosa Luxemburg realised that a period of political calm offered reformism the best chance of extending its influence, and she was anxious to cut out the canker before it had seized irremediably on the party organism. She therefore uncompromisingly demanded the expulsion of Bernstein from the party, and reproached the party leaders with making concessions to him although they knew better than anyone else the real truth about his position. In a letter to Bebel on October 31st, 1898, she wrote:

" It is quite clear to me, of course, that Bernstein's attitude can no longer be reconciled with the programme of our party, but, nevertheless, it would be very painful to have to abandon all hope. However, I must say that I was rather surprised that, if you agree with me, you and comrade Kautsky did not utilise the favourable atmosphere created by the party congress to open an immediate and vigorous discussion on the matter, and that instead you caused Bernstein to write a pamphlet, which can only drag out the discussion. . . . If Bernstein is really irrevocably lost, then the party must get used to the idea of treating him just like any other mischief-maker and banal social reformer."

However, the leaders of the party were not prepared to adopt energetic measures. They were anxious to uphold " the old victorious tactics ", but they felt more dismay than confidence at the idea of the upheavals Rosa Luxemburg prophesied. The rank and file of the party were ninetenths behind the radicals, and opposed to Bernstein, but they did not realise the magnitude of the differences. However, things seemed to be going well, and after the Dresden Congress of the party in 1903, even Rosa Luxemburg believed that Revisionism had been defeated, but she insisted that the party should be " cleansed of all elements of degeneration ". The most favourable time for such a cleansing had been let slip. Reformism was already strong amongst the officials of the party, and it held key positions in the trade unions. An operation such as the one proposed threatened to lead to a split, and the party was not prepared to take the risk, because, despite differences of opinion, it was still possible to act more or less in concert in practical matters. Con-

stitutional conditions in Germany prevented reformist experiments such as were possible in democratic countries,
and the reformists had therefore to be content with pro-
voking the party by useless compromises with leading capitalist National Liberals and with the Catholic Centre Party,
by budget voting, lunching with the monarchs of South
German States, and similar humbug. As a result there were
never-ending and disagreeable debates in the party Press
and at party congresses, but they led to nothing.

Rosa Luxemburg took part in these verbal engagements
only when they offered her an opportunity of laying down
general principles, and, for the rest, she worked hard for the
Polish movement, which since 1898 had again begun to
show signs of vigour. Her personal life was subordinated to
her writing, to her work at national and international congresses, and to her speaking. There were no dramatic
incidents. In November 1899 the leadership of the party
offered her a place on the editorial board of the *Vorwärts*,
but she rejected it; her experience in Dresden had made
her chary of accepting any such position. In addition, her
relations with the chief editor, old Wilhelm Liebknecht, were
still strained, and it was quite clear to her that if she accepted
the offer she would soon come into conflict with his very
impressionist policy. That would have been a much more
serious matter than a brush with a mediocrity like Gradnauer,
not only on account of the objective consequences, but also
because, despite their differences, she deeply respected the
old " Soldier of the Revolution ". When Liebknecht made
her a peace offer in the last year of his life she was delighted
to accept, and it always gave her deep satisfaction to know
that their old conflict was buried before his death.

Bruno Schönlank died in 1902, and she then took over
the editorship of the *Leipziger Volkszeitung*. She had already
made a reputation for herself in German political life, winning
deep admiration on the one hand and arousing lively aversion
on the other, and when the news of her appointment became
known the whole of the *bourgeois* Press burst into protest.
The extreme conservative newspapers howled for police
measures to put the inconvenient woman over the frontier;
the left-wing *bourgeois Vossische Zeitung* recommended the
leadership of the Social Democratic Party to expel " Donna

Rosa, who feels herself predestined to be the banner-bearer of red revolution "; the Christian imperialist parson Naumann and the *Frankfurter Zeitung* called her " Bloody Rosa "; and her reformist opponents in the party joined in the chorus in a vengeful undertone. They were at least gratified a few months later to learn that Rosa Luxemburg had resigned the post. The Press Commission refused to give her—a woman!—the same liberty of action which had permitted Schönlank to make the paper the leading organ of the international socialist Press. Rosa Luxemburg regarded this liberty as essential if the paper were to be the vigorous and coherent organ she had in mind, and without it she could do nothing. The Leipzig socialists were always inordinately proud of their " fluttering red banner ", but they revealed that in the depths of their hearts they agreed with the Gallant Soldier Schweik that " moderate progress within the limits of party discipline " was really the thing to be aimed at.

In October 1902 Rosa Luxemburg refused even to contribute any longer to the paper. Her reasons are not quite clear, though it is known that many of her articles found their way into the wastepaper basket. She accused her successor in the editorial chair, Franz Mehring, of not having defended her interests with sufficient vigour, and she wrote him an icy letter breaking off relations. This was the first violent disagreement between the two, and later she reported it lightly and incidentally to her friend Diefenbach when telling him how she had made the acquaintance of the poet Hebbel:

" I know Hebbel longer than I know you. I borrowed him from Mehring at a time when our friendship was very warm and the neighbourhood between Steglitz and Friedenau [1] (in which agreeable neighbourhood I was still living) was a sunny paradise. . . . I read Agnes Bernauer, Maria Magdalena, Judith, Herodes, and Mariamne, but I didn't get any farther because the sun went in and the temperature dropped with the approach of the first glacial period, and my corpulent Gertrude had to make a pilgrimage to Steglitz carrying a washing-basket full of his presents and borrowed books in answer to a

[1] Both suburbs of Berlin.—TR.

similar transport which had arrived in Friedenau, a thing
that invariably happened every time we got disengaged.''

With friendships, as with politics, Rosa Luxemburg's motto
was: all or nothing! And Franz Mehring was a man of
extraordinary sensitiveness. Small wonder that the two
often came to loggerheads and fell out! Even the difficult
period of the World War did not pass without trouble between
them, but their mutual respect for each other, their related
temperaments, and, finally, their common enemies brought
them together again and again. The first coolness lasted
almost a year, and the breach was healed only when Rosa
Luxemburg abandoned any ill-feeling she may have felt
and came forward vigorously in his defence when he was
the victim of a long-prepared attack which left him almost
alone at the Dresden Party Congress.

Her relation to Jean Jaurès was of an entirely different
character, and her friendship with him rebuts an assertion
which has often been made that she had no understanding
for anyone who did not share her own political opinions,
and had nothing for them but hatred, poison, and rancour.
It is true that she could be merciless towards anyone whom
she suspected of cloaking intellectual nonentity or a scheming
character behind arrogance and bounce, but where a worthy
enemy was concerned she could take even excessive asperity
in good part: *à la guerre comme à la guerre.* It might be said
that she had almost nothing in common with the ideas and
policy of Jaurès, and she attacked him repeatedly. Politically
her attacks were sharp, but the tone of them had something
unusually conciliatory in it. She respected his personality
and she admired the sweep of his ideas, even when she felt
they were wrong, and, above all, she admired his great
enthusiasm and his unswerving devotion to the cause of
the working class. After one of his speeches she observed
(as though to placate her own rebellious conscience): '' What
the man says is altogether wrong, but there's nothing for it—
you've just got to applaud. He carries you away.'' At the
International Congress in Amsterdam in 1904 she crossed
swords with him on the question of class collaboration, but
when Jaurès had spoken there was no translator for him, so
she immediately sprang into the breach and gave a brilliant

rendering of a speech directed against herself. Jaurès thanked her publicly, and observed, " Comrades, you will have seen that political disagreement is not always a hindrance to co-operation." And Rosa Luxemburg was more than willing for co-operation with a man of the calibre of Jaurès.

Naturally, it was not long before the Public Prosecutor began to cast a baleful eye on a woman who showed such scant respect for the gods of respectability, and his first chance came in 1900, when she issued a pamphlet in Polish entitled " In Defence of Nationality ", vigorously condemning the attempts of the authorities to Germanise Prussian Poland. Proceedings were started against her on a charge of having insulted the Prussian Minister for Cultural Affairs. It is not possible to discover at this time of day what her punishment was for that, but in July 1904 she was sentenced to three months' imprisonment for " insulting " a much more highly-placed personage—none other than Wilhelm II himself. The " insult " consisted in her observation that " any man who talks about the secure and good living of the German workers has no idea of the real facts ". She had served the greater part of her sentence when the King of Saxony died and she was included in an amnesty which followed the melancholy happening. She was indignant at the idea that a republican should be compelled to accept mercy from a king, and she therefore refused to leave her cell, but, willy-nilly, she was restored to the freedom of the outer world. That was three months before the first great storm swept over absolutist Russia, " the prison of whole peoples ".

CHAPTER FIVE: FULL-DRESS REHEARSAL, 1905

1. RUSSIA AWAKENS

THE FIRST Russian Revolution dates from Bloody Sunday, January 22nd, 1905. Russian Marxists were not taken by surprise: they had prophesied its coming and indicated its character. At the inaugural congress of the Second International in Paris in 1898, Plechanov declared that the coming revolution against Tsarism would be a workers' revolution or no revolution at all. That was at a time when it was still a moot point whether capitalism would make progress in Russia. The Russian working class was only just beginning to develop, and the only real traces of a modern working-class movement were observable in Poland, and, economically speaking, Poland was almost foreign territory. In Russia proper socialist ideas were confined to small circles of intellectuals and still smaller circles of workers.

The turning-point came in 1896. The coronation of Nicholas II proved the occasion, and the finger of history wrote a double *menetekel* on the wall: the crumbling away of mass devotion to Absolutism, and the first appearance of the proletariat in Russian history. On the great Hodinka Field near Moscow a panic occurred amongst the vast masses who had assembled to greet the new Tsar (in the hope of receiving presents), and hundreds of men, women, and children were trampled to death, whilst in Petersburg 40,000 workers went on strike for the first time as a protest against the loss of three days wages during the coronation festivities. The strike was brutally repressed. However, in January 1897 a second strike broke out and the first great working-class victory was won: the introduction of a legal maximum working day of eleven and a half hours. The barriers were down and social-democratic propaganda began to spread amongst the workers. Socialism in Russia had advanced from the sphere of pure theory into the sphere of practical action; it was developing from an affair of tiny, illegal circles of idealists into one of mass movements. In 1896 a small group of Socialists founded the Russian Social Democratic Party.

Years of underground work followed throughout the country, and their fruits showed themselves suddenly in violent outbreaks. In March 1902 a mass strike broke out in Batum, and immediately afterwards mass demonstrations took place in Nizhni-Novgorod and Saratov. In December 1902 there was a general strike of the workers in Rostov-on-the-Don. For the first time in Russian history the right to hold public meetings was won by the determination of the masses. 1903-4 saw social convulsions which shook the whole of South Russia.

General strikes of the workers spread from town to town: from Baku to Tiflis, Batum again, Yellisavietgrad, Odessa, Kiev, Nikolaiev, and Yekaterinoslav. These strikes differed from the normal strikes of Western Europe by their suddenness, their extent, the rapid submerging of all craft barriers, and their speedy development from purely economic into political movements. They all bore a revolutionary character, not always in their origin, perhaps, but in their impetuous force and the inevitable clash with the State power. Most of these strikes led to pitched battles with the police and military, and they were accompanied by numerous local peasant insurrections against the landowners. 1902–4 saw the Russian Revolution on the march.

The outbreak of the Russo-Japanese War in 1904 caused a new wave of patriotism and chauvinism to rise, and for a while the working-class movement was pushed into the background, but with the news of defeat after defeat on the plains of Manchuria the wave quickly began to ebb, and the hopeless rottenness of the absolutist régime manifested itself. The Liberal *bourgeoisie* came into the open, and at numerous banquets and congresses resounding speeches were delivered and long manifestos and addresses adopted demanding (though not too exigently) various democratic liberties. At first it seemed that the leadership of the democratic movement was to pass into the hands of Liberal landowners, capitalists, and lawyers, but when, in December 1904, Absolutism recovered sufficient courage to utter a few vigorous threats, the whole respectable opposition collapsed and the after-dinner atmosphere became more sober.

On the other hand, the working class answered with a general strike in Baku. In January 1905 a strike took place at the famous Putilov works in Petersburg against the dismissal of two workers. It spread rapidly, and by January 20th, 140,000 workers had come out and the strike had taken on a clear political character. Ironically enough, history willed that this great movement should originate from a trade-union organisation which was really the creation of the Moscow Police Chief, Subatov, as a counterblast to social-democratic influence. It was led not by any of the known revolutionary leaders, but by a dubious adventurer, the priest Gapon. However, despite Subatov and Gapon,

social-democratic agitators worked actively in the movement
and spread revolutionary ideas and demands amongst the
rebellious masses.

At that time even the workers still regarded the Tsar as the
Father of his People, and it was to him they naïvely turned
to remedy their wrongs. They decided to make a mass
pilgrimage to his palace to tell him of their troubles and to
receive justice from his hands. On Sunday, January 22nd,
1905, 200,000 people carrying portraits of the Tsar and holy
pictures at their head set off for the Winter Palace. They
took with them a petition in which they described the wrongs,
oppression, and humiliation suffered by the people, and asked
for redress: a general amnesty, democratic liberties, the
disestablishment of the Church, the eight-hour day, fair
wages, the land for the people, and the calling of a constitutional assembly on the basis of a general franchise. They
went to him as loyal supplicants confident in his redress, but
nevertheless they were very determined, and the peroration
of their address contained a clear threat, if a passive one:

> " These, Your Majesty, are our chief wishes. Order that
> they be fulfilled, and swear to fulfil them, and you will
> make Russia happy and glorious, and your name will be
> written on our hearts and on the hearts of our children for
> ever. But turn a deaf ear to our supplications, and we shall
> die here on the square before your palace. . . . May our
> sacrifice save Russia, who has suffered too much; we will
> make it readily."

They made their sacrifice. They marched into a carefully
prepared ambush. 2000 men, women, and children were
butchered and 4000 wounded. But the blood-bath which
was to have washed away all ideas of violent rebellion was the
baptism of the revolution. The volleys which thundered
through the great square awakened the whole proletariat of
Russia, and by the end of January over a million workers
were on the streets as a wave of huge strikes rolled over the
whole country. The first great rehearsal was in full swing.

Under the immediate impression of these events Rosa
Luxemburg wrote an article in the *Neue Zeit* in February 1905
entitled " The Proletariat Pleads ":

D

" History, like nature herself, is strange and fantastic in its pranks. . . . The humble ' plea ' of the masses of the people to the Tsar was in reality nothing but a request that His Most Gracious Majesty would condescend with his own royal hands to decapitate himself as Tsar of all the Russians. It was a request to the autocrat to destroy autocracy. . . . It was the modern class urge of a determined and mature proletariat clothed in the fantastic quip of an old wives' tale. . . . It was enough that the excited masses should conceive the idea, formally childish, but in reality fateful, of approaching their Little Father face to face, and of testing the myth of royal benevolence, for the struggle to develop with iron logic into the death-lock of two irreconcilable enemies: the war of two worlds, the battle of two centuries."

Rosa Luxemburg enthusiastically greeted the awakening of the Russian people, rudely shaken from their slumber by the volleys before the Winter Palace and by the slashing whips of mounted Cossacks, and protesting fiercely in vast strikes. Everything she had done in scientific investigation, in intellectual struggle, in organising and training revolutionary groups, in obstinate struggles against the State power to bring a little light into the mind of the working masses, had been done with the one idea of revolution. And now the revolution was on the march. She dearly wanted to be there, to be one in the mass which was making history, but even if she had not been confined to a sick bed, as she was at the time, she knew that she could not give way to that desire. She had already learned to control her impetuous temperament and to crush romantic impulses. She belonged to the party leadership, and conditions would not allow its transfer to Poland. Her special task could not be performed in the front line, where local conflict obscured the view over the process as a whole. Her task was to interpret the meaning of events, to set up the next aims of the movement, to examine the tactics and methods used in the struggle, and, whilst learning, to teach. And part of that work must be to examine the ideas which had guided the Polish and Russian movements, and to see how far they had stood the test of revolutionary reality.

2. Problems of Organisation

Russian Social Democracy had longed for the great day, had prophesied it, expected it. However, it had not been adequately prepared for it organisationally, politically, or strategically. In fact, when the preliminary skirmishes of the revolution were already taking place it broke into two parts which were never really forged together again and which finally formed two irreconcilably hostile camps.

The fine proclamation of Russian Social Democracy in 1898 was no more than the beginning of the task of creating a party. Small circles continued to be spread over the country without any real cohesion, with only very little connection with each other, and without any uniform theoretical viewpoint. When Lenin left Russia it was with a firm determination to remedy this situation. In 1900 *Iskra* (" The Spark ") was founded, and its editorial board consisted of the " older generation ", Plechanov, Axelrod, and Vera Sassulitch, and the " younger generation ", Lenin, Martov, and Potressov. Later Trotzky joined the board after his flight from Siberia.

The main aim of *Iskra* was to organise a new congress to create a really strong and cohesive party with a Marxist programme. Clarity on theoretical matters was urgently necessary, and, as a first step, accounts were settled with the Narodniki, who were anti-Marxists denying the necessity of capitalist development in Russia and chasing after a Utopian Socialism based on the peasant commune. However, the Marxist camp itself was far from united, and after the strikes of 1896–97 one group began to insist that Social Democracy should confine its activities to organising the workers for the economic struggle, and that politically it should not go beyond reforms which could be granted within the framework of the existing régime. In this way, it was argued, the working-class movement could at least remain in socialist hands. The general political struggle and the carrying out of the *bourgeois* revolution should be left in the hands of the *bourgeoisie*, and when it had been successful, there would be a basis for a working-class movement along normal Western European lines. This tendency received the name " Economism ".

The *Iskra* group, and in particular Lenin, strongly condemned these ideas, regarding them as a denial of the socialist and revolutionary nature of the class struggle, in which the daily battle for wages, social reform, etc., was a means to an end only, a preparation of the working class for still greater tasks. The *Iskra* group declared that the chief task of Social Democracy was to give the working class a consciousness of its great mission, to prepare it for its rôle as the champion, over and above its own immediate interests, of all oppressed classes, and the protagonist of historical progress as a whole; only a political struggle with revolutionary aims could give the working-class movement a social-democratic character.

Rosa Luxemburg supported the *Iskra* group in these discussions, though one of the leaders of the Economists, Kritchevski, had belonged to her intimate circle of friends in Zurich. However, she strongly disagreed with Lenin with regard to the form the Russian social-democratic organisation should take. Lenin had set down his ideas on the point in many articles and in a pamphlet entitled " What is to be Done? ", and it seemed as though the *Iskra* group was in complete agreement with him. However, at the second Congress of the Russian Social Democratic Party in the summer of 1903 in Brussels and London, Lenin's ideas provoked such violent opposition that finally the party split on the point. A terrific battle took place, and dragged its lengthy way through countless debates around " Paragraph One " of the proposed statutes. To the Western European reader of the debates and of the literature subsequently published by the disputants the point at issue must appear absurd, and the debates themselves nothing but obstinate quibbling and hairsplitting.[1]

In order to understand the dispute it is necessary to remember the state of the social-democratic movement of the day, with its loose and rather anarchical organisation of circles, and the conditions in which an illegal party organisation had to work under Absolutism. At the same time it must

---

[1] There were two proposals before the Congress, one from Martov and the other from Lenin, and they read respectively: " Membership of the Russian Social Democratic Workers Party is open to anyone who accepts its programme and is prepared to take an active part in the performance of its tasks under the control and leadership of the organs of the party," and " Membership of the party is open to anyone who accepts the programme of the party and is prepared to support the party both by contributions and by personal co-operation in one of the party organisations."

be remembered that deep political differences were expressing themselves in the debate on the statutes, differences which as yet were more felt than clearly expressed. Lenin could see serious dangers approaching, and he wished to counter them by giving the party a firm and disciplined organisational form. He was well aware that in the coming revolution the party would be faced with tremendous tasks, and he wanted to forge it into a weapon of iron. And, finally, he was quite certain that he alone amongst the *Iskra* circle would be able to lead the party with the necessary firmness and determination. His opinion was the result of objective and impersonal thought, and it explains his obstinacy.

The text of the two proposals hardly reveals the real difference of opinion. Martov wanted a party without any clearly defined limitations in accordance with the real condition of the movement of the day; a party in which the individual groups would enjoy a very considerable degree of autonomy; a party for broad propaganda, with a loose form of organisation embracing practically everybody prepared to call himself a socialist. Lenin's idea was very different: he wanted a party which would be the advance guard of the class and closely connected with it, but at the same time with clearly defined limits, hierarchically organised, and having very definite bodies—i.e., party committees, factory committees, educational circles, etc.—and the core of his party was to be formed of professional revolutionaries devoting their activities entirely to the movement, taking the initiative in all party matters, and enjoying prior rights in the party. Such a party would be organised from the top downwards, and headed by a Central Committee responsible to the party Congress only, and possessing almost unlimited political and organisational powers. This omnipotence of the Central Committee was stressed still further by the Statutes Commission of the Congress, which gave the Central Committee the power to organise the lower party committees at its own discretion, to dissolve them at will, and to decide on the tasks to be performed by the members of such committees (the professional revolutionaries). In the end this might well have made the responsibility of the Central Committee even towards the Party Congress a fiction.

Martov was victorious at the Congress, and Lenin gave way

on the point. But when the radical wing of the Congress proved victorious in the discussion on the party programme, various reformist groups left the Congress altogether, and the result was that the Lenin group obtained a majority at the election of the Central Committee. After the Congress a further change of alignment took place in this body, and Plechanov went over to the side of Martov, thereby giving him again the majority, but soon after this the final split took place. In accordance with the ultimate voting at the Congress, the two groups which had been formed were called Bolshevists, from the Russian word for majority, and Menshevists, from the Russian word for minority.

After the split Lenin published a book entitled " One Step Forward; Two Back ", in which he vigorously criticised the proceedings of the Congress, and dealt in particular with the organisational question, arguing uncompromisingly in favour of his centralistic standpoint. It would almost seem as though he intended to anger and provoke his opponents, and he uses such formulations as: " Bureaucracy against Democracy; that is the organisational principle of revolutionary Social Democracy against the organisational principle of the Opportunists ". Rosa Luxemburg answered him in the *Iskra* and in the *Neue Zeit* in July 1904, with an article entitled " Organisational Questions of Russian Social Democracy ". At the time the discussions attracted very little attention in Western Europe, where chiefly they caused astonishment that the Russians should think such things worth fighting about. Later on, however, after the seizure of power by the Bolshevists in Russia, these ideas were to become the centre of fierce discussions in the whole working-class movement.

Rosa Luxemburg was in agreement with Lenin that the revolutionary party must be the advance guard of the class, that it must be centrally organised, and that the majority will be carried out always in the strictest discipline. However, when he went beyond that, they parted company She declared that Social Democracy was the first political movement in history depending in everything on the independent action of the masses of the people, and therefore it must create an organisational form for itself very different from that of the conspiratorial Jacobin–Blanquist organisation. When Lenin declared that revolutionary Social Democracy represented

" the Jacobins indissolubly connected with the organisation of the class-conscious proletariat ", he forgot, she declared, that the difference between Social Democracy and Blanquism was not exhausted in the antithesis between the organisation and class-consciousness of the proletariat on the one hand and the conspiratorial activity of a small minority on the other.   The difference between Blanquism and Social Democracy was rather that there was no inherent connection between the conspiratorial activity of Blanquism and the daily life of the masses of the people, and for this reason Blanquism could, and was, in fact, compelled to cut off its organisation from the masses of the people.   Further, the activities of the Blanquists were based on a previously arranged plan, and in its execution they necessarily became the tools of a previously determined Will—of a Central Committee enjoying almost unlimited powers and demanding blind obedience from all subordinate organs :

" The conditions of social-democratic activity are fundamentally different. This activity develops historically from the elementary class struggle, subject to the dialectical antithesis that the proletarian army recruits its forces only during the course of the struggle itself, and realises the true nature of its final task only in the course of the struggle. Organisation, education, and struggle are thus not mechanically separated elements, nor are they separate in time, as they would be in a Blanquist movement; they are various aspects of the same process. On the one hand, and apart from the general principles of the struggle, there can be no complete and previously-accepted fighting tactics drilled into members of a social-democratic organisation by its Central Committee, and on the other hand the very process of struggle which creates the organisation causes a continual fluctuation of the social-democratic sphere of influence. From this it follows that the social-democratic form of organisation cannot be based on blind obedience and on the mechanical subordination of all members to some centralised power. . . . Social-democratic centralism must therefore be fundamentally different to Blanquist centralism. This social-democratic centralism can be nothing but the categoric embodiment of the will of the enlightened and

militant advance guard of the working class as against its
separate groups and individuals. This is, so to speak, a
sort of 'self-centralism' of the leading group of the proletariat: its majority rule within the framework of its own
party organisation."

Rosa Luxemburg regarded the existence of an all-powerful
Central Committee as a danger to the development of the
struggle itself. Experience in Russia and in other countries
had shown, she declared, that new forms had never been
"invented" by leaders, but developed from the creative
initiative of the masses themselves. Unconscious action
preceded conscious action; the logic of the objective historical
process preceded the subjective logic of its supporters. In the
discussion she also made the very significant observation
that in this process the organisational leadership naturally
tended to play a conservative rôle. It developed the newly-
adopted forms to their final consequences, and then turned
them into a barrier against further progress. As an example
she cited German Social Democracy, whose leadership raised
almost insurmountable objections to anything not already
laid down to the last detail in its ordinary parliamentary
routine.

"This inertia is explained to a great degree, however,
by the fact that it is very difficult to present the contours
and tangible forms of a not-yet-existing, i.e., imaginary
political situation in the empty air of abstract speculation.
In any case, it is not so important for Social Democracy to
foresee and draft formulas for future tactics as it is to
preserve a correct historical understanding of each prevailing
form, to preserve a genuine feeling for the relativity of the
given phase of the struggle and for the necessary intensification of revolutionary factors from the standpoint of the
final objective of the revolutionary class struggle. However,
to provide a party leadership with such absolute powers of a
negative character as Lenin suggests, would artificially and
most dangerously intensify the conservatism which naturally
belongs to every such body."

There is no doubt that Rosa Luxemberg attached considerable importance to this argument against Lenin. She

thought to observe in him an obstinacy in argumentation which was dangerous, a certain scholasticism in his political ideas, and a tendency to ignore the living movement of the masses, or even to force it into preconceived tactical channels. This violated her dialectical sense of the political process, and she had already seen amongst the French Guesdists how such obstinacy and rigidity easily became a big hindrance to political action. As a matter of historical fact Lenin showed himself tactician enough to avoid such dangers, and it is possible that he adopted extreme arguments and formulations in order the better to hammer home his decisive points. In any case, in all situations calling for quick tactical decisions he revealed himself to be a master of tactical elasticity —a thing that no one would have suspected from his writings. On the other hand, his followers manifested that conservative inertia against which Rosa Luxemburg had warned the movement almost every time they were left to make their decisions on their own initiative—for instance, when the workers' soviets began to spring up in 1905, and prior to Lenin's arrival in Russia in 1917.

Rosa Luxemburg believed that the only guarantee against socialist tactics becoming rigid was to give those forces in the party capable of exercising Marxist criticism every possibility of development, and to ensure that the leading organs of the party were subject to an effective control by the membership:

> " The ultra-centralism demanded by Lenin develops, it seems to us, not from positive creative ideas, but from a sterile, bureaucratic attitude. Its chief aim is to control the activity of the party rather than to fructify it, to limit rather than to develop it, to dragoon the movement rather than to educate it."

She attached great importance to the creative rôle of the masses, and she believed that it could be developed in the party only if there were wide freedom of criticism. She regarded this freedom to criticise the leading organs of the party as a guarantee against excessive rigidity, as the living source from which all errors and abuses which might develop in the party could be remedied. In her opinion it was the duty of the party leadership to execute the will of the party majority; perhaps to influence the formation of this will by enlightenment, but

D 2

never dictatorially to force its own will on to the party. She had no sympathy whatever with the suggestion that an omnipotent Central Committee could play the part of an infallible providence, and she declared roundly:

> " Mistakes made by a really revolutionary working-class movement are historically incomparably more fruitful and and valuable than the infallibility of the best Central Committee that ever existed."

3. LENIN AND LUXEMBURG

Lenin answered her criticisms of his ideas in an article intended for the *Neue Zeit*. Unfortunately he failed to deal with the positive content of her criticism, and contented himself with denying its validity. He was not in favour of absolute centralism, but of the elementary discipline necessary in any organisation. In her analysis Rosa Luxemburg had ignored the Party Congress and the facts of the party struggle.

The chief part of his reply was devoted to a description of Russian internal struggles, and it was completely incomprehensible for anyone not already well versed in the subject. It is not surprising, therefore, that the editor of the *Neue Zeit*, Kautsky, refused to print the article, and it finally saw the light of day twenty years later in *Leninski Sbornik*.

Later Lenin often ridiculed what he called " Luxemburg's idea of the organisation as a process ", but he was fated to experience the truth that the development of organisational forms was subject to the development of the movement as a whole. When the Russian Revolution of 1905 won the right to organise for the masses, he gave the party a form which had little in common with the ultra-centralism he had recommended, and, under pressure from the greatly increased membership of the party, he even agreed to the re-establishment of unity, though in the process the majority passed once again into the hands of the opportunists, to whose decisions he then submitted in a number of very important matters indeed.

The question immediately arises as to whether the present form of rule in the Soviet Union and the condition of all the parties of the Communist International are the result of

Lenin's organisational principle. One or two observations are necessary before this question can be answered. Lenin has himself admitted that in his book " One Step Forward . . ." he deliberately exaggerated his demand for centralism in order to fight better against the anarchical conditions which existed in the Russian party at the time. When the organisational theses were laid down for the parties of the Third International, it was Lenin who insisted that they were " much too Russian " to be suitable for Western European conditions. These theses were, in fact, founded on " democratic centralism ", and provided for freedom of criticism within the parties, and for the control of the party leadership from below. It is true that in Lenin's own party—the leading party of the Communist International—centralism was very highly developed, but that was because the civil war demanded a semi-military form of organisation. However, whilst Lenin was at the helm all the great political decisions of the day were not dictated from above, but hammered out in vigorous intellectual discussion. The centralist dictatorship and the blind obedience which prevail in the Russian and other Communist Parties to-day are nothing but an evil caricature of Lenin's organisational principle.

The symptomatic rôle of Lenin's opinions on organisational matters is exaggerated and misrepresented when passages are taken from his writings in 1902 and 1904 and coupled with three decades of development. On the other hand, it would be entirely wrong to imagine that Rosa Luxemburg wished the party to be a mere loose organisation of people with similar ideas. She insisted that freedom to criticise and to express opinions must exist within the party as a guarantee against its ideas becoming hidebound and mechanical, but she insisted also that this freedom must find its limit in the necessity for maintaining Marxist principles. At the same time she valued highly the unity of the party and of the working class, and she welcomed the fact that there was room in the ranks of German Social Democracy for very varied opinions: " A great party will not split as a result of newspaper articles or even as a result of individual divergences." However, general agreement on the ultimate aim of the party was not sufficient as the basis for party unity; some measure of unity was necessary in the joint political endeavours of the day, and she strongly opposed all attempts " to obliterate the distinction between the conscious advance guard of the working class and the unorganised masses of the people ". Democratic centralism was a very serious and important matter for her. She strongly opposed all the attempts of the parliamentary fraction to evade the control of the party as a whole, and as the leader of the Polish Party she insisted energetically that the will of the Central Committee should be respected.

This first difference of political opinion between her and Lenin also revealed differences of character. Rosa Luxemburg under-estimated the power of organisation, particularly when the organisation was in the hands of her opponents. She believed, rather too optimistically, that the pressure of the revolutionary masses would correct any political errors of the party leadership. Lenin's general political opinions prior to 1917 reveal unmistakably Blanquist influences and an exaggerated Voluntarism, though he quickly abandoned it when faced with practical necessity. With certain reservations it may be taken that Rosa was more strongly influenced by the historical process as a whole, and arrived at all her political conclusions exclusively from this source, whereas Lenin's eye was more concentrated on the aim before him, for whose achievement he then sought the necessary political means. For her the decisive factor was the mass : for him it was the party, and he aimed at forging into the spear-head of the movement as a whole. He resembles the Chief of Staff of a highly organised army, she rather the standard bearer in the front rank of a broad class host.

4. The Character of the 1905 Revolution

To the outsider the split in Russian Democracy which took place in 1903 seemed due to personal rivalries and to greatly exaggerated differences on organisational matters. However, when the revolution finally broke out, it was seen that the cause of the split was in reality a very deep difference of principle which up to then had been felt rather than form-ulated. The revolutionary movement was compelled to make up its mind clearly concerning the character, objectives, and strategy of the revolution.

General opinion in and beyond the ranks of Russian Social

Democracy held that the revolution would be a *bourgeois* one, aiming at the overthrow of Absolutism and the introduction of *bourgeois*-democratic liberties. However, behind this general agreement there were véry deep-lying differences of opinion. The various *bourgeois*-democratic groups, the Social Revolutionaries, and certain representatives of the Polish Socialist Party let themselves be carried along with the tide, and made no attempt to analyse social relations. Most of the Menshevist leaders concluded that as a *bourgeois* revolution was approaching the leadership of the revolutionary movement belonged quite naturally in the hands of the *bourgeoisie*, and also governmental power after the successful revolution. The working class must therefore confine itself to seconding the efforts of the *bourgeoisie*. Any attempt on the part of the working class to overstep this limit would prove fatal, because it would drive the *bourgeoisie* into the camp of the reaction, and thus spoil the chances of the revolution altogether. And Plechanov, the very man who in former years had proclaimed that the Russian Revolution would be a workers' revolution or nothing, now insisted that the prime tactical rule of social-democratic action should be unfailing tact and discretion in all dealings with the *bourgeoisie*.

The social-democratic Left Wing, including the Bolshevists, Parvus, Trotzky, Rosa Luxemburg, and Kautsky (who was strongly under Rosa Luxemburg's influence), condemned this " tactic of tact " as reactionary and Utopian. They pointed out that the Great French Revolution was carried to victory only because under the Jacobin dictatorship the plebeian element (the proletarian and *petit-bourgeois* masses) seized political power and destroyed feudalism root and branch even against the opposition of the *bourgeoisie* itself. The Revolution of 1848 in Germany failed because the *bourgeoisie* was mortally afraid of the German proletariat (which was just beginning to make its first tentative political steps), and therefore fled for safety after the first storm into the camp of Absolutism, which it thereby saved from destruction. The Russian *bourgeoisie* would inevitably take the same course, and it would take it still more quickly because the strength of the international, and even of the Russian proletariat, was much greater than in 1848.

The lessons of history suggested that the Russian Revolution could be victorious only if the proletariat succeeded in obtaining the leadership, and an analysis of the given situation confirmed this conclusion. Tsarism harboured the most glaring social contradictions; in agriculture a whole scale of productive methods existed, from the tiny plot of land tilled with the ancient timber plough of the Middle Ages, up to the modern large-scale farm of the " Liberal " landowner; in the towns there was a *petit-bourgeoisie* which had never known the normal flourishing phase of handicraft because it had been unable to compete with the cheap domestic industriousness of the peasants: and finally there was a modern and highly-concentrated industry [1] which had been artificially fostered by Tsarism. This very general sketch of the economic structure of Tsarist Russia is sufficient to indicate that there were very important differences in class relations as compared with former revolutions. The Liberalism of the *bourgeoisie* in Russia would obviously prove even shorter-lived than that of the West European *bourgeoisie*; it would quickly seek some compromise with the old powers because of its own close connections with them and because of its deep-seated fear of the working class. The urban *petit-bourgeoisie* was not in a position to play the leading rôle it had played in all former revolutions, because it had no conscious political will and took little or no part in the political struggle. The most that might be expected was that it would be swept along in the general current of the revolution once the dams broke. In other countries and in former times the *petit-bourgeoisie* had done much to educate the working class politically, but in Russia this had been done by the revolutionary intelligentzia, organised in various socialist parties and groups. The peasantry, on the other hand, was driven by a fierce hunger for land, and by a burning desire to throw off the oppressive

---

[1] The large-scale industrial undertaking was more highly developed in Russia than in Germany, although Germany led the rest of Europe industrially. The following comparative table illustrates this fact:

Undertakings employing:	Germany 1895 Census.		Russia 1902 Census.	
	No. of Undertakings.	No. of Workers employed.	No. of Undertakings.	No. of Workers employed.
Between 50 and 1000 Workers	18,698	2,595,536	6,334	1,202,800
Over 1000 Workers	255	448,731	458	1,155,000

burdens of feudalism. It was therefore revolutionary. However, peasant action was necessarily local, and the peasantry was not in a position to take over the leadership of the whole struggle. On the contrary, it needed leadership itself. Rosa Luxemburg realised quite clearly that once its immediate and pressing social requirements were satisfied, it would again fall under the influence of the reaction. Thus, the only class which remained to carry through the revolution was the working class. The Russian working class was not so strong relatively as the working class of Western Europe, but at least it was concentrated in large masses at the points of chief political importance, and it had already proved its fighting value in great struggles. In addition, international social relations had their effect on Russia. The affiliations of the international *bourgeoisie* with Tsarism depressed the Liberal *bourgeoisie* of Russia and robbed it of much of its courage, whilst at the same time the attitude of the Russian working class borrowed something from the power and maturity of the international proletariat.

" The Russian Revolution will, formally speaking, bring about in Russia what was brought about in Western and Central Europe by the February and March Revolutions half a century ago, but at the same time, and just because it is a belated fragment of the European revolution, it represents a type of its own. Russia comes on the revolutionary stage as a politically-backward country. . . . However, quite against general belief, for that very reason the Russian Revolution will have the most clearly defined proletarian character of all. It is true that the immediate aims of the present upheaval in Russia do not go beyond the limits of a *bourgeois*-democratic constitution, and it is quite possible that the final result of the crisis (which may, and probably will, hang on for years, sometimes at ebb-tide, sometimes at the flood) may be no more than a paltry democratic constitution. Nevertheless, the revolution which is condemned to bring forth this puny changeling will be more decidedly proletarian in character than any revolution preceding it." [1]

Thus Rosa Luxemburg was far more sceptical about the

[1] Rosa Luxemburg in an article in the " *Neue Zeit* ", January 1905.

immediate result of the revolution than the Menshevists, but this scepticism did not weaken her revolutionary ardour, because for her the revolutionary process itself was more important than its immediate practical results. For the first time the proletariat would play the leading rôle, and its class interests and its fighting methods would determine the whole character of the revolution. She thus gave the proletariat a much higher task than that of acting as the auxiliary troops of the Liberal *bourgeoisie*: it was to come forward as the advance guard of the revolutionary movement as a whole, acting as a class which, whilst determining its policy together with that of other classes, nevertheless formulated that policy exclusively on the basis of its own class interests and class tasks. Thus in a revolution which was formally speaking a *bourgeois* revolution, the antithesis *bourgeoisie*-Absolutism would be overshadowed by the antithesis proletariat-*bourgeoisie*.

The character of the revolution would naturally express itself in the strategic aim put forward by the Social Democratic Party: a revolutionary government. For the Menshevists there was no question at all that after the revolution and the overthrow of Tsarism, the new government would be a *bourgeois*-class government and nothing else. In adopting this attitude they felt themselves very Marxist indeed, and they even appealed to the decision of the Amsterdam Congress of the International in 1904, which had condemned the participation of Socialists in the government of *bourgeois* States. With particular smugness they quoted Engels' observation that if Socialists came to power in a situation which was not ripe they might easily :

" in the interests of the movement, represent the interests of another class whilst fobbing off their own class with phrases and promises, and with the assurance that the interests of the other class were in reality its own interests. Whoever lets himself slide into this false position is hopelessly lost." [1]

It was Lenin who drubbed the Menshevists out of their Marxist camouflage. How on earth could they talk as though socialist participation in a democratic revolution and

[1] Friedrich Engels, " *Der Bauernkrieg* ".

in the administrative organs of such a revolution were the same as socialist participation in a government which strenuously opposed a socialist transformation of society? Engels' words of warning would, however, prove very useful to prevent any error in estimating the situation as a whole; they would assist in limiting aims and propaganda to the practically attainable. " A revolutionary democratic dictatorship of the proletariat and the peasantry ", a revolutionary government consisting of the Socialists and representatives of a peasant party which would undoubtedly be formed, must create dictatorially the basis for a *bourgeois*-democratic State.

Parvus, Trotzky, and Rosa Luxemburg were in complete agreement with Lenin in his attack on the Menshevist programme of total abstinence from the affairs of government, but they disagreed with him in methods, and they regarded his " democratic dictatorship " as an attempt to wrench the revolutionary process into the desired channels by violence. Parvus declared, with Trotzky's agreement:

" The proletarian revolutionary government will be a government of workers' democracy. If Social Democracy is at the head of the revolutionary movement of the Russian proletariat, then this government will be a social-democratic government."

Rosa Luxemburg dealt exhaustively with the points at issue in the Polish socialist publication *Przeglad Socjaldemokraticzny* (" Social-Democratic Review "), and she declared that Lenin's proposal would prove inoperable for two reasons. He was certainly right when he attacked the Menshevists for their hidebound scholasticism in regarding the peasantry as a reactionary class in defiance of the plain facts of the Russian situation, but he overlooked the very considerable social differentiation within the peasantry as a class, and also the fact that it would certainly, and probably very soon, go over again into the camp of the reaction. Above all, he was wrong with regard to the attitude of the working class: no power on earth could dissuade the proletariat from using its political power in its own interests, irrespective of the limits of the *bourgeois* social order. A government of socialists which attempted to limit the action of the working class in this way would necessarily have to fight against its own class, and it would inevitably prepare the way for the triumph of the counter-revolution. Social Democracy must therefore seek allies amongst the peasantry and support their revolutionary action to bring about the overthrow of Tsarism. It must take the reins of government into its own hands without hesitation, arm the revolutionary masses of the people, and organise the armed working class. This provisional government must carry out as quickly as possible, and by dictatorial means, all the fundamental measures necessary for the political and economic transformation of society. Once this was done a Constitutional Assembly could be called on the basis of the general franchise, but whilst this body was drafting the new constitution, power must remain firmly in the hands of the revolutionary government, and the masses of the people must retain their arms in order to ensure that parliament did not backslide towards the counter-revolution, and if necessary to intervene energetically against it. Rosa Luxemburg was thinking here of such historical events as the Long Parliament in England and the Convention in France. She regarded the political aims of a class as the result of a very complicated process of development and struggle, and as a general rule she was therefore unwilling to make any attempt to reduce them to the limits of a slogan, but this time, and probably as a counterblast to Lenin's " revolutionary-democratic dictatorship of the proletariat and the peasantry ", she formulated the slogan " Revolutionary Dictatorship of the Proletariat based on the Peasantry ".

She was very well aware that conditions in Russia were not sufficiently mature to permit the proletariat to retain power in its hands indefinitely, but at the same time the overthrow of Absolutism seemed possible to her only as the result of the class victory of the proletariat, which would inevitably lead to the seizure of power. She believed, therefore, that Absolutism could be overthrown only if the working class and its leading party directed their whole policy towards this aim. Undoubtedly, once in possession of power, the proletariat would adopt measures transcending the limits of the *bourgeois* social order, and in doing so it would overtax its strength and come into conflict with social " possibilities ". As a result of this policy it would provoke the hostility of the other social forces, and in the end succumb to the counter-revolution. The only way to avoid this fate would be to abandon revolutionary politics altogether. Social Democracy would succeed in leading the revolution to victory only if it submitted consciously to these historical necessities; at the same time it would free Russia from the trammels of absolutist reaction, give an impetus to historical progress beyond Russia's frontiers, and win gains of lasting value for the international working-class movement.

5. Skirmishing in the Rear

Her daring conception of the course of events in Russia was confirmed step by step throughout 1905. During the whole year the working class laid down the law of action for all other social forces. Immediately after the events of Bloody Sunday a vast wave of political strikes swept over the country, and in the name of society as a whole the Russian proletariat raised its fist against Absolutism. Demands for democratic liberties and a Constitutional Assembly spread like wildfire. The authorities were taken completely by surprise and stood helpless in face of the upheaval. Victory seemed almost at hand, and barricades appeared on the streets of Warsaw. However, it was no more than a beginning. The great wave of strikes broke up into innumerable smaller local actions, whose aims ceased to be political, and became economic: higher wages, shorter hours, and improved working conditions. The antithesis Absolutism-*bourgeoisie* was overshadowed by the antithesis capitalism proletariat.

In March the movement received a new impulse as a result of the Russian defeat in Manchuria, and it began to embrace wider and wider sections of the population. A new wave of strikes swept over the country, accompanied by students' strikes, whilst in the rural areas peasants began to set fire to the property of the rich landowners. In Tiflis the first military mutiny occurred. In April the sailors of the Baltic Fleet demonstrated on the streets of Petersburg. Peasant unrest broke out in the Baltic provinces. Strikes, demonstrations, and street-fighting took place in the towns.

On May-Day there was a general strike and big demonstrations in the industrial districts. Collisions occurred between the demonstrators and military in Warsaw and Kalish. The Russian Fleet was destroyed by the Japanese at Tsushima. The " League of the Russian People ", alias the notorious Black Hundreds, was founded. Pogroms broke out. In June there was a general strike and barricade fighting in Warsaw; the famous armoured cruiser *Potemkin* was seized by its crew; troops mutinied in Libau, Riga, and other towns, peasant disturbances occurred in many places, and acts of terrorism took place. In July there was a mutiny in Cherson; strikes of the railwaymen; peasant revolts in the Baltic provinces. In August Minister Bulygin issued a manifesto announcing the calling of a new Duma, which was to have very limited powers and to be elected on the basis of a franchise excluding the majority of the workers and peasants. In September Russian Social Democracy decided to boycott the new Duma. In October a political general strike began in Moscow and spread throughout the country, embracing millions of workers and paralysing economic life and political administration. It ended in the first great victory: on October 30th the Tsar issued a manifesto announcing the introduction of certain democratic liberties and the calling of a Duma based on an indirect franchise graded in assemblies.

In this period the whole Tsarist Empire was a seething cauldron in which all social elements, workers, peasants, students, and soldiers were in violent movement. But the *bourgeoisie*, which was, according to the Menshevists, predestined to take the leadership of the movement and to enjoy the obedience of the other revolutionary classes, was torn between fear and hope, and its representatives trotted around with petitions drawn up at various congresses whose proceedings were so unimportant that history has ignored them. The working class was the power which swept all other forces into the revolution, and the general strike of the workers was the effective weapon of the revolution. On October 26th the hegemony of the proletariat was documented in the formation of Councils of Workers' and Peasants' Deputies in Petersburg. These councils became the central leadership of the revolutionary struggle, and proved to be the embryo of the future public organs of revolutionary power. Up to this point the prophecies of the revolutionary socialist Left Wing were borne out with astonishing accuracy, and the sceptical leaders of the Menshevists let themselves be carried along with the tide, whilst the rank-and-file Menshevists co-operated with the Bolshevists in thousands of committees and worked with them to lend added impetus to the movement and to guide it towards its goal.

Rosa Luxemburg was living in Berlin at the time, and working with an almost feverish concentration of all her energies. Although some of the plans she mentions in her correspondence were not carried out, the amount of work she performed was remarkable. She closely studied political events in order to learn from the historical process at first hand, and in a brilliant series of polemical articles, pamphlets, etc., she interpreted the significance of contemporary events to those who were experiencing and making them. She brought some order into the chaos of apparently contradictory happenings, indicated the next stages of development, vigorously attacked illusions and false ideas about the situation amongst the revolutionaries, cold-douched romanticism, calmed down impatience, and brilliantly utilised the still-sparse experiences of the preliminary struggles to solve the burning question of revolutionary tactics with creative foresight and to concentrate the energy of the party on to its most urgent and immediate tasks.

And at the same time she was even more active than usual in the German and in the international socialist movements in order to make them realise the real significance of the events taking place in Russia. The Russian Revolution strengthened the confidence of the German workers and made them eager for action. In January the miners of the Ruhr district, who had remained passive in face of the overwhelming power of industrial capital, went on strike. The great struggle was fought around purely economic demands, but it had nevertheless a political character, because it aimed beyond Stinnes and Thyssen at the State itself, and after four weeks it won at least a promise of serious reforms. Throughout the country the German workers were showing a lively interest in Russian affairs, and everywhere there were demands for Rosa Luxemburg. She spoke at innumerable meetings up and down the country, and everywhere she was regarded as the living representative of the revolution, and her meetings developed into a tour of triumph. Under irresistible pressure from the enthusiastic masses, who would brook no refusal, she was allowed to speak even on trade-union platforms, which up to then had been closed to her. Clara Zetkin did much to make this possible, and in general she devoted herself with tireless energy to propagating the ideas of the Russian Revolution.

Another result of the happenings in Russia was that the old antagonism between reformists and revolutionaries broke out again, but this time the revolutionaries took the offensive. The Right-Wing elements revealed a symptomatic inability to understand the problems of the revolution. They were not, of course, opposed to the Russian Revolution, on the contrary, they declared themselves enthusiastically in favour of it, but although they prided themselves on their Marxism, they were unable to use it as a key to interpret the happenings in Russia, and they were therefore compelled to fall back on the old stand-by of all political ignoramuses: " the Russian Soul ". They justified the revolution in Russia, but only as an exceptional case, pointing out that any such thing would be impossible, and senseless in any case, in a constitutional State. In other words, the Russian Revolution was an interesting spectacle to be regarded sympathetically by European socialists, but having not the slightest bearing on their own future. The policy of Russian Social Democracy (their brother party in the International) was a closed book to them, and their real heroes were the Liberal Cadets (Constitutional Democrats) and (not so extraordinary as it may seem) the terrorist Social-Revolutionaries. They passed over the mass strikes of the proletariat almost without notice, but they were moved to the depths by dramatic effects such as the emptying of revolvers at Grand Dukes and Governors.

As might be imagined, this attitude provoked Rosa Luxemburg's fierce anger, and she poured bitter scorn on those who sought to explain the Russian Revolution " with banal phrases about bursting ice, endless steppes, tired, passive, and weeping souls, and all the other tomfoolery of bourgeois journalese whose exponents gather their entire knowledge of Russia from the latest performance of Gorki's ' Casual Ward ' or from Tolstoi's novels, and who ignore the social problems of two hemispheres with complacent fatuity ".

It caused her deep chagrin that the columns of the *Vorwärts* should overflow with such turgid bilge, but at least her incidental criticism of such miserable journalism provoked a half-humorous, half-serious polemic on the Marxist *versus* the " ethical aesthetic " conception of history, in which her brilliant friends Mehring and Kautsky led the attack in defence of the former. The important thing for her was to learn the lessons of the Russian Revolution with a view to putting them to some practical use in the struggles of the Western European proletariat. She regarded the political mass strike as used in the Russian Revolution as containing the most valuable lesson for the next stage of the German and Western-European working-class movements. For years she had striven to obtain recognition for this weapon, but without success. As late as 1904 the Congress of the German Social Democratic Party had rejected a motion by Karl Liebknecht that the party should consider the mass strike as a political weapon, but now the Russian example had won masses of workers over to the idea, and a big discussion on the point resulted. The trade-union leaders did their utmost to dissuade the workers from " playing with fire ", as they termed even a discussion of the problem, and the Trade Union Congress in Cologne condemned the idea of the mass strike almost unanimously. In the end, however, the Social Democratic Party Congress in Jena in the autumn of 1905 sanctioned the political strike as a weapon to be adopted under certain circumstances.

This decision was a personal victory for Rosa Luxemburg, but it did not entirely satisfy her. Although the resolution indicated that the militancy of the party was increasing, the formulation was disappointing, and it represented no more than a supplementing and guaranteeing of parliamentarism as the predominant weapon. In addition, it was seen that those who shared her views were in a very small minority, and even Bebel was against her. In her speech to the Jena Congress she declared:

" Listening to all the previous speeches on the question of the political mass strike it becomes difficult to believe that we are living in the glorious days of the Russian Revolution. They were more appropriate to the situation ten years ago. . . . Previous revolutions, and in particular the revolution of 1848, have shown clearly that in revolutionary situations it is not the masses who have to be held in check, but the parliamentarians and the lawyers, for fear that they will betray the masses and the revolution. . . . In face of all this mean spiritedness we must stress once again that the final words of the ' Communist Manifesto ' are not merely a fine-sounding phrase for use at public meetings, and that we are in deadly earnest when we declare: ' The workers have nothing to lose but their chains; they have a world to gain '."

Her uncompromising words irritated Bebel, and in his answering speech he declared ironically: " When I listened to all that, I found myself involuntarily looking down at my boots to see whether we were already wading through pools of blood." Occasionally the fiery old revolutionary forgot his own past, and became the perfect proper citizen. The same uncompromising words also disturbed the Public Prosecutor, and Rosa Luxemburg was arraigned for incitement to violence. A year later she was sentenced to two months imprisonment for the offence.

However, the Russian Revolution had goaded even the Central Committee of the German Social Democratic Party into a more exalted mood, and under the pressure of the Berlin district organisation, which had become actively discontented with the shilly-shallying of the *Vorwärts*, it launched, for the first time, a blow against the Right Wingers. Six editors of the *Vorwärts*, including Kurt Eisner and Gradnauer, Rosa Luxemburg's old enemy, were dismissed, and their places taken by Left Wingers, including Rosa Luxemburg herself. In a letter to Leo Jogiches, who was leading the Polish movement from Cracow at the time, we find her very doubtful about the real value of the new editorial board:

" It will consist of very mediocre lights, but they'll all be koscher enough. This is the first time since the world began that the *Vorwärts* has seen an entirely Left-Wing cabinet on the premises. Now they've got to show their ' ability to govern '. . . ."

Their "ability to govern" became only too obvious, and so did their determination not to displease the party leadership, but by that time Rosa Luxemburg was already at work in a very different quarter.

Chapter Six: ROSA LUXEMBURG IN ACTION

1. On the Revolutionary Front

"Rosa Luxemburg, a heroine with her tongue, does not think it right and proper to expose her own valuable carcase to the dangers of the Polish Revolution, but on the platform she will no doubt continue to screech revolution. . . . We can quite understand that she considers the risk not worth while, but what a colossal piece of impudence it is when a woman who takes good care to keep herself well away from the dangers attending the revolution in her own country, nevertheless makes it her business to incite the German workers to Revolution! What on earth would she do in the unlikely event of her speeches really causing a conflagration here? No doubt she would remember that she is an 'Internationalist', and leave us hurriedly for less dangerous climes."

That was Pastor Naumann, leader of the Monarchist Democratic Imperialists; the man who a few years before, himself well away from the danger zone, had frenziedly urged on the " Bearers of German Kultur " to emulate the Huns in their crusade against the hapless Chinese. The same melody " Get to Poland! " was sung in numerous keys for Rosa Luxemburg's benefit, and her reformist colleagues exultantly joined in the chorus. Even long after she was actually running the risks they were so anxious that she should take, echoes of the refrain could still be heard here and there.

Naturally such things had no effect on her, and they had not the slighest weight in her decision to go to Poland. However, when her health had sufficiently improved to make it at all possible for her to rough it, and when it became clear that she could do useful work on the actual scene of operations, she left Germany. She did so against the urgent advice of her friends, and without the permission of the party leaders, who, both for political and personal reasons, would hardly have granted it. With the passport of a Berlin party member, named Anna Matschke, she smuggled herself over the frontier into Russian Poland in December 1905.

It proved an adventurous journey. The decisive struggle had opened up between Revolution and Absolutism. As soon as it became clear that the October Manifesto of the Tsar was nothing but an attempt to gain time for a counter-attack, the working class again declared a general strike. Insurrection broke out in Moscow. The railway service was paralysed. The Government was mobilising all the troops which appeared still reliable, and concentrating them against the big towns.

At the frontier railway traffic ceased. An attempt to get to Warsaw along the direct route via Thorn and Alexandrovo failed, and Rosa Luxemburg was compelled to travel along the frontier in a wide circle as far as Illovo. At Illovo there were no trains running either, and no possibility of obtaining horses to go by road—which would have been a very dangerous proceeding in any case. One train did leave Illovo for Warsaw, a military train packed with troops on their way to bring the rebellious capital of Russian Poland to reason, and Rosa Luxemburg travelled with it. It was bitterly cold and the train was not heated. It was also in darkness in order to escape the observation of the people, and it crawled along for fear of derailment. At every station the soldiers stood to arms in readiness for a possible attack. The journey lasted two days, and all the time she lived in fear of discovery, but luck was with her, and the leader of the revolution arrived in the capital escorted by the counter-revolution with military honours.

Warsaw was under martial law. The streets of the inner city were almost deserted except for regular patrols of military. The workers were still on strike, but they had suffered a defeat, and the insurrection in Moscow was crushed. Rosa Luxemburg was not dismayed, and in a letter to Kautsky written on January 2nd she declared:

" The cause of the defeat is quite clear: the general strike alone is no longer enough. Only a general armed rising can obtain a favourable decision now, but that must be better prepared."

No one, either in the camp of the counter-revolution or in the ranks of its enemies, recognised that the culminating point of the revolutionary movement had already passed. The masses were still active, but they had become hesitant, and tended to wait for a move from their enemies. All public meetings were forbidden, but the workers met in the factories without interference and heard the speakers of the various parties. The factories were their strongholds. All working-class organisations were also forbidden, but the trade unions were growing by leaps and bounds. All working-class newspapers were suppressed, but the organ of Polish Social Democracy, *Czerwony Sztandar* (" Red Flag "), appeared daily. It was printed in secret, and the printing premises were frequently changed. Very often printing-works were raided and the paper was set and printed at the point of the revolver, and those master-printers who were willing to print the paper demanded that they should be raided and " forced " to do so in this fashion. And every day, despite both police and military, the newspaper boys ran through the streets shouting out the latest edition.

However, the difficulties of the revolutionaries increased. The failure of the strike and the defeat of the insurrection in Moscow heartened the reaction. The State apparatus recovered from the first shock, and the police, who had become hesitant in face of popular indignation, now noticed the uncertainty of the workers, and became more vigorous again. They were wholeheartedly supported by the *bourgeois* Press, which now violently attacked the revolutionaries, even in Poland. A fierce campaign was launched against the Social Democratic Party. Raids and arrests took place almost every day, and there were threats of summary executions. The task of the revolutionary leaders became daily more difficult: speeches in the factories; propaganda in the barracks; the issue of newspapers, leaflets, and pamphlets—a dozen and one organisational and political tasks. In the general confusion and bustle Rosa Luxemburg took it upon herself to contribute to a better understanding of the movement as a whole and to lay down its next aims. For this purpose she wrote a pamphlet entitled " The Revolution has Struck; What Next? " This was the third of three pamphlets issued by her under the same title. The two previous ones had been written in April and May 1905 in Berlin.

2. THE PROBLEM OF ARMED INSURRECTION

The revolutionary movement had developed even more vigorously in Poland than in Russia, and the industrialisation of the country gave it greater impetus, whilst the existence of national antagonism to Tsarism made the *petit-bourgeoisie* more active. As early as March 1904 big demonstrations began and gradually increased in size. Police and military proceeded against the movement with the added brutality of foreign oppression, so that in the autumn of 1904 the Polish Socialist Party decided to offer armed resistance, and on November 13th fierce fighting took place on the streets of Warsaw. At the beginning of January 1905 big movements broke out in Lodz, Radom, Siedlce, and other towns, and after Bloody Sunday they began to develop into armed conflicts—for instance, in Lodz, Vilna, Kovno, Byelostock, Dombrovo, Zavierce, and Czenstochau. The Polish Socialist Party claimed to have the leadership in these struggles, and probably it had. It enjoyed the support of big sections of the working class, and its membership was larger than that of the Social Democratic Party. Events seemed to justify its strategy of fighting for the national independence of Poland, and with its successes it began to adopt a boastful and aggressive tone: " The Polish Socialist Party will settle accounts with its external and internal enemies. It will also settle accounts with those individuals who have come in uncalled from abroad, people who cannot even speak Polish, and their disruptive cliques." [1]

The leaders of the Polish Socialist Party were over-confident and very contemptuous of their rivals in the working-class movement, but they were romanticists rather than real-

[1] Ladislaus Gumplovitcz in the " *Sozialistische Monatshefte* ", March 1905. The nationalist sneer was directed, without factual justification, against Leo Jogiches.

ists, and they saw things as they wanted to see them, and not as they actually were. For years they had insisted that the Polish people were the real revolutionary nation *par excellence*, and they arrogantly ridiculed any suggestion that the barbarian Russians, Ukrainians, Georgians, etc., might also be capable of revolutionary action. For this reason they considered the overthrow of Tsarism impossible and saw Poland's only hope in forcible separation from Russia. They placed no reliance on class forces within Russia, and they regarded emancipation as a military action to be carried out along the lines of the 1863 revolt. All their speculations were therefore based on a favourable foreign-political juncture. This was the policy which sent the leader of the Polish Socialist Party, Josef Pilsudski, hot foot to Tokyo on the outbreak of the Russo-Japanese War in order to beg the Mikado for arms and financial assistance.

When, directly contrary to the expectations of the leaders of the Polish Socialist Party, a revolutionary movement against Absolutism broke out throughout the whole of Russia, they let themselves be carried along with the tide; but the entire character of the movement was foreign to them and their ideas, and immediately the first big happenings took place their revolutionary romanticism boiled over. In the spring of 1905 their party organ *Robotnik* (" Worker ") announced enthusiastically: " Now we have revolutionary forces we must also have revolutionary weapons. Let us form fighting detachments and obtain arms and other weapons and we shall soon have political freedom." The great need of the moment as they saw it was to arm their own followers, and, if they could, the entire Polish people, to purchase arms from abroad, and to manufacture as many bombs as possible.

Rosa Luxemburg regarded these ideas as a danger to the revolution, and she said so in her first pamphlet: they were typical of parties whose attachment to the working-class was artificial and incidental; such parties shared the general idea of the *bourgeoisie* that only physical force decided the fate of social struggles; they were transferring the ideas of conspiratorial terrorists circles to the working-class movement: just give the workers arms, and everything would be all right. Absolutism would certainly be overthrown only by a general insurrection, but the arms would have to be won by the masses in action, by disarming the military and the police, by storming arms depots, and by similar actions:

> " It is not the party committee, not the all-powerful and brilliant ' leader ', and not the little circle of conspirators calling itself a fighting detachment, which count in the revolution, but the broad masses of the people prepared to shed their blood. The ' socialists ' may imagine that it is the duty of the masses to take orders from them and to be trained by them for the armed struggle, but in reality and in all revolutions it is the masses who adopt the ways and means best suited to the conditions of the moment."

Social Democracy must realise the limits of the given situation. In the best case individual workers and groups of workers could be, and certainly should be, armed, in order to resist the brutalities of the police and military; but to tell the workers that the party would provide them with sufficient weapons to fight a pitched battle with the standing army would be to deceive the working class to a dangerous extent.

On the other hand, Rosa Luxemburg did not suggest that the workers should wait patiently for the outbreak of street-fighting, and then leave the lives of thousands to mere chance. She had her own method of preparation, and it must have proved surprising to all those who denounced her as a Blanquist, a Bakuninist, and a blood-wader. Her method was agitation: agitation, above all, in the country districts. Win the peasants and day-labourers for Socialism first, awaken their determination to resist oppression, awaken a desire for emancipation:

> " We must unfurl the banner of the class struggle in the rural areas, and our political demands must not be cloaked with the unclear and cowardly phrases of ordinary patriotism. We must show them their proletarian and semi-proletarian conditions of life, make them realise their own real interests, and, above all, the primary interest they have in common with the working masses of the whole of Russia : the overthrow of Absolutism."

In this way the revolutionary movement could be made general; it would spread everywhere and compel the enemy to dissipate his forces. The primary task of the socialist movement was not the formation of fighting detachments, but agitation amongst the soldiers. It was precisely here that all social-patriotic proposals failed. Russian soldiers stationed in Poland could not be moved by any cause not obviously their own, and socialists must therefore appeal to their class interests as workers and peasants. Socialist agitation would win over a section of the military and make others hesitant, thus weakening Absolutism and undermining the discipline of its armed forces. Socialism should arm the proletariat, both in uniform and out, with the one weapon it could offer: enlightenment on the economic and political interests of the workers and peasants. Enthusiasm for mere acts of violence was misplaced:

"There are two ways of accelerating the revolution and disorganising the government. The government is being shaken by the war with Japan, by the Tchunguses in Manchuria, by famine and bad harvests, and by the loss of credit on the stock exchanges of Europe. These factors are beyond the scope of the working masses. Bomb-throwing is in the same category. Mass action is a very different matter, and it is not dependent on accidents: mass strikes; the dislocation of industry, transport, and commerce; military mutinies; the stopping of trains by strikers, etc. Bomb-throwing has about as much real effect as gnat bites. . . . Only people incapable of political thought imagine that acts of individual terrorism have anything but a passing effect.

"Disorganisation by mass action: that is the real danger for Absolutism. Mass action not only disorganises the ruling system, but it also organises at the same time the political forces which are predestined to overthrow Absolutism and create a new social order. This is the only course for Social Democracy. . . . Agitation will win over the countryside. It will undermine discipline in the army and draw great masses into action. It will generate the forces to throw up barricades, seize the necessary arms, win first a victory here and then a victory there, and finally draw the whole people into the struggle and overthrow Absolutism."

For Rosa Luxemburg the tasks of a revolutionary party went far beyond the heroism of individuals and far beyond the scintillating coups of small minorities: mass agitation, the winning of people's minds for Socialism so that their socialist will could then develop into mass action for Socialism. It was the attitude adopted by Marx at the beginning of the 1848 Revolution, when he vigorously opposed Herwegh's adventurous plan of raising an army of volunteers to carry the revolution into Germany at the point of the bayonet. Rosa Luxemburg's chief anxiety was to ensure that the revolution should reach organic maturity, that the dynamic of events themselves should be utilised by the working-class movement. That was the task of leadership. She was well aware that the party would have very definite technical tasks to perform in preparation for mass insurrection, and in January 1906, at a time when she realised that the mere general strike as such was no longer sufficient to carry the movement to victory, she wrote in her third pamphlet:

" The stage of open struggle which has now begun, makes it the duty of Social Democracy to arm the most advanced workers as well as possible, to prepare plans for street fighting, and, above all, to utilise the lessons of the Moscow struggle. The technical preparations for the armed struggle are tremendously important and absolutely necessary, but they must not be taken as the chief guarantee of victory. In the last resort it will not be the fighting detachments of an organised minority which will carry the day, though they also have their special tasks in the revolutionary struggle, but the broad masses of the proletariat. It will be their readiness to fight and their heroism which will carry the day on the streets. However, these masses cannot be organised in fighting detachments; they can be organised and prepared only on the basis of the daily class struggle both economic and political. Social-democratic trade unions and social-democratic organisations in the army—these are our chief tasks in the preparation for victory."

Armed insurrection was not a frontal attack upon the armed forces of the State, and it was possible at all only if the troops were already partly demoralised, and there were some hope of the process being completed in the fighting itself, leading to the defection of sections of the troops to the side of the people

All this is in diametrical contradiction to the version of her ideas given by certain malicious " Bolshevist " critics.[1] On the other hand, although a textual comparison of Rosa Luxemburg's and Lenin's writings on the point would often reveal agreement, it would be wrong to imagine that they were in agreement in every respect. They approach the question from different angles—for instance, Lenin writes:

" There is no doubt that much, very much, still remains to be done for the enlightenment and organisation of the working class, but now it is a question of knowing where the fulcrum of this enlightenment and organisation must lie: in the trade unions and the legal organisations or in the armed insurrection and the creation of a revolutionary army and a revolutionary government? "[2]

The same can be seen from a passage in Lenin's " What Next? ", in which he declares that the party must create a network of organised military agents whose activity at the moment of insurrection would offer the greatest probability of success:

" The ability to estimate the general political situation correctly, and in consequence also the ability to chose the moment for insurrection opportunely, would be developed precisely in such work. . . . At the same time precisely such work would also compel all revolutionary organisations throughout Russia to maintain permanent and at the same time strictly conspiratorial relations with each other. . . . Without this it is impossible to discuss plans for insurrection collectively and to take the necessary joint measures on the eve of insurrection, both of which must be kept a jealously guarded secret."

History has pronounced judgement on both these conceptions of armed insurrection. Fighting detachments organised on conspiratorial lines have never been able, even in the best case, to do more than stiffen the fighting masses, whilst in the worst case they have often become a danger to the party

[1] E.g., Yaroslavski's " Rosa Luxemburg on Armed Insurrection ", in which the author quotes one or two passages torn from their context, and reveals utter ignorance, feigned or real, of her two fundamental writings on the point.

[2] Lenin, " Two Tactics ", July 1905, Geneva.

E

itself, threatening to launch putschist actions on their own account, whenever they felt the crucial moment for insurrection was being passed, so that the party has often had to dissolve them altogether. On the other hand, the insurrections of 1905–6 approached nearer to what Rosa Luxemburg had in mind. The Moscow Soviet issued the order for the December insurrection, and it issued it quite openly, but in doing so it followed the masses rather than its own free choice. The beginning of the struggle was spontaneous, and the leadership of the insurrection played more the part of a military adviser. The insurrection of November 7th, 1917, on the other hand, was carefully prepared by the Bolshevist Party according to a definite time-table, and it was carried out almost exclusively by regiments which had gone over to the Bolshevists.

The same thing can be seen in the Great French Revolution: a spontaneous action on July 14th, 1789, shook Absolutism to its foundations, and a planned action on August 10th, 1792, brought the final victory. From this one may assume that first of all spontaneous outbreaks such as Rosa Luxemburg had in mind break out during the course of a revolution, but that the final victory can be achieved only by a well-prepared and organised insurrection such as Lenin had in mind from the beginning. A characteristic feature of Rosa Luxemburg's treatment of tactical problems is that she invariably has the next stage of the movement in mind. For instance, when she was interpreting the lessons of the Russian Revolution for the proletariat of Western Europe, she attached more importance to the question of the mass strike than to the actual insurrection. In her theoretical writings intended to serve directly the cause of the revolution in Poland we can observe exactly the opposite, however. Thus there was no absolute difference of opinion between Lenin and Luxemburg on this question.

3. Social Democracy and the Socialist Party in Poland

In the second of her " What Now? " pamphlets (published in May 1905) Rosa Luxemburg deals with the remarkable fact that the first great political mass strike, which broke out in January 1905, finally disintegrated into innumerable small strikes of an economic nature which then dragged on for many months. She raised a question which was occupying the minds of all revolutionaries at the time: " Does this transition from a mass political strike into a number of minor economic strikes represent a temporary decline in revolutionary energy, a retreat, an aimless skirmish with capitalism? And ought we in the future to oppose such a development, to call off the political strike itself whilst it has still all the power of a political demonstration? "

Rosa Luxemburg regarded the solution of the problem as lying in an understanding of the double character of the revolution. It was a *bourgeois* revolution as far as political liberties, the republic, and parliamentary democracy were concerned, but at the same time it had a proletarian character because the working class took the lead in revolutionary action, because its methods dominated the struggle, and because it had developed into the strongest and most important social factor. This new-found force must necessarily express itself in a direct struggle against capital for the improvement of working-class conditions, irrespective of the effects this might have on the political attitude of the *bourgeoisie*. Social Democracy should therefore not oppose these economic strikes under any circumstances, but rather seek to guide them into the main channel of the revolution. The outbreak of economic strikes was also a proof that it would be impossible to keep working-class action within the framework of the *bourgeois* social order once power came into the hands of the working class during the course of the revolution.

At the same time Rosa Luxemburg warned the socialists against tarring all economic strikes with the same brush. Strike fever suddenly seizing hold on great masses of workers was something quite different from a strike in a single factory. Far more important than the fact that the recent strike wave had won improvements in working-class standards, was the fact that new strata had been drawn into the strike movement for the first time: the army of industrial workers in the provinces, the clerical workers, the members of certain professions, and the great mass of the landless proletariat with the proletarised peasantry. Thus for her the economic strike represented a tremendous extension of the revolutionary sphere of action. The task of Social Democracy was therefore to encourage these strikes round the central slogan of the eight-hour day, in order to develop a united mass movement, which would then in its turn develop into a political struggle.

This also represented an important point of difference with the Polish Socialist Party, which participated in economic strikes against its will and only in order to avoid losing its influence on the masses, whilst at the same time bemoaning the " degeneration " of the revolution into a mere bread-and-butter question. It insisted that it was the only revolutionary party, and condemned the Social Democratic Party for misleading the workers. This question really represented the core of all differences in the Polish socialist movement since 1893 : the ideas of the Polish Socialist Party (P.P.S.) which aimed at securing the political restoration of an independent Poland, and the ideas of Rosa Luxemburg, who declared that the overthrow of Absolutism would come through a revolution in which the Polish proletariat would ally itself with the Russian proletariat, and in which the two proletariats would establish their political hegemony over all other revolutionary forces. From the standpoint of the working class it became abundantly clear that the former conception was the wish-dream fulfilment of *petit-bourgeois* nationalist intellectuals, whilst the latter was the logical result of the historical process.

It quickly became manifest that the real revolution was not a matter of bomb-throwing and other putschist undertakings, but one of mass action by millions of people; but the Polish Socialist Party insisted on closing its eyes to the plain facts, and, as a result, it soon lost the leadership of the struggle, and was dragged along in the wake of the Social Democratic Party, because the rank and file of the P.P.S. followed the social democratic slogans, and thus compelled their leaders to do the same. Trouble developed in the leadership of the Socialist Party; the purely nationalists, the " social patriots ", observed with horror that their hopes of an independent Poland disappeared as rapidly as the Russian revolution advanced, and in consequence they opposed the revolution itself.

As early as June 1905 the leadership of the Socialist Party opposed the general strike which broke out in Warsaw and Lodz, and denounced the Social Democratic Party for driving the workers into the strike for " senseless self-advertisement ". This was an admission that the Socialist Party leaders had lost their influence on the working class and even on their own party members. However, worse was to come, and after the great all-Russia general strike in December 1905, Dashinski, the leader and deputy of the Galician Socialist Party and recognised leader of the Polish Socialist Party, published an " Open Letter " in the Cracow *Naprzod* (" Forward ") which was circulated in all three parts of Poland. In this letter he thundered against any general strike on Polish territory, declaring that at a time when the Russian State was suffering a severe crisis the Poles should follow their own aims and use their own methods. They must emancipate themselves from movements of foreign origin having other aims and threatening to corrupt and destroy Polish life. The only aim of the Poles was to win Polish independence. Victory was possible, and the Polish people must prepare for the struggle, and not dissipate its forces prematurely for foreign aims—namely, the attainment of an All-Russia revolution. A general strike might be a suitable and even a victorious weapon in Tsarist Russia, but in Poland it must prove fatal. What was the sense of a strike on the Warsaw–Vienna line, which was not in State hands, but in private Polish capitalist possession?

Chasing after the phantom of national independence, Dashinski trampled over working-class interests, and, in defiance of obvious facts, he assured the Poles that not classes but peoples were engaged in combat in Russia. He dreamed of the unification of the whole Polish people in the struggle for national independence, and his dream was made still more fantastic by the circumstance that the loyalty of the Polish *bourgeoisie* to Russian Absolutism did not waver for one moment and even the National Democrats abandoned the idea of a national insurrection for Polish independence. It was quite clear that a national revolution was possible only within the framework of a social revolution, and, as far as the working class was concerned, class interests were victorious over national interests; but the Polish Socialist Party clung on to the idea of national independence, and placed it above all else. Dashinski, Pilsudski, and their friends now demanded absolute independence of the Russian Revolution and a national insurrection at the moment of Russian revolutionary victory. Thus the leaders of the Polish Socialist Party, who a year before had proclaimed themselves the real leaders of the Polish proletariat, were now compelled by logical necessity to turn away from the proletariat and abandon the cause of Socialism. Their rabid nationalism had condemned them to utter confusion and political impotence.

Dashinski's " Open Letter ", which was answered by Rosa Luxemburg with great trenchancy, brought the crisis in the Socialist Party to a head, and a split took place at its Congress in 1906. The overwhelming majority of the party supported the Left Wing, which then abandoned the slogan of Polish independence and adopted what was practically the programme of the Social Democratic Party. Under the leadership of Pilsudski, the " Fighting Detachments " separated from the party and called themselves the Polish Socialist Party—Revolutionary Fraction. Rosa Luxemburg's strategy had proved completely successful: twelve years of intellectual struggle had brought the whole Polish working-class movement over to her standpoint.

Pilsudski's " Revolutionary Fraction " degenerated into a clique of adventurers. The " Fighting Detachments " adopted " a policy of expropriation " and made armed raids on railway stations, post offices, etc., finally becoming little more than bandits. Rosa Luxemburg was deeply horrified at the degeneration of this movement, and writing in 1909 she describes the scenes before the courts-martial in 1907–8:

" Common bandits appear before the courts-martial side by side with revolutionary workers. They claim membership of the class movement of the proletariat, are included in the common statistics of the counter-revolutionary terror, sit together with revolutionary workers in the prison cells, and die on the gallows singing the anthem of the revolution. Many of these bandits were once revolutionary workers and members of socialist organisations. The mixture of revolutionary activity, banditry, provocation, and spying revealed at some of the proceedings is terrible, and very often the same proletarian strata are involved. How was it possible that the inspiring drama of proletarian revolution could ever have anything in common with this anti-revolutionary individualist struggle of the slum elements against private property? "

The only explanation she could find was in the terrible privations of great masses of workers during the period of reaction, and in the political spinelessness of Pilsudski's so-called " Revolutionary Fraction ", which rapidly caused it to sink completely into political terrorism.

After the utter bankruptcy of this sort of " revolutionary action " had been made undeniably manifest, its inspirer and leader, Josef Pilsudski, cast around for other means of attaining his political aims. When war between Tsarist Russia and Austria-Hungary seemed imminent in 1909 as a result of the annexation of Bosnia by Austria-Hungary, Pilsudski became the Polish agent of the Austro-Hungarian Government, and founded Polish rifle clubs as recruiting units for a Polish Legion to be attached to the Habsburg Army. This action represented the final breach with the working-class movement, and Pilsudski and his followers joined the camp of imperialism.

Seldom has a political conception been so thoroughly justi-fied in the event as Rosa Luxemburg's Polish policy. In the spring of 1906 the Polish Social Democratic Party became affiliated to the Russian Social Democratic Party, and thence-forward the proclamation of the right of self-determination by Russian Social Democracy represented no danger for proletarian strategy in Poland: the principle of national self-determination and the policy of the Polish working class now represented a dialectical unity.

4. In Prison in Poland

The Polish Social Democratic Party became the undisputed leader of the working class in 1905, and Poland marched in the van of the revolutionary movement, outstripped only from time to time by the workers of Petersburg and Moscow. The chief reason for this was, of course, the more advanced industrialisation of Poland, but at the same time the political firmness of the Social Democratic Party under the leadership of Rosa Luxemburg played a great rôle. Leo Jogiches (whose party name at the time was Jan Tyszka) had come to Warsaw under the name of Otto Engelmann, where he had ample opportunity of using his great organising ability. Rosa Luxemburg and Jogiches enjoyed the support of a splendid group of revolutionaries: Djerjinski, who led the military organisation of the party in co-operation with the Russian

Petrienko, Varski, Karski, Radek, Aussem, Hanecki, Malecki, Domski, Unschlicht, Leder, and Brodovski, who were all men who rendered great services in the Russian Revolution of 1917 and the subsequent years. In 1901 the party had hardly 1,000 members, but by 1905 it had grown to 25,000, and by 1907 it even reached 40,000. It issued newspapers in Polish, Yiddish, and German, distributed leaflets in Russian amongst the army of occupation, organised trade unions, and led both strike and barricade struggles.

Naturally, the work entailed sacrifices, and after the December strike the persecutions intensified and arrests became increasingly frequent. On March 4th Rosa Luxemburg and Leo Jogiches were arrested in the house of Countess Valevska. The Warsaw police were put on the track by reports from Germany, and after the arrest of Rosa Luxemburg the German reactionary Press began a campaign of incitement against her and did its best to provide the authorities with material for her prosecution. At first the two were held under their assumed names, Matschke and Engelmann, but the police had an inkling of the truth, and a week later they found a photo of her in the possession of her sister, and she was unable to deny her identity. It was June, however, before the police discovered the real identity of Jogiches, and then it was owing to the denunciation of the German newspaper *Die Post*.

Rosa Luxemburg was first held in the police prison in the Town Hall of Warsaw. Conditions were terrible. The reaction had set in, and the police were out on the hunt. Day after day they emptied their net into the prison. Rosa Luxemburg describes her experiences in a letter to Kautsky:

" Here I am in the Town Hall where ' Politicals ', common criminals, and lunatics are all cooped up together. My cell, intended for one person, now has 14 guests, fortunately all political. On either side of us are two ordinary double cells with about 30 prisoners in each. . . . We sleep all over the floor, packed together like sardines. . . . Such a thing as exercising in the open air seems to be quite unknown here, but during the day the cell doors are left open and we are allowed to walk in the corridor and mix with the common prostitutes, enjoying their conversation and the smell from the open lavatories."

Her health had been undermined by the incessant strain of the previous months, and the conditions she describes soon made her seriously ill, and, in addition, she was further weakened by hunger strikes, which represented the only weapon of the prisoners in their struggle for better conditions. On April 11th she was removed to the notorious " X Pavilion " of the Warsaw Fortress, where conditions were a little better. In February 1917 she again mentions her prison experiences, in a letter to Sonia Liebknecht, the wife of Karl Liebknecht:

"Nothing has affected me so much for a long time as Martha's short description of your visit to Karl. Why didn't you tell me about it? I was vividly reminded of my brother's first visit to me ten years ago in the Warsaw Citadel. There one has to receive visitors in a double cage. A smaller cage stands in a larger one and the prisoner has to talk to his visitors through a double wire network. In my case it was just after a week's hunger strike and I was so exhausted that the warder had practically to carry me into the cage where I clung to the wire netting with both hands to keep myself upright, and I suppose that intensified the impression of a wild animal in the Zoo. My cage was in a rather gloomy corner of the room and my brother pressed his face to the netting. ' Where are you? ' he kept asking, polishing his glasses because the tears blurred his vision."

But there were still worse experiences. There were days when gallows were erected in the prison yard, and then a leaden silence fell until the condemned prisoner began his last journey and the funeral march sounded from all the cells. And sometimes revolutionary prisoners were blindfolded and taken from their cells never to return. Their lives were blotted out without previous legal procedure and sentence. Once this fate seemed about to be Rosa Luxemburg's. Leo Jogiches, reserved and unsentimental, described the incident after her death. The cell door was opened, her eyes were bound, and she was led away, but fortunately it proved to be only an examination, and the sinister procedure was due either to an error or to a deliberate act of mental cruelty. Asked what she felt at the time, Rosa replied: " I was ashamed because I felt myself blanching."

E 2

To use her own expression, she knew that her situation was " rather serious ", but she was not cast down by the sufferings and horrors of prison life. She was sick and she began to go prematurely grey, but her letters from prison are invariably cheerful and full of humorous anecdotes and self-irony. Although she was physically weak and a complete breakdown in health seemed imminent, her indomitable spirit rose to the threat and transcended the sufferings and the menace of the future. She even enjoyed the constant struggle with the prison authorities, and was delighted when she succeeded in besting them. All visits took place in the wire cage she has described; the supervising warders were forbidden to speak to their prisoners under threat of transfer to a punishment battalion. The prison itself was within the walls of the citadel, and the authorities were at great pains to cut it off entirely from the outer world. However, Rosa Luxemburg remained in constant touch with the struggle outside. Not only did she receive regular information concerning the activities of the Social Democratic Party, but she was able to give both advice and instructions. She even received reliable information concerning the happenings in Petersburg social-democratic circles, and it was of such a nature that she exclaimed in despair:

" What confusion! What a lack of determination and energy! ' But let me be there, be there! ' Heavens above! I'd wake them up, if I had to knock their heads together first."

Not only was she able to obtain information and send out instructions to the party, but after four weeks in the citadel she reported that she had written three pamphlets and succeeded in smuggling them all out. At the same time she wrote regular articles for the party Press, though she could work only from 9 p.m. until 2 a.m., so that the work was done chiefly at the cost of her sleep.

Her relatives were, of course, doing their utmost to secure her release. They had got into touch with the Central Committee of the German Social Democratic Party, and hoped that Rosa Luxemburg's German nationality would prove sufficient to secure a weighty *démarche* from the German Government. Rosa complained bitterly about this, and demanded that no appeal should be made to the German authorities, pointing out that if they did anything for her she would not be able to speak her mind about them so freely in

the future.   Her nationality was, as a matter of fact, causing
the Public Prosecutor in Warsaw some anxiety, because
politeness between nations had not yet died out.   In the end
the authorities had resort to a trick: Rosa Luxemburg's
marriage with Lübeck was valid in Germany, but as it had
not been solemnised before a Rabbi it was not valid in Russia,
so that although she was a German in Germany, she was still
a Russian in Russia.   However, in June a medical commission reported: "Luxemburg suffers from anaemia,
hysterical and neurasthenic symptoms, catarrh of the stomach
and the intestines, and dilation of the liver.   Hydropathic
and spa treatment seems desirable together with a strict
diet."   On June 28th she was released on the basis of this
report, but ordered to remain in Warsaw.   Bail in the sum of
3000 roubles had to be found for her, and it seems likely that
the Central Committee of the German Social Democratic
Party put forward the money, because after that she was
accused of base ingratitude whenever she dared to involve the
Central Committee in disagreeable discussions.   Some further intervention appears to have been made, and a second
medical report advised treatment at a foreign spa.   On July
31st she was permitted to leave Warsaw.   There were, however, other reasons for her unexpected release than those set
down in the official records of the case.   During the revolution
the police force was demoralised to a very considerable extent.
High officials had been bribed, and, in addition, the Fighting
Organisation of the Social Democratic Party had let the
officials of the Ochrana know that in the event of anything
serious happening to Rosa Luxemburg, vengeance would be
taken.

She first went to Petersburg, where she met Axelrod and
became involved in violent arguments about revolutionary
tactics.   After that she stayed a month in Kuokkala in Finland,
and from there she visited Parvus and Leo Deutsch in the
notorious SS. Peter-Paul Prison, where they were preparing
to make the journey into Siberian banishment.   It was in
Kuokkala that Rosa Luxemburg wrote her pamphlet "The
Mass Strike, the Party and the Trade Unions", in order to
interpret the lessons of the Russian Revolution for the German
working class.   She was now eager to get back to the political
struggle in Germany, but there was one hindrance.   She

knew that a prosecution for her speech at the Jena Congress of the Social Democratic Party in 1905 was pending, and she also knew that an arrangement had been made between the German and the Russian police that she should be sent over the German frontier before the beginning of the next parliamentary session. That looked as though her immediate arrest was intended, and she had no desire to return to State custody so quickly. In September she left for Germany, and travelled almost direct to the Congress of the Social Democratic Party in Mannheim. After that she was able to recuperate for a time in Maderno on the Lago di Garda : " Sun, peace, and liberty ; the finest things in life—apart from sun, storm, and liberty."

In the meantime Leo Jogiches remained in the Warsaw Citadel. At one time it was even agreed to release him on bail, but for some reason the authorities thought better of it. On November 14th, 1906, Skalon, the notorious commandant of the Warsaw Military District, announced his intention of bringing Jogiches and Rosa Luxemburg before a Military Court :

> " According to an investigation conducted by the Gendarmerie authorities Leo Jogiches, alias Otto Engelmann, and Rosalie Luxemburg, alias Anna Matschke, joined the Fighting Organisation of the Social Democratic Party of the Kingdom of Poland and of Lithuania, an organisation intended to overthrow by armed violence the monarchical form of government in Russia as laid down in the Constitution, and in this way obtain the independence of Poland, thereby violating Paragraph 102 of the Penal Code."

Rosa Luxemburg refused to appear before the court at all, and the trial of Jogiches alone began on January 10th, 1907. At the very beginning of the proceedings an incident occurred which determined the attitude of Jogiches throughout the trial. In accordance with the old caste system in vogue in Tsarist Russia, the President of the court addressed him with the appellation " Du " [1] because in the indictment he was described as a member of the lower-middle class. Leo Jogiches and his lawyer protested against the indignity, but

[1] " Du—Thou ", used as a familiar form of address amongst friends, or, formerly, by superiors towards their inferiors.—Tr.

the court decided that as Jogiches was regarded as a Russian subject the appellation must stand. Jogiches thereupon refused to take any further part in the court proceedings and remained silent throughout the three-day trial. He was convicted of military desertion (committed in 1891) and high treason, and sentenced to eight years hard labour. Rosa Luxemburg would have received a similar sentence, and it would have been a death sentence for her. On April 5th, 1907, just before he was to be sent to Siberia, Jogiches escaped from prison. The flight, which was carried out with the assistance of Hanecki and of a gendarme who had been won over by Jogiches, was a masterpiece of ingenuity.

5. Criticism of the Revolution

When Rosa Luxemburg drew up the balance of the first year of revolution she was full of confidence in the future. She expected a further increase in proletarian activity, further demoralisation in the Tsarist State and its military apparatus, and insurrections in town and country finally developing into a general mass insurrection strong enough to overthrow Absolutism. The events of 1906 seemed to justify her hopes: demonstrations, strikes, peasant revolts, insurrections, and mutinies broke out again and again, and proved that the fire of revolution had not yet died down. However, official terrorism intensified, and there were pogroms, punitive expeditions (particularly in the Baltic provinces), mass shootings, summary courts-martial followed by executions, and wholesale banishments to Siberia. The workers were steadily deprived of their revolutionary gains, and they lost one position after the other, and in the end the mass strikes gave way to mass lock-outs.

December 1905, with its general strike and the insurrection in Moscow, had been the highest point of the revolutionary wave. The revolutionary masses were still active, but it soon became clear that they had lost the initiative, and the centre of events then shifted from mass action to parliamentary politics. Despite the reactionary electoral law, the Liberal Party, Constitutional Democrats (Cadets), won a big victory, and its attempt to uproot Absolutism by parliamentary means caused new hopes to spring up amongst Right-Wing socialists. Rosa Luxemburg had prophesised that the Duma would become the fig-leaf of Absolutism, and that it would be a Cossack Duma. She was right, and the parliamentary politics of the day reflected the revolution in defeat. Absolutism went over to the attack and dissolved the first Duma in July 1906, ruled without a Duma until March 1907, dissolved the second Duma in June 1907, and then caused a third Duma to be elected on the basis of an even more reactionary franchise, so that this time it was controlled by arch-reactionaries. The counter-revolution had spread its shroud over the whole of Russia.

Later, in the *Juniusbroschüre*, Rosa Luxemburg deals with the decline of the revolution:

" Two causes explain why, despite its unexampled display of revolutionary energy, clear-sightedness, and tenacity, the Russian Revolution of 1905–6 suffered defeat. One of these causes lies in the inherent character of the revolution itself: the vast historical programme it brought with it; the volume of economic and political problems it unrolled, some of which, like the agrarian question, were insoluble altogether within the framework of our contemporary social order; and the difficulty of creating a modern *bourgeois* class State against the counter-revolutionary resistance of the whole *bourgeoisie* of the empire. From this angle the revolution was defeated because it was a proletarian revolution with *bourgeois* tasks, or, if you prefer, a *bourgeois* revolution with proletarian-socialist fighting methods, i.e., a collision of two epochs . . . a result of the delayed development of class relations in Russia and of their over-ripe development in Western Europe. Similarly, from this angle the defeat of 1906 does not represent the bankruptcy of the revolution, but merely the inevitable close of its first chapter, which will just as inevitably be followed by subsequent chapters. The second cause was external; it lies in Western Europe: European reaction once again hurried to the assistance of its threatened protégé. . . ."

The defeat of the revolution caused great confusion in the socialist movement of Russia, and to a lesser degree in the socialist movement of Poland, where the Social Democratic Party was more firmly organised and ideology more coherent. It was quite natural that in the new period of illegality the party membership should decline very considerably and that great masses of workers should fall back into political apathy. Much more disturbing, however, was the fact that large numbers of intellectuals, who had previously been the backbone of the revolutionary movement, gradually retired from political life altogether. In addition, all sorts of aberrations began to show themselves in the social-democratic ranks. Amongst the Bolshevists some groups took refuge in philosophical speculations (Machism), and even in mysticism. Theories were mooted which in practice must have developed into sheer adventurism. Otsovism demanded the recall of the party Duma fraction and a boycott of the Duma on principle. The Menshevists, who had not been given the chance of demonstrating their tactical ideas during the revolution, now succumbed to defeatism, declaring that the revolution had been repulsed once and for all, and that socialists must now make the best they could of the new situation. A strong group even demanded the liquidation of the illegal party organisations, though that was practically synonymous with demanding the dissolution of the party altogether.

Debates on fundamental revolutionary problems now reopened with redoubled violence, and old theories had now been enriched with the practical experience of 1905–6. Rosa Luxemburg took a greater part in them than the needs of the Polish movement really demanded. Amongst the Menshevists it was Tcherevanin who did most to examine the lessons of the revolution, publishing two books on the subject. He came to the conclusion that the working class, and with it Social Democracy, had not sufficiently respected the *bourgeois* character of the revolution; their violent attacks on capital had driven the *bourgeoisie* into the arms of the reaction, and thus caused the defeat of the revolution, though he admitted that, in view of the given class relations, it was too much to expect the working class to content itself with the rôle of mere henchman to the *bourgeoisie* and to sacrifice its own class interests. Logically, therefore, a " correct " Menshevist tactic would have failed too. He came to the despairing conclusion that in the given circumstances no correct working-class policy was feasible at all, and thereby amply demonstrated the helplessness and uselessness of Menshevist ideas.

In this period Lenin maintained his demand for a " demo-

cratic dictatorship of the proletariat and the peasantry ".
Trotzky continued to develop his theory of permanent
revolution, and devoted a series of articles to the question in
the organ of Polish Social Democracy in 1908. He came to
the conclusion that although the revolution was directly
faced with *bourgeois* tasks it could not remain satisfied with them.
In fact, the revolution could perform these tasks at all only
if the proletariat seized power. If the proletariat seized
power, however, it could not confine itself to carrying through
the *bourgeois* revolution, and in pursuing its own aims it would
interfere not only with feudalist property, but with *bourgeois*
property as well. It would then come into conflict not only
with the *bourgeoisie*, but also with big sections of the peasantry.
Thus, the contradictions facing a workers' government in a
backward country could be solved only internationally, only
by the proletarian world revolution. Compelled by historical
necessity to burst the *bourgeois*-democratic framework of the
Russian Revolution, the victorious proletariat would also have
to go beyond its national limits—i.e., deliberately strive to
make the Russian Revolution the prelude to world revolution.

Rosa Luxemburg discussed these various ideas in a number
of exhaustive studies, analysing the course of the revolution
and the counter-revolution. She condemned the ideas of the
Menshevists in two speeches delivered to the Congress of the
Russian Social Democratic Party in London in May 1907,
and they were masterpieces of political polemics. Her ideas
were also excellently set out in a speech delivered by Leo
Jogiches in 1908 at the Congress of the Polish Social Democratic Party. After summarily dismissing the Menshevist
ideas, he dealt with Lenin's standpoint.

According to the Bolshevists the interests of the proletariat
and the peasantry in the revolution were identical. If this
standpoint were to be logically maintained, then, for a time
at least, all efforts should be concentrated on the formation of
a workers' and peasants' party. But then at a certain stage of
the revolution " the dictatorship of the proletariat and
the peasantry " might turn into a weapon against the proletariat and against the achievements of the revolution. The
Bolshevists were ahead of the Menshevists, thanks to their
greater sense of historical development. They were no doc-
trinaires, and took into account the great potential strength of

the peasantry. Their error, however, was that they saw only the revolutionary aspect of the peasantry, and in this respect they represented the antithesis of the Menshevists, who, in order to justify their own conception of a revolution led by the *bourgeoisie*, could see only the reactionary aspect of the peasantry. However, history could make nothing of mechanistic formulas. In reality he and his friends, the Bolshevists and a section of the Menshevists, were all working for the dictatorship of the proletariat—the Menshevists despite their erroneous ideas. It would be difficult to formulate the position more abstractly and less dialectically than the Bolshevists did. At the bottom of their conception was something like a military advance according to a previously prepared plan, but in reality the vital content of the historical process would be determined by its own course and by its own results—i.e., objectively, despite the subjective aims of its participants. The character of classes and parties changed under the influence of momentary happenings and new situations. In the last resort, however, there was little fear that the policy of the Bolshevists would lead to dangerous concessions to the peasantry, thanks to the common-sense proletarian spirit which pervaded all their ideas. He and his friends were in favour of the dictatorship of the proletariat based on the peasantry. The ideas of Parvus and Trotzky were closely related to the ideas of the speaker's party, though the party did not accept the idea of permanent revolution, which based its tactics not on the Russian revolution, but on the effects of that revolution abroad. It was not possible to base tactics on combinations which could not be properly estimated.

Thus both Leo Jogiches and Rosa Luxemburg were more reserved in their judgement than Trotzky, though Rosa Luxemburg readily admitted that the proletariat dictatorship she had in mind could be guaranteed only by the victory of the working class in the big capitalist countries; failing this, it would inevitably succumb to a counter-revolution.

Her attitude to the peasantry is important because certain of her enemies have again and again wrongly charged her with under-estimating, and sometimes even ignoring, the importance of the peasantry for the revolution. In reality she stresses again and again in her writings that the agrarian question is the crux of the revolution, and that the peasants are of primary importance in any proletarian seizure of power. At the Congress of the Russian party in 1907 she vigorously denounced the ideas of Plechanov and the Menshevists on the peasant question as sterile and mechanical, and although she often compared the Bolshevists to the French Guesdists, finding their theories too narrow and rigid, she agreed step by step with their practical policy throughout those years. She also agreed with them with regard to future revolutionary prospects. She knew that an upheaval of such magnitude could not attain its end in one quick rush, and she reckoned with a protracted period of revolution in which there would inevitably be times of ebb and flood. In particular, she stressed the fact that the victory of reaction in 1905–6 could not re-establish the old power of Absolutism or the old relation of the classes. She knew that the revolution was not dead, and that it would rise again more powerful than ever. In 1912 she was one of the first to recognise the gradual rise of the new revolutionary tide. It was thrown back once more at the outbreak of the World War, but only to reappear more powerful than ever in 1917 when it swept all before it.

Chapter Seven: A NEW WEAPON

1. Disappointment

" I AM DYING to get to work, and imagining how grand it will be to plunge into the discussion on the general strike. . . . I had to laugh at the recent discussions in the party; it seems that current events have even proved important enough to shake the world between the Linden Strasse and Engel Ufer.[1] We are living in grand times; I call them grand times when the masses are faced with problems, big problems which make them use their brains and their critical faculties; times which arouse deep emotions, and are therefore fruitful because every hour brings something new and creates something fresh; not

[1] The headquarters of the Social Democratic Party of Germany were situated in the Linden Strasse and the headquarters of the A.D.G.B. (German Trade Union Federation) on the Engel Ufer.—Tr.

mice but mountains, great events and great crimes (e.g., our own government). . . . I am agog with excitement at the idea that I shall soon have an opportunity of describing these gigantic events." [1]

This was the exalted state of mind in which Rosa Luxemburg prepared to return to Germany after her release from prison in Warsaw. Her enthusiasm did not flag as far as it concerned the Russian Revolution, but the nearer she came to her second home the more she was troubled with doubts. In Finland a copy of the *Vorwärts* was her first taste of Germany. The pettiness of the squabbles, the narrow-mindedness of the combatants, and the mediocrity of the ideas expressed by the " koscher " Left-Wingers she had left behind in the editorial offices made her sigh: " I began to feel queer near Plevna." And when she finally arrived in Germany and breathed the stuffy atmosphere in which the leaders of the German Social Democratic Party moved, she felt like a fish out of water. That was at the Party Congress in Mannheim.

The fresh breeze from the East which had aired the party headquarters for a while had dropped, and, naturally inclined to defeatism, the party leadership had reacted like a sensitive thermometer to the fall of temperature in Russia after the December struggles, and signs of working-class militancy in favour of the general franchise in the " Red Kingdom of Saxony " [2] and in Hamburg were immediately suppressed. And when the authorities exercised a little gentle pressure the party leaders immediately rendered a great demonstration on the anniversary of Bloody Sunday quite innocuous by depriving it of all revolutionary significance. In February 1906 the Central Committee of the party had discussed with the trade-union leadership the implications of the general-strike resolution of the Jena Congress, and agreed in secret that it should remain a dead letter. In practice the trade-union leaders were controlling the party, and the Mannheim Congress only confirmed the general tendency.

Rosa Luxemburg took the matter very seriously. Even

[1] Rosa Luxemburg in a letter to Emmanuel and Mathilde Wurm on July 17th, 1906.

[2] At the Reichstag elections in 1903 the Social Democratic Party won all the seats in Saxony with one exception, but in Saxony itself—i.e., for the Saxon Diet elections—the three-class franchise still existed, and it effectively excluded social-democratic candidates from the Diet.

in Jena she had realised that the leaders of the party were very far from sharing her views, but at Mannheim August Bebel had declared quite openly that if Wilhelm II decided to send an army against a victorious Russian Revolution, the German Social Democratic Party would do nothing. After this she realised that it was no question of temporary disagreement on details, and that in future she would have to reckon Bebel and the great majority of the party officials as enemies. Replying at the beginning of 1907 to Clara Zetkin, who had expressed anxiety at the trend of party policy, she declared:

" Since my return from Russia I feel rather isolated. . . . I feel the pettiness and the hesitancy of our party régime more clearly and more painfully than ever before. However, I can't get so excited about the situation as you do because I see with depressing clarity that neither things nor people can be changed—until the whole situation has changed, and even then we shall just have to reckon with the inevitable resistance of such people if we want to lead the masses on. I have come to that conclusion after mature reflection. The plain truth is that August,[1] and still more so the others, have completely pledged themselves to parliament and parliamentarism, and whenever anything happens which transcends the limits of parliamentary action they are hopeless—no, worse than hopeless, because they then do their utmost to force the movement back into parliamentary channels, and they will furiously defame as ' an enemy of the people ' anyone who dares to venture beyond their own limits. I feel that the masses of the people, and, of course, still more the masses who are organised in the party, are tired of parliamentarism, and would welcome a new line in party tactics, but the party leaders and still more the upper stratum of opportunist editors, deputies, and trade-union leaders are like an incubus. We must protest vigorously against this general stagnation, but it is quite clear that in doing so we shall find ourselves against the opportunists as well as the party leaders and August. As long as it was a question of defending themselves against Bernstein and his friends,

[1] Bebel.—Tr.

August & Co. were glad of our assistance, because they were shaking in their shoes. But when it is a question of launching an offensive against opportunism then August and the rest are with Eddie,[1] Vollman, and David against us. That's how I see matters, but the chief thing is to keep your chin up and not get too excited about it. Our job will take years."

In this long struggle Rosa Luxemburg reckoned with the support of the masses and with the objective development of the home and foreign situation. Some reflection of the spirit of the party rank and file had found expression at the Jena Congress, and at many public meetings she addressed on the Russian Revolution she could see, from the deep interest and enthusiasm of the audiences, that there was more revolutionary spirit in the lower regions of the party than in its leading circles. In Austria the Russian Revolution had caused a mass movement of such vigour that even Victor Adler refrained from his usual delaying tactics, with the result that at the end of 1906 the Austrian proletariat won its first great political success: the general franchise.

Rosa Luxemburg was more cautious than Trotzky in estimating the effect of the Russian Revolution on the capitalist countries of Europe, but at the same time she was firmly convinced that the rising of the Russian proletariat had ushered in a new epoch for Europe as a whole. The catastrophes prophesied in her analysis of social forces in the capitalist world had come visibly nearer, and 1905–6 had shaken more than the Empire of the Tsar. In Morocco a dispute between France and Germany raised the spectre of European war. International imperialist politics revealed their true character. The period of wars and revolutions had opened up, and with it the period of mere agitation and organisation had closed for the working class. It was already clear that sooner or later it would be faced with the necessity of action, and Rosa Luxemburg concentrated her attention on assisting its intellectual and organisational preparation for the coming struggles.

[1] Bernstein.—Tr.
[2] In " Social Reform or Revolution ".

2. The Political Mass Strike

Above all, she assisted it to learn the lessons of the Russian Revolution as far as they were of value for the proletariat of Western Europe, and in particular of Germany. The Russian Revolution, unlike all previous revolutions, was characterised by mass action with a typical proletarian weapon: strikes in which millions took part not merely to win improvements in their standards of living, but also to gain great political objectives. Rosa Luxemburg had always favoured the political mass strike, but now she realised its full significance as the specific weapon of the proletariat in times of revolutionary ferment.

The idea of the general strike is old. Some English Chartists regarded it as their weapon to force the Government to grant a general franchise, and thus open up the way to Socialism. At its Congress in Brussels in 1868 the First International proclaimed " the strike of the peoples " as a weapon against war. The Geneva Congress of the International Alliance of Bakuninists in 1873 proclaimed the general strike as a weapon for starving out and overthrowing the *bourgeoisie*: if all work ceased for ten days, the existing social order would collapse. And the French Syndicalists declared that the general strike was the chief weapon of the proletariat: not the barricade struggle of *bourgeois* revolutions, and not the parliamentarism of politicians, but the peaceable action of folding arms would carry the working class to victory. Courageous illusions! They failed to judge the real relation of forces correctly, and they imagined that mere propaganda would prove sufficient to bring about a general strike and maintain it until the *bourgeoisie* had capitulated.

The mass strike came about in a very different fashion. In 1891 125,000 workers went on strike in Belgium; not in order to overthrow *bourgeois* society, but to obtain greater political freedom within the framework of that social order by means of the general franchise. Their first attempt failed to achieve its object, but a second strike in 1893, in which 250,000 workers took part, succeeded in obtaining improvements which opened the doors of parliament to representatives of the working class. In 1902 the Belgian Labour Party, acting in concert with the Liberals, launched another strike, in which 350,000 workers took part. However, the Liberals pusillanimously left their allies in the lurch, and the strike was a failure. In the same year Swedish workers carried out a great demonstration strike in favour of a general franchise. In France 160,000 miners went on strike, and drew many other workers into the struggle. In 1903 Dutch railwaymen began a political strike, which quickly developed into a general strike. In September 1904 a wave of violent strikes swept over Italy, and in a number of towns street-fighting took place. Thus the mass political strike was no entirely new weapon, but its full significance was revealed by the Russian Revolution.

However, in the two most important capitalist countries of Europe the working-class movements maintained a very cool attitude to the idea of a general strike. In Great Britain the idea seemed to have been buried with the Chartist movement. In Germany, after the Belgian strike of 1893, both Bernstein and Kautsky broached the idea of the general strike as a defensive weapon against reactionary attacks on working-class political rights, and when in 1896 putschist tendencies began to manifest themselves in German reactionary circles, Parvus propagated the political mass strike as a means of leading the workers from the defensive to an offensive struggle for power. However, these were little more than academic discussions, and the overwhelming majority of social-democratic leaders still mouthed the catch-phrase: " General Strike is General Nonsense ". And when they considered it necessary to put forward arguments in favour of their attitude (which was not often), they appealed to Engels' rejection of the anarchistic idea of a general strike to starve out the possessing classes. In 1873 Engels published his pamphlet " The Bakuninists at Work ", pointing out that even the Bakuninists themselves admitted the necessity of a carefully prepared organisation with well-filled coffers. Here was the cardinal weakness of the scheme, because no government would permit such preparations to proceed:

" On the other hand, political development and the excesses of the ruling classes would bring about the emancipation of the workers long before they would ever be in a position to create this ideal organisation and to accumulate such colossal reserve funds. If it ever had them it would not need the detour of the general strike before obtaining its ends." [1]

When the Belgian general strike of 1902 ended in defeat, most German social democrats who concerned themselves at all with tactical questions considered that Engels' verdict had received new confirmation, and even radical social democrats declared the experiment to be the last kick of Bakuninism: such experiments were useless, they led to armed conflicts and to the abandonment of peaceable means, and, further (so they distorted Engels' idea), the working class would have power long before it had sufficient strength to conduct a victorious general strike. Rosa Luxemburg did not share these views. At the beginning of the Belgian general strike she severely criticised the conditions under which it had been launched, declaring that it was not wrong to launch a general strike, but fatal to let the Belgian Liberals determine the way in which it should be conducted, because as a result the striking workers were degraded into mere supers of a parliamentary action. In addition, an exaggerated legalism had renounced all strike meetings and demonstrations, and cooped up the strikers in their own homes, thereby robbing them of that important feeling of strength and solidarity which resided in masses. The essence of a general strike was that it represented the first stage of a wider struggle, but it was just this character which the organisers of the Belgian general strike had zealously emasculated:

"A general strike pledged to remain within strict legal limits is like a military demonstration with unloaded guns. The 'Hands in Pockets' slogan issued by the *Peuple* will frighten no one, and certainly not a class fighting to maintain its political domination. The strikes of the Belgian

[1] For a long time this was held to be Engels' final verdict on the general strike, but that this was not the case has since been shown by the publication of letters written by him to Victor Adler and to Kautsky in 1893. At the time there was strong support in the Austrian party for a general strike to enforce a general franchise, but under existing conditions Engels was decidedly opposed to any such experiment, but the crucial point is that his letters show that he by no means opposed the general strike on principle.

workers in 1891 and 1893 were sufficient to break down
the resistance of the clericalist reactionaries, but only
because the latter had good reason to fear that if they
did not give way violent unrest would follow and the
strike movement take a revolutionary turn. This time,
too, it might have been quite unnecessary to use actual
violence to attain the desired end—if only the leaders had
not solemnly ejected all their cartridges in advance, turned
the military demonstration into a pleasant Sunday afternoon parade, and forgone the thunder of the general strike
for the fizzing of a damp squib." [1]

Rosa Luxemburg's attitude towards the problem of the
political strike again demonstrates that she was never prepared to accept the traditional interpretation of authority
uncritically. She carefully examined Engels' words on the
subject, and found that they were " coined to deal exclusively
with the anarchist theory of the general strike as a means of
introducing the social revolution instead of obtaining the
same end through the daily political struggle of the working
class ". She regarded the two things as complementary, and
she recognised the deeply revolutionary character of the
general strike. A general strike assumed more than ordinary
militancy amongst the workers expected to take part in it;
it could not be organised according to ordinary everyday
rules, and it involved revolutionary consequences which, if
overlooked, might result in a demoralising defeat.

The general development of revolutionary feeling which
began as a result of the Russian Revolution, and its object
lessons in the use of the strike weapon, broke down barriers
which had previously prevented the German working
class from feeling any sympathy for the idea of the political
strike.

With few exceptions, the trade-union leaders obstinately
continued to reject the political strike on principle. Up to
that time they had never regarded the political strike as
anything but an idiosyncrasy of the Latin temperament,
and as such to be ignored completely by the shrewder spirits
of the sober North; but when the German working class
was seen to be far from immune from these dangerous ideas,

[1] Rosa Luxemburg, " Collected Works " (German), Vol. IV., pp. 341–42.

they opened up a fierce attack on " the Mass-Strike Apostles and Romantic Revolutionists ". The campaign reached its culminating point in the Trade-Union Congress in Cologne in 1905 under the slogan, " The Trade Unions Need Peace and Quiet! ", and even a theoretical discussion of the general-strike problem was condemned as playing with fire. The motives of the trade-union leaders were evident: they feared to lose their tactical independence of the party, they feared that their well-filled coffers would be plundered, and that the authorities would take measures against their organisations in the event of political strikes. In general, they were opposed to any " experiments " which threatened to disturb the carefully organised routine of daily and more or less peaceable skirmishing with the employers. A comparatively small group of reformist party leaders supported them because it smelt the revolution behind the political strike and wanted the maintenance of legal barriers at all costs. One of the leaders of this group, the lawyer Wolfgang Heine, carefully consulted the Penal Code, and then declared the political strike to be illegal because it came within the provisions against breach of contract and high treason, and was thus both a venial and a mortal sin against the *bourgeois* social order.

On the other hand, a number of reformist politicians vigorously supported the idea of the political strike because they regarded it as a weapon to defend the existing Reich's franchise (which was constantly being threatened), and perhaps win a similar franchise in the German States. Some of them even hoped that its use might result in the final consolidation of the parliamentary régime, and thus clear the way for the fulfilment of their cherished dream: the stage-by-stage attainment of political power through a coalition policy. The three most prominent members of this group were Eduard Bernstein himself, Friedrich Stampfer, and Kurt Eisner. They supported the idea of the political strike because they regarded it as a substitute for street-fighting, as a peaceable means of exerting extra parliamentary pressure on the authorities.

Then came the majority of the deputies, editors, and officials, who rallied round the Central Committee, and later termed themselves the " Marxist Centre ". They

rejected the idea of co-operation with *bourgeois* parties in a
coalition government, and believed that on the basis of a
really democratic franchise they would be able to obtain a
majority in parliament to carry out the socialist transformation of society. For them, too, the political strike was a
peaceable substitute for street-fighting. As early as October
1903 Rudolf Hilferding expressed the ideas of this group in
the *Neue Zeit*: Since barricade fighting had become impossible, the withholding of labour-power was the only means
the proletariat possessed of exerting pressure on a tyrannical
State. The workers must always be prepared to launch a
general strike in defence of the general franchise, or one day
the enemy might suddenly render all parliamentary activity
impossible. The political general strike must become the
regulator behind social-democratic tactics: every worker
must be prepared to defend the achievements of his class by
using his power over the vital productive processes of society
if necessary; the political general strike must not replace
parliamentarism, but merely protect the political activities
of the working class from attack; and, finally, the idea of
the political general strike must never develop into anything
beyond an idea.

These ideas turned the general strike into an exclusively
defensive weapon, into a policy of clenching the fist whilst
hoping anxiously that no occasion would ever arise for its
use. All these people had the same sort of general strike
in mind: one which would be decided on, organised, and
directed according to settled rules, whilst the strikers would
maintain strict discipline and never move hand or foot
except at the behest of their leaders.

Kautsky's ideas were rather different: it would never be
possible to enforce political concessions by a general strike
in a rigidly organised State like Germany, or even to ward
off reactionary attacks; if the political strike was to be
used, then the party must be prepared to accept the final
consequences and seize power. The general strike was a
revolutionary weapon, and applicable only in a revolutionary
situation. When he first began to express these ideas (in
the *Neue Zeit* in February 1904), Kautsky also believed that
the general strike would take the place of armed insurrection, but after the Russian Revolution he realised that armed

insurrection was not played out as a political weapon, and that a general strike might easily develop into an armed insurrection. His ideas thus seemed to have much similarity with those of Rosa Luxemburg, and, in fact, he was strongly under her influence; but there was one important difference: Kautsky was always willing to accept revolutionary conclusions provided only that they applied exclusively to other countries, or to the past or the far-distant future; his theory of the general strike as a revolutionary weapon meant renouncing the use of it until, in some far-distant future, the historical process would automatically bring forth the revolution.

3. " THE MASS STRIKE, THE PARTY, AND THE TRADE UNIONS "

As we already know, Rosa Luxemburg was deeply disappointed with the spirit which prevailed at the Jena Congress of the party. She did not agree with Bebel's resolution limiting the use of the mass strike to the defence of the general franchise, or that the party should pledge itself to use the strike weapon in defence of the franchise. However, with the rest of the Left Wing at the Congress, she voted for the resolution. She explains her attitude in a letter written to Henriette Roland-Holst on October 2nd, 1905:

" I am quite in agreement with you that Bebel's resolution gives a shallow and one-sided interpretation of the mass strike. When we first read it some of us agreed to oppose it at the congress on the ground that the mass strike should not be regarded merely as a means of political defence, but as an elementary form of revolutionary action. However, Bebel's speech at the congress, and still more the attitude of the opportunists (Heine, etc.), altered the situation, and once again we ' Left-Wing extremists ' found ourselves fighting not Bebel, with whom we have important differences of opinion, but with him against the opportunists. . . . As a matter of fact, in the discussion the mass strike was treated (even by Bebel, though perhaps he didn't quite realise it) as a form of revolutionary mass struggle, and the spectre of revolution was clearly visible then and throughout the whole congress. . . . I

think we are entitled to be satisfied with this tactical
result."

Rosa Luxemburg hoped that the subsequent discussion in
the Press would still further develop the inherent logic of the
mass strike as a political weapon, but the Russian Revolution
gradually ceased to exercise its inspiring influence, and she
was disappointed. The understanding come to between the
party leadership and the leaders of the trade unions made
the Jena decision on the general strike into a knife without
a haft, and in autumn 1906 her pamphlet " The Mass Strike,
the Party, and the Trade Unions " appeared very opportunely
to raise the discussion of the political strike to a rather higher
intellectual level. The work was born of her experience on
the revolutionary front, and the hammer-blows of the Russian
Revolution re-echo in it. The mass struggles which raged
throughout Russia over a period of many years unroll once
again with their fantastic and sudden changes of position,
the rapid advance of the struggle, and then its equally rapid
recession, the remarkable lack of proportion between the
unimportant occasions and the enormous extent of the
struggles, the indissoluble mixture of economic and political
motives in the great strikes, the successes and defeats. The
book gives a vivid and extraordinarily vital picture of the
great struggle of two diametrically opposed social forces, and
in no other description of the 1905 Revolution is there such
power of delineation and such dramatic intensity.

At the same time it reveals to us how Rosa Luxemburg
formed her opinions on the tactics of the many-sided struggle
of the working class, and how she succeeded in solving
problems at a time when the elementary conditions for their
solution were only just developing—for instance, the question
of the relation between the daily struggle of the working class
in defence of its interests and the greater struggle for the
realisation of Socialism. The discussion on the mass strike
showed that most theoreticians of the Social Democratic
Party had developed schemes in their heads to overcome all
possible difficulties with ease, provided only that previously
formulated regulations were strictly complied with. Rosa
Luxemburg's methods were very different. She appeared
with no carefully calculated patent method for the solution

of all future difficulties. She based her theories on living experience and on a detailed analysis of the historically formative process of class struggle, never for one moment losing sight of the process as a whole. And at the same time she was able to raise herself, with almost visionary power, above the ordinary events of the day, to exclude accidental circumstances due solely to the given situation, and to sum up the factors generally valid for a particular phase of development in such a fashion that the picture she developed pulsed with life.

Her analysis of events led her to certain general conclusions which are fundamental for her special conception of the mass strike:

" Instead of the rigid and empty formula of a mechanical political ' action ' carried out at the orders of the higher party authorities and according to a previously prepared plan, we see a section of reality which cannot be taken out of the great framework of the revolution, because it is bound up with all the rest of the revolution in a thousand ways.

" The mass strike as we saw it during the Russian Revolution is such a changing phenomenon that it reflects all phases of the political and economic struggle, and all stages and factors of the revolution. Its application, its effect, and its origins alter continually. It opens up sudden and unexpected possibilities at times when the revolution seems to have exhausted itself, and, equally, it is liable to fail when its success is reckoned on with absolute certainty. At one time it floods like a broad wave over the whole country, and at another it breaks up into a network of small rivulets. Sometimes it gushes forth with tremendous force, and at others it sinks back into the ground and disappears. Political and economic strikes, mass strikes and partial strikes, demonstration strikes and militant strikes, general strikes in one branch of industry, and local general strikes in individual towns, peaceable wage struggles and street fighting on the barricades—all these forms are mixed together, inextricably tangled, running side by side, crossing each other, and developing into each other in a constantly and rapidly changing kaleidoscope. But the motive power of it all is clear enough. It is not to be found in the mass strike as such, or in its technical peculiarities, but in the relation of social and political forces in the revolution itself. The mass strike is nothing but the form of revolutionary struggle at a given moment; and every change in the relation of the opposing forces, in party developments and class differences, and in the position of the counter-revolution affects the strike action at once through a thousand invisible and uncontrollable channels, though the action itself hardly pauses for a moment; it changes only its forms, its extent, and its effects. It is the strongest pulse of the revolution, and at the same time its most powerful impulse. In other words, the mass strike as we saw it in action in the Russian Revolution was not a cleverly concocted recipe for heightening the effect of the proletarian class struggle, but the law of proletarian mass movement itself, the form taken on by the proletarian struggle in the phase of revolution." [1]

Rosa Luxemburg has been accused of generalising too freely on the basis of Russian revolutionary experience, of incorrectly identifying mass strike and revolution, of arbitrarily confusing two fundamentally different things: the economic and the political strike. Naturally, she was well aware that demonstration strikes and isolated mass strikes conducted with a definite political end in view are of great importance, but a demonstration strike whose duration is previously limited by its sponsors is no more the fully-developed revolutionary class struggle than a naval demonstration is naval warfare. As a naval demonstration may be used to support diplomatic action, so the demonstration strike may be used to support parliamentary pressure at a given moment of social tension. On the other hand, individual mass strikes not organised and carried out according to a previously arranged plan (for instance, the Belgian strikes in 1891 and 1893, and the great wave of strikes in Italy in 1904) all bore clear evidence of a revolutionary character and arose out of a situation which was revolutionary even though it did not develop its potentialities to the full. For Rosa Luxemburg they were preliminary phases of the real revolutionary strike, and therefore of great im-

[1] Rosa Luxemburg, *ibid*., pp. 437–38.

portance. The mass strike was not the artificial product of a deliberate tactic, but a natural, historical happening, and therefore she regarded " the purely political mass strike they talk about so much as a lifeless and mechanical theory ". She also rejected the idea of using the mass strike as a means of rescuing the movement from an *impasse*, because " in reality it is not the mass strike which produces the revolution, but the revolution the mass strike " :

" If the mass strike is not an isolated phenomenon but the expression of a certain phase of the class struggle, and if this phase is identical with the revolutionary phase of that struggle, then it is clear that the mass strike cannot be conjured out of nothing even by the leaders of the strongest socialist party. So long as Social Democracy does not possess the power to arrange and postpone revolutions at will, not even the greatest measure of enthusiasm and impatience on the part of the social-democratic masses will prove sufficient to inaugurate a period of mass strikes, because they are powerful mass movements of the people. . . . A mass strike brought into being exclusively as the result of party discipline and party enthusiasm would, in the best case, prove no more than a passing incident, a symptom of the fighting spirit of the working class, and afterwards the situation would quite naturally revert to normal. Naturally, mass strikes don't fall ready made from heaven even in revolutionary periods. In one way or the other they are the product of the workers who take part in them. The decision is taken by the workers, and in this respect, and also in the subsequent leadership of the strike, the initiative will rest with the organised and enlightened social-democratic core of the working class. However, this initiative and this leadership have a margin of influence chiefly affecting particular strikes and actions when the revolutionary period has already opened up, and then usually within the limits of a single town. . . .

" Spontaneity played a great rôle in all Russian mass strikes without exception, whether as an accelerating or retarding element. The reason for this is not that Social Democracy in Russia is young and inexperienced, but that in each particular action so many differing and uncon trollable factors are at work: economic, political, social, national, local, material, and psychological. In consequence no such action can unroll like a Euclidian problem. . . . In short, the spontaneous element has played a great rôle in the mass strikes in Russia not because the Russian proletariat is ' untrained ', but because the revolution refuses to let itself be dragooned into any particular previously determined form." [1]

However, if the mass strike is not an artificial product and cannot be decided on at the will of its organisers, but is something which arrives as a historical necessity, with all the power of mass spontaneity behind it, it is idle to worry much beforehand about the means to support the strikers and succour the victims of the strike, for history will not ask whether these preliminary preparations have been made or not:

" Once a really serious period of mass strikes opens up, all such ' costing operations ' are something like an attempt to measure the ocean with a bucket. And it is an ocean, a sea of terrible troubles and privations for the proletariat— that is the invariable cost of every revolution. The solution which a revolutionary period brings with it for this apparently insoluble problem of providing material support for the strikers, is to generate such a tremendous volume of idealism amongst the masses that they appear to become almost immune to the most terrible privations."

It might appear, therefore, that the whole discussion could be of little more than academic importance if the outbreak of the mass strike was so far beyond the will of the leadership to control, if its course was determined by so many unpredictable factors, and if it was entirely the product of objective historical development. Rosa Luxemburg certainly believed that it was absurd to decide beforehand to answer an attack on the franchise with a general strike, because it was quite impossible to prophesy how the masses would react to such a situation. Further, she regarded the attempt to confine the use of the mass strike to a purely defensive action as an attempt to avoid the real duty of the party, because although the mass strike

[1] Rosa Luxemburg, *ibid.*, p. 444.

F

would come as a result of the spontaneous decision of the masses, and this in its turn would depend on innumerable factors, one important factor at least the party could make itself responsible for—namely, the existence of clarity on the character of the proletarian class struggle in general and of the mass strike in particular, and the cultivation of a fighting spirit in the ranks of the workers. The party should make it its business to ensure that the masses were aware beforehand of the probable consequences of such an event, and to plan its own policy in a far-sighted fashion:

" Social Democracy is the most enlightened and class-conscious section of the proletariat. It cannot and must not fold its arms and wait with fatalistic resignation for the arrival of a ' revolutionary situation ', for a spontaneous mass action of the people to fall from the clouds. On the contrary it must always forge ahead of events and seek to accelerate them. It will not do this by suddenly, whether opportunely or not, issuing the slogan for a mass strike, but only by making it quite clear to the broadest masses of the proletariat that a revolutionary period is inevitably approaching, by explaining to them the inherent social factors leading to this period, and pointing out what its political consequences will be."[1]

And again:

" The most important task of the party leadership in the period of mass strikes is to give the struggles an aim and a direction; to adopt such political tactics that at each moment of the struggle the totality of the existing, active forces of the proletariat can be effectively applied; and to ensure that they are expressed in the militant attitude of the party and that social-democratic tactics never sink below the level of the actual relation of forces, but rather forge ahead of them. This leadership will then more or less naturally develop into the technical leadership of the struggle. Logical, determined, and progressive tactics pursued by Social Democracy gives the masses a feeling of security and confidence, and intensifies their fighting spirit, whilst weak and vacillating tactics, obviously based on a low

[1] Rosa Luxemburg, *ibid.*, p. 457.

estimation of proletarian strength, necessarily paralyses and confuses the forces of the proletariat. In a serious situation mass strikes break out ' spontaneously ' and always at the opportune moment, whereas sometimes a direct appeal issued by the leadership proves a failure."[1]

It might have appeared from the discussion that Rosa Luxemburg thought leadership in a mass strike of very subordinate importance, but the contrary is true. She did not believe that leadership could go into action in the immediate technical preparation of the strike, but she firmly believed that the character and trend of the party policy in general would be decisive for the course of the great struggles impending throughout the whole period. Would the leaders of German Social Democracy, devoted exclusively to the economic skirmishing of the trade-union struggle and to the political manœuvres of parliamentarism, prove fitted for such a task ? She had no illusions on the point, and it filled her with anxiety for the future. Her chief adversaries in the debate had been the type of labour officialdom she most detested : intellectually complacent, narrow-minded, of mean understanding, and yet arrogant. These mediocre representatives of bureaucratic officialdom, holding themselves to be the only expert authorities, but utterly ignorant of the trend of development, appeared in force at the Cologne Trade-Union Congress. Their appearance provoked Rosa Luxemburg to flay their " self-complacent, beaming, and smug ignorance, sufficient in and a joy to itself, considering itself far superior to the accumulated historical experience of the international working-class movement ". This type of official had undoubtedly obtained increasing influence on the fate of the German working-class movement, and actually captured the Central Committee of the party. When Rosa Luxemburg wrote her pamphlet on the mass strike she felt the urge to castigate these sworn enemies of any revolutionary policy, and she analysed the trade-union leader as a type. Although she kept a curb on herself, occasionally her indignation burst out.

In the discussion on the mass strike it was her main intention to clear up precisely those questions which were of primary importance to the trade unions. Apart from their

[1] Rosa Luxemburg, *ibid.*, p. 446.

mortal fear of anything which might tend to revolution, the trade-union leaders had put forward two objections to the mass strike: first of all, such a strike was not feasible as long as the majority of the working class was not organised in the trade unions, thereby offering some guarantee that whatever decisions were taken would be carried out in a disciplined fashion, and secondly, the trade unions would in all probability break down altogether under such a tremendous task. Such objections were obviously another side of the idea that a mass strike would be previously planned and carefully prepared from above. If the almost perfect organisation of the working class were necessary before a political mass strike could take place, then it would be ridiculous to contemplate such a strike for one moment; and, further, all such strikes which had already taken place must have been begun in complete ignorance of the fact that their *conditio sine quâ non* was not present. At the time the German trade unions had about 1,500,000 members, or roughly one-tenth only of the whole working class. The great mass of unskilled labourers were hardly touched and there were many important sections of the working class whose organisation the labour bureaucrats regarded as entirely beyond the bounds of possibility—for instance, workers and other employees in the pay of the State, farm labourers, etc. Rosa Luxemburg, on the other hand, believed that precisely these sections could prove of very great importance in a mass strike. All the wide-scale experiments with this weapon had shown that it was a powerful lever of mass organisation, and Russian revolutionary experience in particular had shown that the ferment of a mass strike awakened millions of backward and previously inert masses to class consciousness and trade-union organisation. She had no doubt whatever that the mass strike would have the same compelling effect in Western Europe. Whilst the nervous guardians of the German trade unions feared that they would be shattered like fragile porcelain in the storms of a revolutionary situation, she was convinced that they would emerge strengthened and rejuvenated. In addition, a revolutionary period in Germany would alter the character of the trade-union struggle, would develop it to such an extent that the ordinary guerrilla skirmishing of the unions would appear child's play by comparison.

She explained the narrow-minded, mechanical ideas of

the parliamentarians and the trade-union leaders as a result of their specialisation in particular, and often very difficult, day-to-day tasks, which robbed them of the ability to see farther ahead. Her efforts to give them some dialectical understanding of history on a broad scale met with the same obstacle: they regarded everything which went beyond their own limited experience either as the outpourings of exaggerated revolutionary romanticism or as the result of her alleged hatred of the trade unions. Without bothering to reply to her arguments, they raised a tremendous outcry against her. Her pamphlet was first printed in a limited edition for the delegates to the Mannheim Party Congress, and she bowed to party pressure and agreed to delete certain expressions to which objection was taken. The reformist and trade-union Press tried to turn this into a " capitulation ". The matter is interesting even at this distance, because it gave Franz Mehring the occasion to say publicly what she meant to the international working-class movement:

"Rosa Luxemburg displayed that very 'dignified objectivity' her opponents always claim for themselves, when, despite the bitter and unobjective attacks made on her by a certain section of the trade-union Press, she refrained from aggravating the conflict immediately there seemed some chance of reaching an objective agreement. And for this she is now being mocked at, not by the *bourgeois* Press, which usually delights to display its dull idiocy in attacks on her, but by a section of the social-democratic Press. That is profoundly deplorable, all the more so because these irresponsible and petty attacks on the finest brain amongst the scientific successors of Marx and Engels are due in the last resort to the fact that its owner is a woman."[1]

4. THE THEORY OF SPONTANEITY

In her pamphlet on the mass strike, and on many occasions later, Rosa Luxemburg stressed that revolutionary movements could not be " fabricated "; that they could not come about as the result of party decisions, but only spontaneously and under certain definite historical conditions. Her opinion has

[1] Franz Mehring in the " *Neue Zeit* ", July 1907.

been confirmed by historical experience again and again, but this has not prevented a serious charge being made against her in this respect. Her ideas have been completely misrepresented, and she has been accused of inventing a theory of spontaneity, and of falling victim to a mysticism, or even a mythology of spontaneity. Zinoviev was the first begetter of this charge, and at the same time he enumerated certain other features which he declared were peculiar to something he termed " Luxemburgism ". His object was obviously to enhance the prestige of the Russian Communist Party in the Communist International. Those who followed him developed the legend, until to-day it is regarded as a politico-historical axiom unnecessary of proof. In order to make clear the real attitude of a great revolutionary leader towards revolutionary activity it is unfortunately necessary to deal with these attacks. The theory of spontaneity which Rosa Luxemburg is supposed to have developed is said to be the negation, or at least the depreciation, of the rôle of the party as the leader of the class struggle; an uncritical worship of the masses as such; an over-estimation of the impersonal and objective factors of development, and a denial of the importance of subjective factors; a negation, or at least a depreciation, of the importance of conscious and organised action; and, finally, complete abandonment to the mechanical fatalism of the historical process.

In itself such an accusation against a woman like Rosa Luxemburg is an absurdity. If one thing characterised her more than another it was her ceaseless urge to act, and to cause others, both individuals and masses, to act. " In the beginning was the deed ", was her motto throughout life, and if she regretted anything in retrospect, it was only that she had not been able to act still more vigorously. And this woman is supposed to have fallen victim to a philosophy of passivity, to have believed that history takes its course irrespective of human action, and that humanity can but fold its arms patiently and submit humbly to its inexorable fate! Her impetuous urge to action was so obvious and so undeniable that even her critics could not ignore it, but they got over the difficulty by noting wisely that it was interesting to observe that her political activity was in diametrical contradiction to her theories. That is an astonishing thing to say of a woman whose brilliant

mind and sharp logic guided all her actions. One " mistake "
she certainly did make : whilst writing she did not think of the
super-wise critics who would come after her and explain to
the world what she really meant, using dozens of quotations
torn out of their contexts to prove her the founder of a " theory
of spontaneity ". She wrote for her own day and for a working
class whose organisation had developed from a means to an
end in itself. It was this circumstance which compelled her
to stress the factor of spontaneity in all struggles of a revolutionary character, and to warn both leaders and masses of
the great events which were approaching. Even so, an objective examination of her writings would protect her against
all such misapprehension, because she said clearly again and
again exactly what she meant by spontaneity. Opposing the
idea of a general strike carefully prepared in advance by the
party leadership, organised methodically like any ordinary
wage struggle, and deprived of all its impetuous revolutionary
character, she pointed once to the example of the Belgian
strikes of 1891 and 1893 :

> " The difference is that the mass strikes of the nineties
> were spontaneous movements born of a revolutionary
> situation, of an intensification of the struggle and of an
> intense concentration of working-class energy. They were
> not spontaneous in the sense of being chaotic, undisciplined,
> aimless, and leaderless. On the contrary, in both these
> strikes the leadership showed itself to be completely identical
> with the masses ; it marched at their head and controlled
> and directed the movement effectively precisely because it
> was at one with the thoughts and feelings of the masses, and
> in contact with them ; because it was their mouthpiece,
> and the conscious expression of their aims."[1]

Spontaneity in the sense that Rosa Luxemburg uses the
word, therefore, does not exclude conscious leadership but,
on the contrary, demands it, and still further, in her opinion
the spontaneity which her subsequent critics have taken in
such bad part, and described as fatalism, does not fall suddenly
and unexpectedly out of a blue sky, as we have already shown
by several quotations in this chapter. Such quotations could
be produced in profusion. When, in 1910, the German workers

[1] Rosa Luxemburg, "Collected Works " (German), Vol. IV., p. 380.

came into movement in connection with the Prussian franchise,
she demanded that the Central Committee of the party should
draw up a definite plan for the further development of the
action, and she herself made concrete proposals. She vigorously
condemned a "wait-and-see" policy, and demanded the
prosecution of the action as a powerful political offensive.
During the World War she pointed out in her "*Juniusbroschüre*"
the importance of parliament as the one free tribune from which
mass action could be launched once men like Liebknecht had
seized on it and used it systematically and with determination.
The reliance she placed on the masses did not overshadow
the importance of the party and its tasks. Writing against
Kautsky's "tactic of attrition" in 1913 she declared :

> "Leaders who hang back will undoubtedly be pushed to
> one side by the advancing masses, but to wait first patiently
> for this definite sign that the situation is ripe may be all
> right for a lonely philosopher, but for the political leader-
> ship of a revolutionary party it would spell moral bank-
> ruptcy. The task of Social Democracy and its leaders is not
> to let themselves be dragged along in the wake of events,
> but deliberately to forge ahead of them, to foresee the trend
> of events, to shorten the period of development by conscious
> action, and to accelerate its progress."[1]

There is no doubt that she under-estimated the retarding
effect which an organisation can exercise on the masses when
its leaders are opposed to the struggle; and perhaps she
over-estimated the elementary activity of the masses, expected
it earlier than it actually came. However, the over-estimation
of the masses is the unavoidable "mistake" of every real
revolutionary, and it springs from a heartfelt desire for
revolutionary progress, and from the knowledge that the great
upheavals of human history are always the work of the masses
of the people. However, her reliance on the activity of the
masses was very far from being mystical. She was well aware
of the weakness of the masses, and she had ample opportunity
for observing their vices in counter-revolutionary periods. A
letter written to Mathilde Wurm from prison on February
16th, 1917, after she had been tormented for over two years

[1] Rosa Luxemburg, *ibid.*, p. 669.

with the idea that the masses had failed to rise to the historic occasion, is revealing:

" In me there is no element of vacillation, unrest, routine and parliamentary cretinism such as cloud the judgement of many people. Your whole argument against my motto: ' Here I stand; I can do naught else!' amounts to saying: that's all very fine, but people are too base or too weak for such heroism, and therefore we must adapt our tactics to their weakness according to the principle: *chi va piano, va sano*. I find that a very narrow conception of the world.

" There is nothing more subject to rapid change than human psychology. The Psyche of the masses embraces a whole world, a world of almost limitless possibilities: breathless calm and raging storm; base treachery and supreme heroism. The masses always represent what historical conditions make of them at a given moment, and the masses are always profoundly capable of being very different to what they may appear at any given moment. It's a poor navigator who steers his ship by the superficial weather signs around him, and fails to use the means science has given him to foresee approaching storms. ' Disappointment ' in the masses is always a compromising sign for political leaders. A real leader, a leader of real moment, will make his tactics dependent not on the temporary spirit of the masses, but on the inexorable laws of historical development. He will steer his course by these laws in defiance of all disappointments and he will rely on history to bring about the gradual maturing of his actions."

There is not one iota of truth in the allegation that Rosa Luxemburg held a theory of mechanical spontaneity. The alleged theory is itself a legend created for a definite political purpose and used uncritically to-day by bureaucratic officials who are yes-men to those above them, but believe that they can command and dragoon those below them with impunity and without fear of being called to account.

Well-meaning people are often misled in this matter by an inability to recognise the dialectical character of historical necessity. Rosa Luxemburg certainly believed in the existence of " inexorable laws of historical development ", but the executors of these laws are human beings, the masses of the people, their organisations, and their leaders, with all their strength and all their weakness, all their successes, and all their failures. And, further, such laws fulfil themselves more or less quickly, and more or less directly, according to the actions of these human beings, these masses, and their organisations (the party, the State, etc.). And even when the course of history seems to sink away from the heights altogether, it will still create the circumstances which will finally ensure its logical development to its inevitable end. Rosa Luxemburg believed that the next great turning-point in world human history was the overthrow of the capitalist order of society; it was an inexorable historic necessity, and the working class must realise this and aim to bring it about. She had all the impetuous temperament of a Harry Hotspur, but she subjected it to the discipline of her knowledge, and she could summon up sufficient patience to let things and human beings mature to the point at which decisive action might take place.

It was not long before she recognised that the international impetus given to the working-class movement everywhere by the Russian Revolution of 1905 was exhausted, and so, although the discussions on the general strike as a political weapon continued, she took hardly any part in them. Purely academic discussions on tactical questions were never to her liking, and it was only when the masses again came into movement that she returned to the lists—in order to obtain action.

Chapter Eight: CAPITALISM INEVITABLY DOOMED?

1. The Party School

In 1907 the German Social Democratic Party founded a party school in Berlin. Up to the outbreak of the World War about thirty members of the party and the trade unions were chosen annually by their district organisations to take courses throughout the winter in the social sciences and in the practical work of agitation and propaganda. The organisational growth of the working-class movement made such a school necessary in order to ensure a supply of trained editors, speakers, and other officials. Amongst the teachers were Franz Mehring, Rudolf Hilferding, Hermann Duncker, Emmanuel Wurm, Gustav Eckstein, and Hugo Heinemann, most of them members of the Left Wing of the party. It appears that Rosa Luxemburg was chosen too, though at first she took no part, but whether this was because she refused for reasons of her own or because the trade unions objected to her, it is impossible to say now. The Prussian police also caused one alteration in the college of teachers, threatening Hilferding, who was an Austrian, with expulsion if he continued to take his classes, so Rosa Luxemburg stepped into the breach, and from 1908 onwards she lectured on political economy.

She proved a splendid teacher, not only because she had thoroughly mastered her material, but because she possessed very considerable natural talent. As a writer and as a speaker this talent had always been present, but now she had a chance to develop it fully. The task of the teachers at the party school was not an easy one. The pupils came from very varied strata; there were mechanics, carpenters, decorators, miners, party officials, trade-union officials, housewives, intellectuals, very young men who had attracted attention for some reason or the other, and old and experienced party members. Most of them were unused to systematic thought, and their knowledge of Socialism was obtained chiefly from ordinary propaganda pamphlets. Rosa Luxemburg easily established contact with them. She never lectured at them in the usual professorial fashion, ramming the finished results of scientific investigation into them; her method was to make them think for themselves and arrive at their own conclusions, whilst keeping her contribution down to the necessary minimum. It was the task of her pupils to think, and she encouraged them by questioning, showing them their errors in her analysis of their answers. This method of teaching did not lead her to occupy her time with the more promising pupils to the exclusion of the others: her whole class had to work, and she tolerated no shirking. She encouraged their ambition, but gave no quarter to laziness or arrogance. She could often be ironical, but the barbs

never rankled, because she never failed to conciliate the
victim by some humorous and friendly observation, and her
ready wit was renowned. She succeeded in obtaining the
best results from the dullest brain, and she created an atmosphere in which her pupils found it easy to give of their best,
and in which they developed an enthusiastic spirit of rivalry
and emulation. She would apparently accompany them
along their own line of reasoning, and she would compel them
to think out their ideas to their logical conclusions; but at
the same time, and almost unnoticeably, she would guide
them to their aim through their own efforts. After such
intellectual wrestling her students would find themselves the
possessors of new and readily understood conclusions to which
they had fought their own way, and which they accepted
because they had mastered all the stages on the journey, and
not because they had been told by their teachers that they
were right.

Her great ability to handle human beings stood her in good
stead as a teacher. Naturally, she was intellectually head
and shoulders above her pupils, in knowledge and experience,
in brain and personality; but there was not the slightest
arrogance about her; her superiority never cramped her
pupils—indeed, it was generally only afterwards that they
realised how big a share she had had in the successes they had
obtained. She developed a contempt for dilettantism and
loose thinking in them, and inspired them with enthusiasm
and understanding for scientific achievement, and from that
developed their own enthusiasm for creative effort. The
collaboration with Rosa Luxemburg was a gain both mentally
and morally for all her students. Amongst them were certainly some who had come with the determination not to be
won over by the heretic, but one and all they were irresistibly
won over, and even those who afterwards became her opponents
in the movement never lost their gratitude to her or their deep
respect for her. Her aim was to win them for her ideas and
for her cause, and in the majority of cases she succeeded.

2. " Introduction to Political Economy "

Her teaching activities gave birth to two very important
works on socialist theory, the first of which was her " Intro-

duction to Political Economy ".[1] Unfortunately we have it only in a fragmentary form, but from a letter written by Rosa Luxemburg on July 28th, 1916, from prison in Berlin to the publisher, I. H. W. Dietz, we know the general plan of the work. In the summer of 1916 the first two chapters were ready for printing and all the other chapters already in draft. Unfortunately, however, only five chapters could be found amongst her literary remains, and they were published in 1925 by Paul Levi,[2] who unfortunately took it on himself to make arbitrary alterations in the text, to omit important notes, and to insert many errors. If we had the whole book to-day we should have all the material she dealt with in her lectures at the party school. From the torso in our possession we can see that the book was gradually built up in a long process, during which she gradually recognised all the difficulties in day-to-day intercourse with her pupils, and was able to overcome them one by one. The result is a brilliantly clear exposition of economic development and its many problems. The style is popular and leads the reader from stage to stage in a fashion which must delight anyone familiar with the difficulties of the material and open up new and unexpected angles of vision even for him.

From what we have and from the titles of the missing chapters it is clear that the book was to have been a condensed exposition of all the economic teachings of Karl Marx. Popularisations of Marx had been attempted before, but Rosa Luxemburg was not satisfied to follow in the beaten track, or even to keep to the methods of exposition favoured by Marx. She sketches the great stages of the economic and social history of mankind, and combines the whole with a criticism of the social theories which formed the intellectual reflection of those stages. Her style is vivid, and her polemics, where they become necessary, are trenchant. At the party school her favourite method was to work on the wrong or half-true answers of her pupils until the truth finally became

---

[1] Rosa Luxemburg, " *Einführung in die Nationalökonomie* ", issued by Paul Levi in Berlin, 1925.

[2] Paul Levi (1883–1930), lawyer, defended Rosa Luxemburg in the Frankfort process in 1914. Member of the Spartakus League, one of the founders of the Communist Party of Germany, and after the deaths of Rosa Luxemburg and Leo Jogiches, the leader of the party until 1921. Later he returned to the Social Democratic Party.

visible. In her book she adopts much the same method, but here it is the errors, stupidities, and subjective evasions of the great luminaries of political economy which provide her with material. Their smug fur flies, and many of their apparently profound revelations are seen to be nothing but empty phrases. Behind the scientific weakness of her opponents she senses the moral weakness of the class enemy, and takes a joy in trouncing them. At the same time her attacks on the orthodox economists are not mere fireworks to make her matter more compelling, or mere polemical excesses. On the contrary, they are always closely connected with her subject-matter. First of all they serve as proof that the orthodox authorities on the social sciences are deeply influenced in their judgements by the interests of their class, and secondly that economic science has always been a weapon in the hands of the ruling class to consolidate its position.

She demonstrates the necessary development of economic science from the anarchistic mode of production in capitalist society which obscured economic relations or showed them as in a distorting mirror, thanks to competition and the monetary system. She also shows that this science developed originally as a weapon of the *bourgeoisie* against feudalism, and that as such it did splendid scientific service; but that with the rise of the modern working class it developed into a purblind defender of the existing order, whilst its exponents gradually liquidated its greatest achievements and, as far as they still sought to arrive at theoretical generalisations at all, caused it to degenerate into a sort of economic mysticism, and even to the pseudo-scientific tomfoolery of the Sombart school.[1] And finally she shows that whilst Marx's " Criticism of Political Economy " represents a weapon in the hands of the proletariat in the class struggle, in a fully developed socialist plan-economy political economy as a science will be superfluous.

The reader is shown the origin, development, function, and final dissolution of all social and economic orders, beginning with primitive Communism and going on to modern capital-

---

[1] Werner Sombart (*b.* 1863), Professor of Political Economy in Breslau and Berlin. He at first sympathised with Marxism, but gradually tended to defend the policy of German imperialism with pseudo-scientific arguments. Rosa Luxemburg attacked him on many occasions with sarcastic wit. His chief work is " Socialism and Social Movements in the Nineteenth Century ".

ism, whose internal mechanics are laid bare and whose final collapse, as a result of its own inherent contradictions, is shown to be inevitable. Together with her history of theoretical economic problems she also gives an account of *bourgeois* and socialist theories interpreted from the standpoint of Marxist historical materialism—the first attempt on such a scale.

3. " THE ACCUMULATION OF CAPITAL "

Rosa Luxemburg worked on economic problems for a number of years. Her teaching activity at the party school, her ordinary work of agitation and propaganda, long discussions on tactics with her opponents, and a tremendous amount of work for the Polish and Russian movements, postponed the conclusion of her " Introduction to Political Economy " again and again, and when, at the beginning of 1912, she was about to conclude the basic draft she met with an unexpected difficulty:

" I could not succeed in depicting the total process of capitalist production in all its practical relations and with its objective historical limitations with sufficient clarity. Closer examination of the matter then convinced me that it was a question of rather more than the mere art of representation, and that a problem remained to be solved which is connected with the theoretical matter of Vol. II of Marx's ' Capital ' and at the same time closely connected with present-day imperialist politics and their economic roots."

And in this way Rosa Luxemburg came to write her chief work, " The Accumulation of Capital ",[1] the second product of her activity at the party school.

The theoretical problem which she had to master demands

[1] Rosa Luxemburg, " *Die Akkumulation des Kapitals, Ein Beitrag zur ökonomischen Erklärung des Imperialismus*," Berlin, 1913 (" The Accumulation of Capital, a contribution to an economic explanation of Imperialism "), and Rosa Luxemburg, " *Die Akkumulation des Kapitals order was die Epigonen aus der Marxschen Theorie gemacht haben. Eine Antikritik*," Berlin, 1919 (" The Accumulation of Capital, or what the Traditionalists have made of the Marxist Theory. An Anti-critique.") Both books together represent Vol. VI of her " Collected Works ".

a very considerable knowledge of Marxist economic theories for its understanding, and it is not possible to set it down briefly. All that can be done here is to make some attempt to give a general idea of the point at issue, and in this respect the times in which we are now living will assist our understanding. In 1929 the capitalist world economic system was shaken by an economic crisis unparalleled in history. It broke out after the chief damage caused by the World War to the economic system had been made good, after the world market relations broken off and destroyed during the World War had gradually been re-established, and after a short but vigorous boom period had awakened high hopes everywhere in the capitalist world. However, for the expert even the boom period of 1924–28 had many disturbing features which marked it off from former, pre-war, boom periods, and, in particular, in all the most important capitalist countries—in the U.S.A., Great Britain, Germany, etc.—unemployment was several times greater at the peak point of the boom period than it had been at the lowest point of the crisis periods before the World War, and the productive capacity of industry was no longer being fully utilised. The crisis which broke out in 1929 lasted as many years as a crisis formerly lasted months, and it led to unemployment figures ten and twenty times in excess of pre-war figures, and to the closing down of whole branches of industry. Over-production reached such dimensions that public opinion everywhere adopted the phrase " Starvation in the midst of plenty ". At the same time the drop in production and capital which followed, enormous though it was, no longer proved sufficient (as it had always done in former crises) to clear the way for recovery, and the authorities had to adopt the desperate remedy of destroying vast quantities of commodities of all sorts. After the crisis had devastated the world economic system for years a gradual betterment came about, however, and production figures slowly began to rise; but even then one of the most important causes of the recovery (which did not affect the whole world) was the huge work of rearmament which set in after Hitler's rise to power. At the same time all countries erected higher and higher economic barriers against their neighbours, and brutal wars of conquest were launched once again. The spectre of a new world war had arisen, and it soon became clear that even if war were postponed for a long time, the world would in all probability be plunged into a new economic crisis which, in the unanimous opinion of all economists, would prove even more devastating than the last, whose delayed effects were still present.

An important question which immediately arises is whether this catastrophic development was the fault of individual capitalists or groups of capitalists, or individual governments or groups of governments, perhaps; whether, in fact, with greater dexterity on the part of capitalism's leaders the situation could have been avoided. Like all other Marxists, Rosa Luxemburg was convinced that the World War developed from the essential character of capitalist society, and in her investigation of the problem she came to the conclusion that the causes which bring about modern warfare also tend to destroy the conditions for the continued existence of the capitalist economic system. As a result of this she assumed that the final collapse of capitalism would come about in just such economic and political crises as we have witnessed in recent years. However, she failed to prove this point on the basis of Marx's " Capital ". Was her conviction erroneous, or were Marx's teachings inadequate? The question was a very important one for her whole attitude. Her political activity was based on scientific knowledge, and she firmly believed that Socialism could be brought about only if it was possible to prove that capitalism would inevitably be destroyed by its own immanent contradictions.

The difficulty arose with the problem of whether the capitalist economic system (which was characterised above all other economic systems in human history by a tremendous and increasing urge to expansion) would be in a position to develop without hindrance. Economic science admits that this possibility of constant development is an essential condition for the existence of the capitalist system. In former economic systems production took place for direct use, and the things produced were consumed by master and man. Bad harvests, wars, and epidemics sometimes brought catastrophes in their train, but there were no crises arising out of the immanent laws of the economic system: crises of over-production, accompanied by widespread starvation in the midst of plenty, followed by the mass destruction of useful commodities in an effort to re-establish " normal " production conditions by force, were quite unknown. The capitalist economic system must satisfy social requirements in some way or the other, but that is not the main object of capitalist production. This main object is profit, and profit originates in surplus labour—i.e., in that quantity of labour-power expended by the worker over and above the quantity necessary to satisfy his own requirements. However, the profit which results in this way is embodied in the first place in the commodities produced, and it can be realised only when the capitalist finds purchasers for them. The capitalist who has the best chance of selling his commodities, and thus realising his profit, is the one who can produce most cheaply. Competition thus develops, and it compels the individual capitalist to improve and perfect his means of production to the best of his ability; if he fails to do what others around him are doing, he falls back in the race and is lost. Every new stage of technical progress in industry increases the productive forces and the masses of commodities produced, but at the same time the number of workers employed declines, relatively at least, and often absolutely, so that the number of paying customers is reduced. The more powerful the forces of production become the more " hands " are rendered superfluous in industry, and a steadily increasing army of unemployed workers develops. In its turn the existence of this army depresses wages and limits market capacity still further. Thanks to increasing competition, the capitalist economic system is compelled to produce more and more, and the result is inevitably the outbreak of periodic crises, during the course of which productive methods which have shown themselves behind the times are abandoned and great capital values destroyed. Once that has been accomplished the process begins again, but this time the disproportion between the productive forces and the volume of labour-power required to set them in motion is more striking than ever, and thus the dangers increase.

This was the predestined course of capitalist economic development as laid down in Marx's theories: the reserve army of unemployed was to become greater and greater, wages were to be forced down in the end to a mere existence level, and crises were to follow each other with increasing rapidity and increasing violence. However, at first these theoretical conclusions seemed to be in diametrical contradiction to existing reality. From the sixties onwards wages in Europe had been steadily rising, the reserve army of unemployed became smaller instead of greater, and the crises, the apoplectic fits which were to signal the approaching end of capitalism, became weaker and weaker, and capitalist prosperity seemed to be permanently on the increase. In an effort to find a way out of the obvious contradiction, many of the followers of Marx began to give his words concerning the increasing impoverishment of the working classes, the intensification of social contradictions, and the approaching collapse of capitalist society a sense which they obviously could not sustain. Rosa Luxemburg rejected this subterfuge and held fast to Marx's theories, declaring, in answer to Bernstein, that the crises Marx had in mind would set in at a later stage of capitalist development, and that the present period of capitalist progress was a passing phase—although it had already lasted over half a century. She remained unshakably convinced that capitalist development would sooner or later come up against insuperable limits and dash itself to pieces against them.

And then, in Vol. II of Marx's " Capital ", she found a passage which, if correct, would overturn her whole theory. It related to the possibility of a progressive accumulation of capital, a limitless extension of production. The process of accumulation appears at first glance to be a very simple matter. The capitalist uses that part of his realisable surplus-value which he does not consume himself to purchase machinery, raw materials, and supplementary labour-power, and thus new capital is invested in the economic system. However, if the capitalist economic system is regarded as a whole, the simple process becomes a very complicated one, far beyond the control of the individual capitalist. In any particular phase of production, commodities of varying natures must be turned out to meet the market requirements of the population, to renew worn-out means of production, and for re-investment. At the same time these various kinds of commodities must stand in a certain relation to each other in point of value, and they must find a paying demand if they are to be disposed of. Thus the producers of machinery, raw materials, etc., must turn out commodities to the extent and to the value required by themselves and by the producers of consumption goods in each new phase of the process of production. In the meantime the producers of consumption goods must have succeeded in selling their commodities if they are to pay for the means of production and for the labour-power they require in the new phase of production. In the planless, anarchical capitalist order of society these relations and many other equally necessary social relations are regulated by the influx of new capital into certain industries, by price movements, by capital depreciation, bankruptcy, crises, and other such factors.

Marx embodies these manifold and often contradictory relations of value in which the extension of production and the accumulation of capital proceed in capitalist society in a very ingeniously constructed formula. He proceeds, as he invariably does in all his economic investigations, from the assumed existence of a society producing in an exclusively capitalist fashion, having no vestiges of pre-capitalist economic factors to complicate its workings, and consisting exclusively of capitalists (and the dependent throng living on surplus-value) and workers. In this formula each commodity finds its purchaser, and the process of accumulation proceeds in this purely capitalist society without let or hindrance as though obeying an economic law of perpetual motion. However, the formula made his prophecy of progressively devastating crises in capitalist society incomprehensible, and the contention, first advanced by Bernstein, that the trusts could entirely overcome the crises by regulating production seemed justified. Since 1815 economists have violently debated whether a limitless development of capitalism is possible, whether, above all, it will always be possible to find paying customers for the progressively increasing volume of commodities. Just before Rosa Luxemburg came on the scene the optimists seemed to have won a decisive victory— on the basis of Marx's formula. The practical point at issue was whether capitalism in Russia was an inevitable stage of development or not.

This formula of Marx was the difficulty Rosa Luxemburg came up against when she wished to prove the inevitability of capitalist collapse. Until she took up the problem all the theorists had accepted the formula without giving the matter any deeper thought, but she discovered, first of all, that Marx had not concluded his investigation of the problem of accumulation, but had broken off in the middle, and, secondly, that he had failed to take an essential condition into account in his formula: he assumed that the value of labour-power—i.e., the sum of wages—would increase in the same proportion as the value of the means of production. However, the process of production is not extended in each new phase by new machinery, etc., of the same type as the old which it replaces, but by improved machinery, more advanced technique, and more thorough rationalisation; the result is, as we have previously seen, that the value of the means of production increases progressively in relation to the value of the labour-power employed. In fact, the relative depression of the total sum of wages as compared with the total value of the means of production is precisely the sense of technical progress from the capitalist standpoint. This steady change in the relations of value was not taken into consideration by Marx in his formula. Once this factor is included, then the producers of consumption goods are faced with a terrible dilemma: either they must progressively renounce the accumulation of their realised surplus-value, and consume it themselves with the exception of a steadily decreasing part (a proceeding which would invert the whole sense of capitalist society), or they must accept the fact that an increasing volume of the consumption goods they produce cannot find buyers. In other words, there would be steadily increasing volumes of unsaleable commodities on the one hand, and a steadily increasing reserve army of unemployed workers on the other, combining to cause more and more rapid and more and more violent economic crises. And this is exactly true of present-day capitalist society.

Up to the outbreak of the World War the capitalists found a way out of the dilemma created by increasing productive forces and decreasing purchasing power by unloading larger and larger quantities of commodities on to social strata not producing in a capitalist fashion (peasants and urban craftsmen, etc.), or on to areas where the mode of production was backward—for instance, in the colonial and semi-colonial countries. But the more vigorously capitalism drove forward into these virgin territories the more it accelerated the process

of accumulation. At the same time this penetration into
" non-capitalist space " explained the existence of certain
social phenomena which, as they stood, could not be reconciled
with Marx's theories.

Rosa Luxemburg discovered the solution of the problem of
accumulation in this capitalist penetration into non-capitalist
areas, and she showed clearly that capitalism would be unable
to exist at all if it were deprived of this possibility of expansion.
At the same time, and despite the formula we have just dealt
with, she was able to reconcile her ideas with those of Marx.
It is true that in his investigations into the mechanics of
capitalism he always assumed the existence of a purely
capitalist society in order to determine the laws of capitalist
production under the purest possible conditions, just as a
vacuum is necessary to demonstrate the law of gravity,
but at the same time he always stressed the fact that capitalist
penetration into non-capitalist areas would prove the most
effective means of overcoming economic crises, and that
capitalism must perish when there is no longer any possibility
of extending the capitalist market.

Rosa Luxemburg linked this idea to the problem of capital
accumulation, and this represents the great achievement of
her chief theoretical work. It is true that in her argument
she made a number of errors which were subsequently discovered by Bucharin after her death,[1] but he did not disprove
her main thesis, though he imagined he did. Fritz Sternberg[2]
then rectified her theory of accumulation in one or two points
and successfully applied it to other economic questions,
and we have followed his ideas in our general sketch of the
problem.

4. IMPERIALISM AND THE THEORY OF CAPITAL ACCUMULATION

Rosa Luxemburg did not confine herself to an investigation
of the theoretical problem of accumulation. Undoubtedly
she was assisted to a solution of the problem by her studies of
primitive communist societies, their decline, and, above all,

[1] Nikolai Bucharin, " *Der Imperialismus und die Akkumulation des Kapitals* "
(" Imperialism and the Accumulation of Capital "), published in " *Unter
dem Banner des Marxismus* ", 1925.
[2] Fritz Sternberg, " *Der Imperialismus* " (" Imperialism "), Berlin, 1926.

their ruthless destruction by encroaching European " civilisation ". She had already described this process in her " Introduction to Political Economy ", taking as her examples the civilisations of the Incas and of India, and the old Russian *Obshtchina*, and she now returned to the question from the standpoint of the capitalist incursion into non-capitalist areas. She divides the process of development into three phases: the struggle of capitalism against primitive self-sufficing society, which begins with the rise of capitalism under feudalism and soon goes beyond the limits of its own geographical area; the struggle against simple commodity production; and, finally, the fierce rivalry of world capitalism for the last vestiges of foreign markets—i.e., the last chance of accumulation.

She describes the bloody and brutal struggle against primitive society in the colonies, taking India and Algeria as examples, and the conquest of markets by " peaceful penetration ", taking China from the opium wars to the Boxer crusade of the world capitalist Powers as an example. From the history of the U.S.A., Canada, and South Africa she shows how the native Indians and Negroes were robbed of land and freedom, and often of their lives; how simple commodity production squeezed out primitive self-sufficing society, only to be expelled in its turn by modern capital, which drove the natives before it from district to district. All the crimes in the calendar, including slave-raiding, murder, and massacre, were committed in these economic crusades to realise surplus-value. And " the ruin of independent handicraft by capitalist competition is a chapter in itself, a less noisy one perhaps, but no less painful ". And she concludes:

" The general result of the struggle between capitalism and simple commodity production was this: capitalism took the place of simple commodity production after replacing primitive self-sufficing society by simple commodity production. It is said that capitalism lives from non-capitalist societies, but it might more truthfully be said that it lives from their ruin; it is said that capitalism needs non-capitalist areas for its own accumulation, but it might more truthfully be said that it needs to swallow them up before capital accumulation can proceed. Seen historically this capital accumulation is a process of metabolism proceeding between

capitalist and pre-capitalist modes of production. . . .
Capitalism can no more exist without these non-capitalist
areas than the latter can continue to exist side by side with
capitalism. . . .

" Thus the assumption Marx made as the hypothesis of his
formula of accumulation is in accordance only with the
objective historical tendency of the process of accumulation
and its theoretical result. . . . And now comes the difficulty.
Once the final result is reached—it remains merely a
theoretical supposition, of course—accumulation becomes
impossible altogether: the realisation and capitalisation of
surplus-value becomes an insoluble task. As soon as the
Marxist formula of extended reproduction conforms to
reality, it reveals the outcome of the whole process: the
historical limits of the process of accumulation—i.e., the
end of the capitalist mode of production." [1]

As the capitalist incursion penetrates more and more into
non-capitalist areas, its methods become more efficient,
because it not only finds customers for commodities which
would prove unsaleable within the ordinary framework of
capitalist production, thereby fully realising surplus-value,
but at the same time it spurs on the process of accumulation,
thereby increasing the productive forces and reproducing on
a still greater scale the fundamental contradictions which set
the whole process into movement. Capitalism can therefore
not wait until new markets for its commodities have been
won, but side by side with these commodities it begins to
export capital and to set up modern capitalist production in
countries which are still at a stage of primitive self-sufficiency.
In this way, however, it also creates still further competitors
for itself, and the possibilities of expansion are thus supple-
mentarily limited. At first the capitalist robbers hunt each in
his own chosen sphere, but as the area available decreases,
they begin to squabble amongst themselves for possession of
the last vestiges not yet fully under capitalist dominance, or
for a re-division of the booty. This is the phase of fully-
fledged imperialism:

" Imperialism is simultaneously a way of prolonging the

[1] Rosa Luxemburg, " Collected Works " (German), Vol. VI., p. 335.

life of capitalism, and a way of very effectually limiting it. Naturally, this does not mean that the final limits will be reached inevitably and mechanically; however, the tendency towards these final limits is making itself felt already in a way which indicates that the final phase of capitalism will be a period of catastrophes." [1]

And again:

" The more violently capitalism liquidates the non-capitalist strata at home and abroad, and depresses the standards of living of all working people, the more the day to day history of international capital accumulation develops into a never-ending chain of political and social catastrophes and convulsions, which, taken together with periodically recurring economic upheavals in the shape of crises, will render the continuation of capital accumulation impossible, and make the rebellion of the international working class against capitalist dominance necessary even before capitalism has reached the natural self-created limits of its economic possibilities." [2]

5. The Traditionalists enter the Arena

With her " Accumulation of Capital ", Rosa Luxemburg had solved a problem which had haunted economists since the first big economic crisis in 1815, and which had exhausted even Marx's huge powers. The conception of history which gave her confidence in her own theoretical and political judgement had been confirmed: Socialism must come not merely because it was the ideal of increasing masses of human beings, but because capitalism itself was going downhill to its final destruction. The idea of Socialism had shed the last vestige of Utopianism. At the same time imperialism had been recognised as a historically necessary phenomenon, and with this a barrier had been erected, at least theoretically, to the illusions and subterfuges in which even prominent Marxists were indulging. The way had been cleared for an understanding of the tremendous convulsions towards which the capitalist world was moving. Rosa Luxemburg's achievement was all the more remarkable because it was made during

[1] Rosa Luxemburg, *ibid.*, p. 361.
[2] Rosa Luxemburg, *ibid.*, p. 380.

a great period of capitalist prosperity, a period of prosperity caused precisely by a tremendous capitalist incursion into non-capitalist areas, and in defiance of the general expectation that the most dangerous antagonisms between the imperialist Powers were about to find a peaceable solution. In a letter written five years later, on July 12th, 1917, to her friend Diefenbach from prison in Wronke, she describes the creative enthusiasm in which her " Accumulation of Capital " was conceived and carried out:

" The period whilst I was writing the ' Accumulation ' was one of the happiest in my life. I lived almost in an ecstasy, seeing and hearing nothing but the problem I was working on so satisfactorily. I don't know what gave me more pleasure: the intellectual wrestling with a knotty point and its gradual unravelling walking slowly up and down the room, or afterwards the putting of results to paper in a literary form. Do you know I did the lot right off inside four months? A herculean performance! And then I gave the MS. into print without even looking through it again."

The literary form she has given her book is brilliant, but its purely theoretical chapters make very great demands on the intellect of the reader, and assume a wide knowledge of political economy in general and of Marxist theory in particular. She was well aware that she was writing for a very limited public, and that, as she put it herself, " from this point of view the book is a luxury and might just as well be printed on the finest hand-wove paper ". However, she could hardly have expected the reception which was actually accorded the book in socialist and Marxist circles. The only prominent Marxists to recognise its value were Franz Mehring and Julian Marchlevski, and they were both enthusiastic about it, whilst a horde of competent and incompetent critics indulged in an orgy of loud criticism which often degenerated into mere abuse. Very few of them made any attempt to come to grips with the problem at issue, and, in fact, most of them declared without more ado that the problem which had caused her so much trouble did not exist at all. Of course, they brought out Marx's formula as an indisputable proof that the process of accumulation could proceed endlessly under purely capitalist conditions, and they refused to bother their heads about her objection that Marx's formula was not reconcilable with the economic hypothesis of his whole analysis of capitalism. It was not long, however, before the critics came to loggerheads amongst themselves, and their subsequent violent disputes indicated at least that the problem was not quite so unimportant as they would have had the world believe.

Those few critics who made any serious attempt to analyse the process of accumulation on their own fell victim to the grossest errors, and Otto Bauer, who took the problem very seriously, declared that the natural increase in population was the basis for the continued process of accumulation, though that was an idea Marx himself had already rejected with scorn. However, when Bauer went on to extend Marx's formula and adapt it to the real conditions of the capitalist system of competition, he discovered that it was indeed impossible for capitalists to realise the whole of their surplus-value within the framework of a purely capitalist society. Objectively, therefore, he confirmed Rosa Luxemburg's theory, but he tried to escape from his quandary by arbitrarily transferring the unrealisable commodity surplus in the con-sumption-goods sector to the production-goods sector, to which Rosa Luxemburg replied laconically: " One can't buy copper-mine shares with a stock of unsaleable tallow dips, or found an engineering works with a stock of equally unsaleable galoshes." At the critical point Bauer had overlooked the fact that not only values were involved in the process of accu-mulation, but also very tangible commodities of different categories.

In 1915, when Rosa Luxemburg was in possession of very considerable involuntary leisure as an inmate of the Women's Prison in the Barnim Strasse in Berlin, she occupied her time usefully by thoroughly analysing the arguments of her critics, and she showed great acumen and considerable humour, though occasionally some bitterness, in the performance of her task. The result was the second volume of her work, with the sub-title " What the Traditionalists have made of the Marxist Theory. An Anti-critique ", and not one stone remained upon another of the altar painfully erected by her critics for the sacrifice of her theories. At the same time she used this reply to present her own ideas again, but in a more popular form, so as to appeal to a wider circle of readers. Her work is a masterpeice of scientific investigation and scientific presentation of a problem, and her own verdict on it is just: " Form has been reduced to its utmost simplicity; there are no unnecessary accessories, no fireworks and no dazzle; it is unpretentious; everything is reduced to broad outline, naked ; one might say, like a block of marble."

After her death, Bucharin published a criticism of her theory of accumulation. As we have already pointed out, he undoubtedly succeeded in revealing a number of weaknesses in her arguments, and if his objections are granted, then her theories require certain modification. However, Bucharin himself was under the impression that he had refuted her whole theory, but his solution of the problem turned out to be an indirect confirmation of her fundamental theory. In his attempt to present the process of constant capital accumulation in a purely capitalist society he assumed the existence of " State capitalism " producing according to plan, and declared :

" In the event of a miscalculation with regard to consumption goods for workers the surplus could be got rid of by distributing it amongst them, or by destroying it altogether. In the event of a miscalculation in the production of luxury articles the ' solution ' is equally clear. Thus no crisis of over-production can possibly come about here."

Bucharin's " solution " is astonishing. We are presented with a form of " capitalism " which is not economic anarchy, but a planned system, in which there is no competition: a general world trust, and in which capitalists do not have to bother their heads about the realisation of their surplus-value, because all unsaleable products are very simply disposed of. " The process of production proceeds smoothly, generally speaking." In fact, one has only to exclude hypothetically all the ordinary conditions of the problem, anarchical production, competition, and the necessity of realising surplus-value by selling the produced commodities—and, hey presto, the problem no longer exists. " In Rosa Luxemburg's opinion crises would be inevitable even in our hypothetical State capitalist society, but we have shown, on the contrary, that crises could not exist." [1] That was not Rosa Luxemburg's opinion at all—in fact, given Bucharin's premises, she would probably have agreed with him, except that she would never have called a system " pure capitalism " in which capitalists lived in complete harmony with each other, directed society, and consumed the best fruits of its toil, whilst an army of State slaves, and (because, under such circumstances, the reserve army of labour must necessarily increase enormously) a broad stratum of more or less parasitic hooligans represented the ever-open door for all surplus production. Such a society may approximate to the ideal of fascist dictators, but it is not " pure capitalism " in the Marxist sense. Thus in the end Bucharin's criticism of Rosa Luxemburg's theory of capital accumulation develops into a strong argument in favour of her contention that non-capitalist areas are, after all, necessary for capitalist accumulation.

Various critics, and in particular Bucharin, imagined they were playing a high trump when they pointed to the great possibilities of capitalist extension into non-capitalist areas, but she had already cut the ground from under their feet by pointing out repeatedly that capitalism would enter into its final convulsions long before the inherent tendency to extend its markets had reached its objective limits. That was not a subterfuge to save an untenable theory. Dealing with the general contradictions of capitalism in her pamphlet " Social Reform or Revolution " (fifteen years before she brought these contradictions to a common denominator in her " Accumulation of Capital "), she wrote :

" Naturally even the prevailing social-democratic tactic does not consist in waiting for the development of capitalist contradictions to their final intensity, and then waiting still further for the inevitable change. On the contrary, we base our line on the once recognised tendency of capitalist development, and in our political struggle we then endeavour to intensify its consequences to the utmost ; that is the essence of any revolutionary tactic." [2]

[1] Nikolai Bucharin, " *Der Imperialismus und die Akkumulation des Kapitals* ", in " *Unter dem Banner des Marxismus* ", Vol. I., p. 254.
[2] Rosa Luxemburg, " Collected Works " (German), Vol. III., p. 64.

Expansionist possibilities are not a geographical or a demographical conception, and the extent of the process cannot be determined by a comparison of capitalist and non-capitalist populations in the world. A social economic problem is involved, and a whole complex of contradictory interests, forces, and phenomena has to be taken into account: the driving impetus of the productive forces, the political strength of the capitalist Powers, friction between the various branches of production, the acceleration and retarding of expansion by competition between the imperialist Powers, the struggle between the heavy and the manufacturing industries in the industrialisation of the colonies (India), the dominance of the motherlands over the colonies, colonial revolutions, imperialist wars, revolutions in the capitalist countries and all their consequences, the dislocation of the capital market, political insecurity in large areas (China), and innumerable other factors. To-day, at a time when the productive forces have developed tremendously, the factors retarding expansion have become so effective that they have already produced serious economic, social, and political dislocation, and they clearly indicate the decline of capitalist society. Theoretically it is quite possible to imagine a new forward drive on the part of capitalism which would open up new fields for the productive forces and introduce a new period of general progress. However, there is no practical indication of how this could come about. In drawing her conclusions for the working-class struggle, Rosa Luxemburg incidentally demonstrates once again how ridiculous is the suggestion that she was the victim of blind fatalism in dealing with the historical laws of capitalist development:

" Here, as at other times in history, theory does its full service by showing us the tendency of development and indicating the final end to which it is objectively travelling. However, this final and logical end will no more be reached in the present period of development than it was ever reached in any earlier period of historical development. It is unnecessary that it should develop to its final consequences because social consciousness, this time embodied in the social proletariat, intervenes actively in the blind play of forces. And, further, in the present case a correct understanding of Marxist theories offers social consciousness most fruitful assistance and a most powerful incentive." [1]

Chapter Nine: THE STRUGGLE AGAINST IMPERIALISM

1. The Political Problem

ROSA LUXEMBURG's "Accumulation of Capital" did more than solve an abstract theoretical problem: it also showed that imperialism, with all it typical accompaniments (the rivalry of capitalist States for colonial possessions and spheres of influence, for possibilities of capital export, and for raw material resources; protectionism; the increasing dominance of bank and trust capital; the armament race, etc.), was not an accidental result of certain political actions which might just as easily have been avoided, and that it did not serve merely the interests of one small capitalist clique (the armaments industries), but that it was a historically necessary phase of capitalist development—in fact, the final stage of that development. These conclusions were naturally of great importance for the policy of the working class:

> "As always in such cases, the exact theoretical understanding of the problem down to its very roots will give our practical policy in the struggle against imperialism that clearness of vision and that vigour which are essential for a successful proletarian policy."

Lively debates took place in the ranks of German Social Democracy on the point, and the conclusions drawn by the various groups were highly interesting. The frankly reformist group took hardly any part in the discussion on the problem of accumulation, and a number of them (those who accepted and supported German imperialism, like Schippel, Leuthner,

[1] Rosa Luxemburg, *ibid.*, p. 479.

Quessel, Maurenbrecher, and Winnig) gladly accepted the thesis that imperialism was an inevitable stage of historical development, arguing that a real Marxist could not oppose historical progress, but must seek rather to further it, particularly as the free development of the productive forces was the preliminary condition for Socialism. In this, of course, they were confusing the position of the *bourgeoisie* and that of the proletariat in the historical process. They overlooked the fact that capitalist exploitation was also a historical necessity, representing historical progress as compared with earlier and more primitive forms of exploitation, though, despite this, Socialism still resolutely opposed capitalism.

However, the majority of the party leaders took a different stand. The bigger the dangers of imperialism loomed up the more they sought to avoid them by burying their heads in the sand. Kautsky developed a theory of his own to suit the case. He admitted that capitalism was expanding ceaselessly, and he approved of it, but he declared that this expansion was not imperialism; imperialism was merely a particular method of expansion, a violent one, used by certain small but powerful capitalist groups (bank capital and militarism), and it was not in the interests of the capitalist class as a whole, and certainly not in the interests of heavy industry. Political power was becoming a less and less serviceable instrument for economic expansion. Expenditure on armaments only reduced the volume of capital available for investment in Turkey, China, Persia, etc., and therefore the majority of the capitalist class would more and more strongly oppose a policy of imperialist violence. In consequence, the capitalist Powers would turn more and more away from imperialism and return to the policy of the Manchester School, with its principles of Free Trade and the Open Door.

Even when Kautsky began to develop this theory it obviously contradicted the known facts, but his position became grotesque when he clung to it and embellished it even at the height of the World War. His trouble was perfectly obvious; it was a clear case of intellectual flight from disagreeable reality. In searching for the political tendency which united her critics, Rosa Luxemburg was tilting chiefly at Kautsky, " the super-expert behind the scenes ", when she wrote:

" The belief in the possibility of accumulation in a ' pure ' capitalist society, the belief that capitalism is possible without expansion, is the theoretical formula for a certain definite tactical tendency. This conception tends to regard the phase of imperialism not as a historical necessity, not as the final bout between capitalism and Socialism, but rather as the malicious invention of a group of interested parties. It tries to persuade the *bourgeoisie* that imperialism and militarism are deleterious even from the standpoint of *bourgeois* interests, in the hope that it will then be able to isolate the alleged handful of interested parties and so form a block between the proletariat and the majority of the *bourgeoisie* with a view to ' curbing ' imperialism, starving it out by ' partial disarmament ', and ' removing its sting '. Just as *bourgeois* Liberalism in its period of decay appealed from the ' ignorant ' monarchs to the ' enlightened ' monarchs, now the ' Marxist Centre ' proposes to appeal from the ' unreasonable ' *bourgeoisie* to the ' reasonable ' *bourgeoisie* with a view to dissuading it from a policy of imperialism with all its catastrophic results to a policy of international disarmament treaties; from an armed struggle for world dominance to a peaceable federation of democratic national States. The general settling of accounts between the proletariat and capitalism, the solution of the great contradiction between them, resolves itself into an idyllic compromise for the ' mitigation of imperialist contradictions between the capitalist States '." [1]

2. The Danger of Imperialist War

The tactics of German Social Democracy were naturally in accordance with its theoretical attitude towards imperialism. Although social-democratic leaders occasionally thundered against imperialism in general, yet in the Reichstag they invariably supported German imperialism on all decisive questions, and criticised only " the excesses " of imperialism— i.e., the provocation offered to the rest of the world from time to time by Wilhelm II, Kiderlen-Waechter, etc. German Social Democracy followed a policy of " peaceful penetration " because it disliked the bloody consequences of imperialism.

[1] Rosa Luxemburg, *ibid.*, p. 481.

G

The imperialists in the social-democratic camp pursued their course unwaveringly. Some of them spoke quite openly of the coming military struggle with Great Britain, though in 1913 Quessel proposed the conclusion of an agreement with her for the peaceful division of the world, and in particular of Africa. They were quite openly in favour of colonialism, and David even declared that it was an integral part of the universal cultural aims of the socialist movement. At the same time they looked at all imperialist questions exclusively from the stand-point of the dominant race, which, in the best case, was advised to make its autocracy " benevolent ".

The " Marxist Centre " was very lax in matters of foreign policy, but it was full of hope, and as late as 1911 Bernstein announced confidently that war was quite out of the question : the desire for peace was becoming universal, and the peacable assurances of leading statesmen might be accepted with confidence. The armaments race was an anomaly with neither national nor economic justification, and the best way to avoid war was by general disarmament, international arbitration courts, peace alliances, and the formation of a United States of Europe. In short, the " Marxist Centre " appealed to the good-will of the imperialist *bourgeoisie* rather than to the socialist will of the proletariat.

Rosa Luxemburg opposed this policy root and branch, and she enjoyed the sympathy of the Left Wing of the party, though its support was not always discriminating. For her it was a matter of fundamental principle that Social Democracy should never take sides in the foreign-political manœuvres of capitalist Powers, because their aim was always plunder and exploitation, no matter what diplomatic mask they might adopt. The working class must always pursue a foreign policy guided exclusively by its own international and revolutionary interests. The prime necessity in any international conflict was to lay bare the capitalist interests behind it, and show its consequences. She did this herself with extraordinary keenness of vision, keeping always the whole field of world politics in view and unravelling the most complicated problems with a sure hand. She mercilessly trounced both the peace pretensions of *bourgeois* diplomacy and the sheep-like illusions of the social-democratic leaders. When Sir Edward Grey came forward in 1911 with his proposal for a general limitation of armaments, her voice sounded a discordant note in the general chorus of socialist approval:

"Militarism is closely connected with colonialism, protectionism, and world politics as a whole—i.e., if the Great Powers honestly and sincerely want to call a halt to the world armament race they must begin to dismantle their protectionist systems and to abandon colonial robbery and their policy of 'spheres of influence' all over the world —in short, both in home and foreign politics they must begin to do the exact opposite of what is now the very essence of capitalist-class national policy." [1]

Rosa Luxemburg did not often write on foreign politics and she did so only when confusion in the Marxist camp made it necessary to clarify a particular question and rectify party policy. She laid down the general standpoint of Social Democracy to imperialism, and to the economic and political happenings in the struggle of the capitalist Powers for the world market, and also certain tactical principles. Imperialism could not be overcome within the framework of capitalism because it developed from the vital interests of capitalist society. Any struggle against imperialism must therefore be directed against capitalist society as a whole. Imperialism or Socialism were the real alternatives. Any attempt to arrive at partial solutions of foreign-political conflicts would inevitably lead to supporting one group of imperialists against the other, and this invariably meant fraternisation with the national *bourgeoisie* against the foreign *bourgeoisie* and the abandonment of international working-class interests. Such a policy would lead deeper and deeper into the mire of nationalism, and finally end in participation in an imperialist war. Any attempt to guarantee peace on the basis of *bourgeois* society (and in particular the propaganda in favour of peaceful expansion, disarmament, international arbitration courts, alliances, benevolent colonial policy, and such things) was either an illusion or an astute camouflage of imperialism's policy of violence, and in any case it must cloud the vision and weaken the strength of the working class. The real struggle against imperialism (apart from the constant Marxist

[1] Rosa Luxemburg, in the *Leipziger Volkszeitung*, May 6th, 1911.

exposure of the real background of all diplomatic conflicts) must lie in the strengthening of international working-class solidarity, in united action by the international working class in all world political crises, and in a struggle against the domestic effects of imperialist policy: militarism, oppressive taxation, the rising cost of living, and cuts in social policy and democratic liberties. Rosa Luxemburg, and with her the Left Wing of the party, considered social development so progressed that in any future convulsion Socialism—i.e., the conquest of political power by the working class—would become an immediate issue. The party must therefore now go beyond its previous activity of mere agitation and organisation to mass action, and, more than ever before, the party policy must be active and militant.

Following on the Russian Revolution of 1905, the European Powers lined up in two great blocks: the Triple Alliance and the *Entente Cordiale*. The Morocco conflict of 1906 suddenly revealed how close Europe had come to armed conflict, and the fear of war began to spread to wider and wider sections of the population. The threat of war and what to do about it became burning questions for the International, and at its Stuttgart Congress in 1907 they were dealt with practically for the first time. Rosa Luxemburg was present as the representative of the All-Russia Social Democratic Party, and as a member of the War Commission she strongly opposed a suggestion, supported by the British and French delegates, that war should be answered by a general strike and a general refusal to do military service, since it involved a promise which it would hardly be possible to keep, seeing that the ruling classes were not likely to plunge the world into war at a moment when it appeared at all possible that the masses might take strong action against them. She aimed at securing a clear statement against war by the International and persuading the parties of the International to adopt a determined revolutionary policy in accordance with the strength of the working class. Together with Lenin and Martov, she drew up a resolution which was fashioned and re-fashioned in discussions with Bebel, in order to give the German Public Prosecutor no excuse for a prosecution, or perhaps even the suppression of the Social Democratic Party. The decisive passages of this resolution were:

" In the event of a threat of war it is the duty of the workers and their parliamentary representatives in the countries involved to do everything possible to prevent the outbreak of war by taking suitable measures, which can, of course, change or be intensified in accordance with the intensification of the class struggle and the general political situation.

" In the event of war breaking out nevertheless, it is their duty to take measures to bring it to an end as quickly as possible, and to utilise the economic and political crisis brought about by the war to arouse the masses of the people and accelerate the overthrow of capitalist class rule."

In guarded words and without romanticism, but with the necessary clarity concerning its aim and character, the resolution indicated the line of action to be adopted, and it was accepted with great enthusiasm and without a dissentient voice. Did Rosa Luxemburg seriously believe that it would be adhered to ? She was well aware that there were very many nationalists in the International who would consider it nothing but an empty gesture, but she did believe that the radical socialist leaders, particularly in the Central Committee of the German Social Democratic Party, would rise above their weaknesses in a critical situation and prove themselves worthy of their position.

3. THE BREACH WITH KAUTSKY

It was not long before certain events seemed to justify this belief: for the first time in its history, German Social Democracy mobilised the masses of the workers for a political offensive. The point of attack was well chosen. The most modern capitalist country in Europe was ruled by a semi-absolutist government supported by reactionary Junkers, and the anachronism was becoming more and more grotesque. Prussian Junkerdom monopolised the government apparatus and administrative machinery, and entrenched itself behind the Prussian Diet, in which it had an overwhelming majority, thanks to an electoral system which divided the population into three classes according to tax returns, and automatically gave the power to the well-to-do. In 1908 social-democratic candidates polled 600,000 votes, and gained six seats, whilst the conservatives polled 418,000 votes, and held 212 seats.

The same year saw the first non-parliamentary attack of the working class on the positions of Junkerdom, and for the first time workers demonstrated on the streets in defiance of police prohibitions. The immediate result of this action was that in the Royal Speech Wilhelm II promised electoral reform. However, two years passed before any attempt was made to implement this promise, and the Chancellor, Bethmann Hollweg, then produced a so-called reform which seemed like a deliberate provocation of the working class: members of free professions, higher officials, pensioned officers, etc., were to move up a class. That was the net result of the " reform ". The proposal proved the signal for energetic working-class action, with which broad masses of the lower-middle classes openly sympathised. Every Sunday in February and March 1910 great masses of workers demonstrated on the streets of all the big towns in defiance of authority. Bloody collisions took place in the provinces, but police brutalities only infuriated the people, and the demonstrations continued. In Berlin the Police President, Traugott von Jagow (afterwards one of the leaders of the Kapp Putsch against the Weimar Republic in 1920), issued threatening proclamations in Napoleonic style, and troops were concentrated in the town and exercised on the streets to overawe the population. However, the organisers of the demonstrations did their work so efficiently that von Jagow suffered one moral defeat after the other. Hundreds of thousands of workers assembled on the streets, but always where they were least expected, and the Social Democratic Party seemed to have the working class completely in hand. The demonstrations did not gain their immediate objective, the introduction of a modern franchise for Prussia, but at least Bethmann Hollweg's proposals had to be abandoned and the right to demonstrate on the streets was secured.

It was the first tangible political victory of the modern German working class, and it was won by masses in a thoroughly militant mood. Furthermore, it was no passing wave of feeling, because the miners followed up the action by engaging in a big wage struggle, whilst 200,000 building workers fought tenaciously against a lock-out, and by their endurance and clever tactics succeeded in winning a victory.

Rosa Luxemburg considered the situation ripe for a big political test, and the weapon of the political strike seemed a suitable one to intensify the action in favour of a modern franchise and prevent what had already been done from passing away without trace:

> " In a situation like the present, long delays, long pauses between the individual phases of the campaign, and hesitation in the choice of weapons and tactics almost represent a lost battle."

This opinion was widespread in the party, and numerous organisations (Breslau, Halle, Königsberg, the Rhineland, etc.) demanded the calling of a general strike, whilst in Kiel and Frankfort-Hanau short demonstration strikes took place. At the beginning of March the Central Committee of the Social Democratic Party went into council with the leaders of the trade unions on the proposal of a general demonstration strike. The decision was a negative one, but the fact that the proposal was discussed at all was sufficient evidence of the mood of the working class.

Rosa Luxemburg was well aware of the difficulties involved: a class which had never carried out a great action, and which for years had been accustomed to take all its slogans ready-made from the Social Democratic Party, would find it difficult to make the big step from political demonstrations to a political strike. She therefore proposed the organisation of political action accompanied, in the beginning, by demonstration strikes of limited duration, and at the same time she demanded that the general strike should be put forward for discussion, to discover how far the masses would be prepared to take part in it.

It was clear that, despite its vigour, the movement for the franchise would be only a passing phase in the period of great mass struggles which she saw facing the German working class. The Left Wing of the party put forward the alternatives: Socialism against imperialism. That was quite adequate for general anti-imperialist propaganda, because it clearly showed the real significance of the whole historical epoch, but as a slogan for immediate mass struggles, Socialism, and even the seizure of political power, was too far away, and therefore she took an important tactical step and proposed the slogan of a republic as a suitable one for the propaganda and action of the moment:

> " The slogan of a republic in present-day Germany represents something far more than a happy dream, the dream of a democratic ' People's State ', something far more than the demand of doctrinaires with their heads in the clouds. On the contrary, it is a practical war cry against militarism, navalism, colonialism, imperialism, junkerdom and the Prussianisation of Germany; it is the result and the drastic summary of our daily struggle against all these various phenomena of the ruling reaction." [1]

The slogan was, in fact, even more for Rosa Luxemburg than she admitted. It was more than " the acid test of class attachment, the slogan of the class struggle " in the every-day struggle, and if her interpretation of the Russian Revolution were adapted to German conditions, it meant that the first decisive step in a German Revolution would be the abolition of the dozen-and-one little monarchies throughout the country. Afterwards, of course, the revolution would go much farther, and end in the seizure of political power by the proletariat. Her slogan of a republic was thus not merely something invented to fit the situation of the moment: it was the linking up of all the great struggles of the day with the final aim of the proletarian class struggle.

Whilst the franchise demonstrations were still proceeding she summed up her attitude in a long article which she submitted to the *Vorwärts*. It was returned to her at the beginning of March 1910 with the observation that party instructions forbade any propaganda in favour of a political strike. She then sent the article to Kautsky for the *Neue Zeit*, and although he found it " very fine and very important ", he finally gave way to the party leaders, and refused to publish it. In the end the article was divided up and published separately in various party dailies.

Rosa Luxemburg considered Kautsky's attitude a personal affront. She was the chief contributor to the *Neue Zeit*; she had been his permanent adviser and frequently represented him in the editorship; in fact the great reputation which he

[1] Rosa Luxemburg, " Collected Works " (German), Vol. IV., pp. 509 *et seq.*

enjoyed amongst radical socialists was due in no small measure to her intellectual collaboration. Kautsky's attitude was more than mere submission to the party leadership; it symbolised his own political *volte-face* and the fact that his intellectual alliance with Rosa Luxemburg was at an end. This was made quite clear when he published an article in the *Neue Zeit* spitefully criticising the article he had rejected and presenting a viewpoint in sharp contradiction to the ideas previously put forward in the publication and embodied by him in his most important pamphlet " The Social Revolution " and in his famous book " The Way to Power ".[1] In this book he had expressed agreement with Rosa Luxemburg's views and written: " There is every reason to assume that we have now entered a period of struggles around the State institutions and for State power "; but now he condemned the same idea as senseless, and declared that the party must adopt a defensive policy, a policy of avoiding battle, a tactic of attrition—at least until the next Reichstag elections two years later, which would bring a tremendous victory for Social Democracy and " a catastrophe for the whole upper-class governing system ". This victory alone could be the basis for " a strategy of final offensive ", and already it put " the key to the whole historical situation " into the pocket of Social Democracy. Thus, according to Kautsky, the revolutionary situation could not be expected to develop out of the powerful activity of the working masses then making itself manifest, but from a hypothetical catastrophe of the governing system brought about at the ballot-box. When Rosa Luxemburg expressed her fears to Clara Zetkin in 1907 that the party leaders would try to divert any great action into parliamentary channels, she mentioned Bebel, and though she probably had no idea that Kautsky would do the same, her fears were justified in the event.

The irreconcilable nature of the breach, both political and personal, between her and Kautsky was soon revealed. At first he advanced various transparent excuses for not publishing her reply to his attack, and energetic pressure was necessary before he finally agreed to do so. Caught in his own contradictions, he then began to accuse her of falsification, using all those literary subterfuges which are the

[1] Karl Kautsky, *Der Weg zur Macht*, Vorwärts-Verlag, Berlin, 1909.

G 2

invariable resource of renegades. The dispute went on from May to August 1910, and although Rosa Luxemburg displayed her usual brilliant polemical ability, it was apparent that this time she was moved rather by resentment at Kautsky's attitude than by her usual delight in intellectual combat.

Franz Mehring was also opposed to her in this particular question, and even Lenin defended Kautsky against a " wrong interpretation " of his " strategy of attrition " which the Menshevists claimed as a justification of their own policy. Mehring soon came round, however, and after the outbreak of the World War Lenin realised with a shock that from 1910 onwards there had been more in the disagreement than different estimations of the given political situation; that, in fact, Kautsky's policy had been profoundly reformist. More than the friendship between Kautsky and Luxemburg was broken: the unity of the radical majority fell to pieces too, and the party split up into three separate tendencies: the reformists, who progressively adopted an imperialist policy; the so-called Marxist Centre, which outwardly maintained the traditional policy but in reality tended more and more to adopt Bernstein's views; and the revolutionary wing, generally called the Left-Wing radicals, under the leadership of Rosa Luxemburg, Clara Zetkin, Franz Mehring, Karl Lieb-knecht, Karski, and Pannekoek.

The whole policy of the German Social Democratic Party in the pre-war period consisted of evasions and retreats, and in the creation of one illusion after the other. In 1911 Germany's Foreign Minister, Kiderlin-Waechter, sent the *Panther* to Agadir and brought Europe to the verge of war. The Bureau of the Second International thereupon appealed to all affiliated parties to organise a joint action against the danger of war. The Central Committee of the German party refused, declaring that it had been informed by the Ministry for Foreign Affairs that Germany did not intend war, and pointing out that if the party took a strong attitude against colonialism it would prejudice its chances at the coming elections. Rosa Luxemburg sounded the alarm at this monstrous piece of treachery, and as a result an action, though a very lame one, was actually organised against the Morocco adventure. The Reichstag elections in 1912 greatly increased the number of social-democratic seats, but for the

second stage of the elections the Central Committee concluded a miserable compromise with the Liberal Progressives,
involving the toning down of the election campaign and the
abandonment of any independent social-democratic propaganda in a number of important constituencies, and this
caused confusion and disappointment in the party ranks.
Kautsky justified the compromise by announcing a regeneration of the Left Wing of the *bourgeoisie* brought about by a
new Liberalism based on " the new middle classes " and he
glorified the election of 110 Social Democrats as an event
of world historic importance, adding: " Although we have
not won that overwheming strength for which we hoped,
still we have condemned the government and the reaction to
impotence."

What actually happened was that, driven by their imperialist interests, the Liberals veered more and more to the
Right, and neither government nor reaction had any further
cause to fear their hostility. Social policy in Germany was
sterile and the Prussian franchise reform was buried, but
every year brought increased armaments and increased
taxation to pay for them. That was the result of sacrificing
everything to the hunt after seats in parliament.

The official policy of German Social Democracy became
more and more a flight from disagreeable reality. Italy
carried out her robber raid on Tripoli, the Balkan War
presaged the still greater conflict under way, and Germany's
foreign policy aggravated political antagonisms and intensified
the danger of war. However, the leaders of the German
Social Democratic Party still dreamt of eternal peace, and
its Reichstag's fraction congratulated the government on its
foreign policy and praised the " Peace Mission " of the Triple
Alliance. At the same time the imperialist wing of the party
became increasingly aggressive, and in the *Sozialistische
Monatshefte* it strongly supported the campaign of nationalist
incitements being waged against Great Britain and Russia.
In the summer of 1913 Ludendorff presented his new armament proposals to the Reichstag, and they put all previous
efforts into the shade, but the Social Democratic Party contented itself with impotent protests in parliament, whilst its
parliamentary fraction even voted for the financial measures
necessary to carry out the proposals. Even members of the

Left Wing of the party (Radek and Pannekoek) fell into the trap prepared for them and supported the action of the parliamentary fraction on the ground that the funds were to be obtained by taxing property. Rosa Luxemburg was able to appeal to former precedents which laid it down that the aim of any particular form of taxation must determine the attitude of the party towards it and not the means, and the aim in this case was increased armament. She knew that nationalist and imperialist motives were behind the party voting, and she laid it down as an unalterable principle that, in view of the rapidly approaching danger of war, the party should do nothing which might be interpreted as a support of the government and its armament policy.

Her opinions met with widespread support amongst the rank and file, but just for this reason the attacks on her became even more violent, and Kautsky denounced her and her followers as " direct actionists ", " anarcho-syndicalists ", and " Russians ", thundering against " putschism ", " backstair intrigues ", and " revolutionary gymnastics ". In March 1913 a national Press conference of the party agreed to refrain from all criticism of the Central Committee, and of the parliamentary fraction. Most of the radical party newspapers refused to be bound by this undertaking, but when Paul Lensch resigned the editorship of the " *Leipziger Volkszeitung* " in the summer of 1913 and Hans Block took his place, the paper (the most important organ of the radical opposition) submitted tamely, and after fifteen years of brilliant collaboration its columns were closed to Rosa Luxemburg. Franz Mehring, Karski, and Clara Zetkin supported her staunchly. Naturally, the breach took place to the accompaniment of a certain amount of personal friction, but the reason was nevertheless purely political. Karski wrote to Block at the end of 1913 :

" The point is that we three (Luxemburg, Mehring, and myself), and in particular I (which I would like to stress) are of the opinion that the party is experiencing an internal crisis far more serious than the time when Revisionism first arose. You may think the expression hard, but I am convinced that the party will fall into a decline if matters go on like this. In such a situation there is only one hope for a revolutionary party: the sharpest and most ruthless self-criticism."

In order to carry out this task and to secure wider publicity for their ideas, the three founded the " *Sozialdemokratische Korrespondenz* " in December 1913. It existed into the war period, and then fell victim to the military censorship. Apart from articles on tacital questions, Rosa Luxemburg wrote chiefly about militarism, on which she now began to concentrate her activities. When the notorious Zabern incident occurred in Alsace-Lorraine, and martial law was declared, she regarded it as a minor prelude to what might be expected in the way of nationalist excesses in the coming war. Her campaign against militarism was so effective that she earned the undying hatred of the militarists, and it was not long before she was persecuted by the authorities.

4. THE COURTS TAKE A HAND IN THE GAME

The first prosecution took place on February 20th, 1914, in Frankfort-on-Main, where she was indicted for inciting soldiers to disobedience. The basis of the charge was a speech delivered in September 1913 in the Frankfort district, in which she had declared, " If they expect us to murder our French or other foreign brothers, then let us tell them: ' No, under no circumstances! ' " The defence was conducted by Paul Levi and Kurt Rosenfeld, and they had little difficulty in showing that there was no legal basis for the indictment, but the Public Prosecutor refused to bother about that and insisted that the accused should be convicted, sentenced to one year's imprisonment, and arrested on the spot. One year's imprisonment for pure propaganda was a sentence which had not been passed in a German court since the days of the Anti-Socialist Laws. Rosa Luxemburg admitted the words complained of, made no attempt to explain away their significance, and defended herself by going over to the attack. She justified the struggle against militarism and war, and delivered keen thrusts against the Public Prosecutor, the officers' caste, and Wilhelm II himself. Referring to the demand for absolute obedience on the part of the soldier as the basis for the whole State, she declared:

" We believe that something more than the Army and
the orders of the ruling classes will decide on the war and the
outcome of it: the great mass of the working people will
decide, and they have the right to decide. We believe that
war will be possible only if the working class wages it with
enthusiasm as a just and necessary thing, or if it tolerates
it passively. On the other hand, if the great majority of
the working people come to the conclusion that war is a
barbarous, deeply immoral, and reactionary thing hostile
to the interests of the people as a whole—and to lead the
masses of the people to this conclusion is just the task we
Social Democrats have set ourselves—then war will be impossible even if, for the moment, the ordinary soldiers still
carry out the orders of their superiors."

Referring to the demand of the Public Prosecutor for her
immediate arrest, she declared:

" And in conclusion just a few words on the baseless attack
made on me, an attack which recoils on its originator.
The Public Prosecutor declared (I made a note of his words)
that he must demand my immediate arrest because it was
inconceivable that I should not wish to escape. In other
words, he was saying: ' If I, the Public Prosecutor, were
faced with a year's imprisonment I should try to escape.'
I am quite prepared to believe that he would, but socialists
do not run away; they stand by what they have done and
laugh at your punishments. And now you may sentence
me."

She was sentenced to one year's imprisonment, but not
arrested on the spot, and she went from the court-room to a
mass meeting in which the workers of Frankfort were awaiting
the outcome of the proceedings. She took the floor with the
feeling that the struggle had only just begun, and she treated
verdict and sentence with contempt by propagating in vigorous language the same ideas which they had tried to suppress,
appealing for a still more determined struggle against militarism and imperialist war. The monstrous sentence caused deep
indignation throughout the country, and she spoke at innumerable meetings, and her audiences were even larger than

usual.   It was the beginning of a great campaign against class-injustice, militarism, and the rapidly approaching imperialist war, but just because the clouds of war were massing, the Central Committee of the party did its best to shackle the campaign.

However, anti-militarist feeling was rising, and when the Erfurt court passed a brutal sentence on certain members of the *Landwehr* [1] for trivial offences, Rosa Luxemburg wrote a fierce article against the brutal treatment commonly meted out in Germany's barracks.   The Minister for War, von Einem, instituted a prosecution for insulting the Army.   The case created a storm.   In answer to an appeal issued by the defence, no less than 30,000 victims of maltreatment in Germany's barracks volunteered to give evidence, and when the case was about to open, the representatives of the War Ministry were at their wits' end, and had to beg for postponement as the only way of preventing the thousands of witnesses to barrack-room brutalities from entering the witness-box.   In the end the process was shelved, but the persecution of Rosa Luxemburg continued.   In June 1914 she put forward a resolution on the political mass strike at a party meeting in Berlin.   The content was nothing out of the ordinary and the text was moderate enough, but the Public Prosecutor swooped.   Rosa Luxemburg and all those who had signed the resolution were indicted, and an attempt was even made to discover and indict all those who had voted for the resolution.   It was quite clear that the authorities intended to gag the revolution, and that they would not be particular as to how they did it.   War came, and with it new prosecutions.   Since the days of Lassalle no political figure in Germany had been so systematically and persistently harried by the Public Prosecutor, and, like Lassalle, Rosa Luxemburg could boast that her escutcheon was picked out with prosecutions.

Despite her poor health, the prospect of a long term of imprisonment did not depress her unduly, and she regarded the persecution as a sure sign that she had done her duty well. But one thing did depress her, and that was the certainty

[1] German Army organisation embraced four stages of military service: the Standing Army, the Reserve, the *Landwehr*, and the *Landsturm*, the last two categories consisting of older men.   Members of the *Landwehr* were called upon at certain intervals to present themselves for control, and on that day they were subject to military and not civil law.—TR.

that the approaching storm would find a spineless and cowardly generation in the leadership of the party. She pinned her hopes on the younger generation, whose best forces she herself had schooled by her work and by her writings, the generation which regarded Karl Liebknecht as its leader. Karl Liebknecht was only a few years younger than Rosa Luxemburg, but as a Prussian lawyer he had been compelled to stay in the background during his period of study and training, and he had therefore entered political life at a considerably later date. And when he did come forward he had to fight against the prejudices and distrust that all sons of great men meet. His passionate temperament, his independence of character, and his tireless activity seemed extravagant to the Fathers of the Party who had watched him grow up as the son of old Wilhelm Liebknecht. Rosa Luxemburg, on the other hand, respected him for just those characteristics, and although he did not always agree with her, this did not prevent her recognising the authentic revolutionary in him. Joint work on two fields brought them closer together: the work for the Russian Revolution (he was not only the legal representative of the Russian Bolshevists, but also their go-between for the illegal work in Russia) and the struggle against militarism. In anti-militarist work in particular they complemented each other excellently. Whilst Rosa Luxemburg gave the struggle its theoretical basis, Karl Liebknecht was undoubtedly the leader in action. During the last few years before the war, during the war itself, and in the early days of the Revolution they stood shoulder to shoulder—unto death.

Chapter Ten : THE CONSUMING FLAME

1. The Woman

THE FIRST of the great catastrophes prophesised by Rosa Luxemburg during the Bernstein debate began to loom up; it was not the final struggle for freedom, which she would have welcomed, but the great mass slaughter of the peoples, for which she was prepared, but which she feared and abominated. And instead of the masses being led to heroism and self-sacrifice in the cause of human emancipation, she saw them deceived, humiliated, brutalised, and led to the slaughter for the cause of their enemies and the triumph of brutishness. A testing time of severe physical and mental suffering began, and she had to exert all her strength to hold on to her chosen course. She stood the test magnificently. Her health was poorer than ever, but mentally she was at the height of her powers. Her great talents had come to maturity. The leading part she had played in practical politics had left her uncorrupted and her enthusiasm undimmed. The precious stone of her character was adamant against the wear and tear of time, and its facets took on an additional polish in adversity. In the supreme test it was to shine out brilliantly.

Throughout her life her character was distorted in the public eye by hatred and prejudice rather than flattered by favour. To her enemies she was " Bloody Rosa ", and she met with bitter hostility equally from the out-and-out defenders of capitalist profit, and from those who prided themselves on their sympathy with the cause of the proletariat, the people who felt that working-class politics should be confined to collecting the crumbs which fell from the rich man's table, though at a pinch they could be revolutionary enough with regard to past times and far-off countries, whilst still regarding any attempt at upsetting the established order of things in their own day and in their own country as criminal anarchy. The *journaille* and the cartoonists zealously fostered the legend of Rosa Luxemburg as a modern fury, a dynamitard, a *petroleuse*, and in the critical months of the revolution in 1918–19 an atmosphere of mass suggestion was created and deliberately whipped up to a pitch of hysteria, until the murderous campaign of incitement bore the desired fruits in the brutal slaughter of Rosa Luxemburg and Karl Liebknecht. There is not a word in anything Rosa Luxemburg ever wrote which could justify the vile campaign of calumny waged against her, though, like all real Marxists, she never hesitated to proclaim the fact that capitalism came into the world oozing blood and slime at every pore, and that it would defend itself fang and claw against the advance of a higher form of human culture, stopping at no crime, and if necessary wading through streams of blood.

When her letters from prison were published after her death, they brought about a revulsion of public feeling. Many men and women, not socialists, have since openly confessed their deep regret that the news of her murder filled them with satisfaction, and they have bitterly reproached themselves for having had any share, even indirectly, in the creation of the savage atmosphere which made the murders possible. But her letters from prison do not present the whole woman; the determined revolutionary recedes into the background, and the sensitive woman and artist is revealed. But both aspects belonged to her nature, and her greatness lies in her revolutionary aspect.

Physically she was not cut out for the rôle of heroine. She was slight of build and her body was badly proportioned; her legs were too short for her torso, and owing to early hip trouble her walk was ungainly. Her features were sharp and pronouncedly Jewish. It was a face indicating energy and determination, and it repelled the one and fascinated the other. Her features were very expressive, and her face would reflect all her feelings from deep thought to unrestrained merriment, from deep sympathy to asperity and mockery. Her forehead was high and well formed, and around her fine lips there was often a line of deep melancholy. Her large, dark, and compelling eyes were perhaps her chief feature. They too were extraordinarily expressive, sometimes hard and keen, sometimes serene and happy, and often sparkling with anger and excitement. They reflected a powerful intellect and an indomitable soul. Her voice was fine-toned and powerful, and she spoke clearly, articulating her words distinctly, so that the whole of an audience, no matter how large, could follow her without difficulty. Her mastery of the German language was complete, and the finest nuances of meaning presented no difficulties. To the end of her life she retained a slight Polish accent, but it lent character to her voice and gave an added zest to her humour. But she knew also when to remain silent and to listen to others. She was a brilliant conversationalist, and she could discuss trivial matters with a charm and wit which made her company a delight to all those privileged to enjoy it.

However, the lighter side of her nature was not expended lavishly—except perhaps with children. All the children in the street in which she lived knew and liked her as a good friend, and with Kautsky's sons she could play and romp almost as though she were one of them, taking part in their games with all due solemnity and zeal. But amongst adults, particularly strangers, she was usually cool and reserved, almost cold. Perhaps it was a guard against losing precious time, perhaps it was to keep her freedom of action where people were concerned with whom she might one day come into political conflict. When she did give her friendship she gave it wholeheartedly, but not before she knew the other thoroughly. It has been said very untruly that her friendships were invariably based on similarity of political opinion, but they were based on character, and any doubt that arose in this respect led inevitably to a breach. The only three people in the Polish movement who could call her their friend were Leo Jogiches, Julian Karski, and Adolf Varski. Karl Radek was perhaps the most talented of her pupils, but she never became friendly with him, and she deliberately held him at a distance because a certain frivolity, not of word, but of political character, made her suspicious of him. In most of the important problems of the Russian Revolution she found herself in agreement with Trotzky, but there was never friendship between them. With Lenin, on the other hand, she often came to blows, and hard words were frequently exchanged, but she always had the highest personal respect for him, and he for her. At the furious height of the Russian factional struggles, when she was overbrimming with anger at the Bolshevists, she could still praise Lenin highly as a real revolutionary, free of all affectation, and a man with whom it was always a pleasure to associate. And then there was Jaurès, the leader of the French Socialists, a man who was her very opposite in socialist politics, and still she never ceased to feel deep friendship for him. What she thought of him she once wrote to Sonia Liebknecht when referring to Rodin: " That must have been a splendid man: frank and natural, with a warmth of character and intellect which reminds me forcibly of Jaurès." Her judgement of human character was thus far from being narrow, and she never demanded strict agreement with her own political ideas. She could judge mildly on personal weaknesses, even amongst her friends, but she did demand unconditional sincerity of character and political principle. Her circle of personal friends in Germany was not very large, but it included such men as Bebel, Singer, Mehring, Karl and Sonia Liebknecht, and a number of artists, and her friendship with the Zetkin and Kautsky families and with the young doctor Hans Diefenbach was particularly close.

It was in this small circle that she dropped the reserve maintained for the outside world, and to each member of it she was a staunch and always reliable friend, giving them of her best, whether it was consolation, encouragement, courage, or companionship. But she had a sharp tongue and a ready wit, and she used them both unsparingly and often embarrassingly. On one occasion she was out for a walk with Clara Zetkin, and, deep in a discussion, they wandered into the danger zone of a military rifle-range. That evening they both went to the Kautskys', where the Fathers of the Party were assembled. The incident was recounted and caused considerable amusement, and speculation as to what might have happened if. . . . Bebel insisted on drafting an obituary for the two, and he proceeded from superlative to superlative, until finally Rosa Luxemburg interrupted him with the dry observation that the best obituary would be the shortest—namely, " Here lie the two last men of the German social-democratic movement." Bebel seems to have felt the gibe keenly, but generally her caustic remarks were taken in good part, particularly as they were often at her own expense, and in her company the atmosphere was generally light-hearted and sometimes high-spirited almost to excess. Politics were not her only interest; she was fond of music, in particular the *Lieder* of Hugo Wolf and the *arias* of Mozart, and she had a very agreeable voice. She could dream at times and give herself up to reverie, but whether she was serious or light-hearted, ironical or humorous, she created an atmosphere around her as effervescent and inspiring as champagne.

At the same time she was a serious worker in the study, though with none of the usual paraphernalia of the solemn scholar, or the unconsciously comic affectations of a Wagner, up to his velvet tammy in the thousand and one unimportant details of his work, and blind to all else. Her nature had nothing of the Faustianism beloved of all German heroes—at least, nothing in the sense that the spectres of the past did not haunt her, and she had no need to occupy herself with internal inhibitions and difficulties. But she did have one thing in common with Faust: the imperative urge to master life, to make the utmost of it, and to make her knowledge as universal as possible; and she had his joy in creative effort too. Her talents would have opened many doors. Politics and the sciences (economics and history) which offer political weapons were not enough, though she worked tirelessly to master them; not merely from a sense of duty, but with a desire to grasp the whole process of social development. She also studied geology and ethnology, and her special favourites were botany and ornithology. She was no mere amateur in these sciences, and she devoted herself to them with an intellectual passion which made her forget all other things, sometimes for weeks and even months together. In the spring of 1917 she wrote to her friend Hans Diefenbach:

" How glad I am that I took up botany three years ago, and did it with my usual passion for thoroughness, with all my heart and soul so that I forgot the world, the party and my work, and thought of one thing only: to wander around in the country with my arms full of flowers and plants, and then to take them home, examine them, catalogue them and note them in my books. I spent the spring in a fever. And what anxiety and frustration I suffered when I sat before a plant and failed to recognise it! I think I almost fainted with chagrin on one or two occasions until my loyal Gertrud was so vexed that she threatened to take the lot away from me. But now I am thoroughly at home in the world of plants and flowers. I won my place with energy and devotion, and things one wins like that strike deep roots."

Sometimes her artistic impulses took hold of her in the same thorough fashion. From childhood she had sketched plants, flowers, animals, landscapes, and portraits in brush and pencil, and suddenly she felt a desire to paint in oils. She set herself to oil-painting in the same determined fashion, and she overcame technical difficulties by sheer talent and industry, and professional painters were astonished at the artistic instinct her work displayed. There is one self-portrait in oils, done with stark realism and showing great ability, though the colouring strikes one as too florid. Whether she turned her attention to politics or to absolutely unpolitical things, her restless energy and her eagerness for experience caused her to do so wholeheartedly. Her desire was to play a creative rôle in life and to urge forward the laggard and the lagging, and of her as of Victor Hugo it might be said:

> *Dans la tête un orchestre*
> *Et dans l'âme une lyre.*

If the sphere of politics had been closed to her, she would probably have turned to poetry for self-expression. Her exercises in rhyme as a child undoubtedly came from an inner urge for expression that sought a congenial outlet. Her first article, an appeal for May-Day, was turned down by Leo Jogiches because unconsciously she had turned it into well-scanned rhythm. It would not be surprising if, even at this date, unknown poetry were still discovered somewhere, written and overlooked in the press of political events. A deep fund of lyricism found expression in her letters, and some of them are pure poetry, particularly those which were written in prison, when, hungry for some of the pleasures of life, she sought and found them in memory. She paints picture after picture; with a few lines she creates a landscape; she describes everyday and insignificant events with such colourful vitality that the brewers' draymen, the newspaper-sellers, the old market-women, and the flower-sellers live as she writes, and her readers can breathe the sun-filled air of a summer's day and feel the compelling influence of the creative artist. She can interpret the sufferings of others in deeply moving words, but about her own she is silent, and there is never more than a halting word or two to her very nearest friends.

There was something manly in Rosa Luxemburg's character, in her clear and logical mind, in her boundless energy, in her determination, in her daring and confidence, but it was never the deliberate maleness of the blue-stocking, never the affectation that plays the man. She was frank and natural, and therefore her essential femininity was beyond all question. With all her strength of character, she could be gentle and sympathetic,

sensitive and helpful.   And sometimes she longed to abandon
the hurly-burly of public life altogether: " I must have someone who believes that I drifted into the whirlpool of public
affairs by accident and not design; someone who knows that
I ought really to be a goose-girl."

She never felt it her destiny to stalk the stage as " a great
woman ". She could play and trifle with abandon. Her
literary taste was sound, but she was not ashamed to devour
thriller after thriller when the mood took her. Her moral
standards were frank and without hypocrisy, but suddenly
and unexpectedly harmless prejudices would reveal themselves.
The younger generation even found her rather narrow in
her moral ideas and were delighted at the opportunity of
smiling their superiority for once.

2. The Fighter

Perhaps the letter from prison which has struck the deepest
human chords is the one in which she describes the wretched
bison, dragged off to Germany as war loot, broken to the yoke,
and stupidly maltreated. The dumb suffering of the unfortunate beast brought tears to her eyes, and made her think
of her own unhappiness, pain, helplessness, and yearning.
Her sympathy for suffering dumb creation is real and deep:
the half-frozen butterflies she puts into the warm sunlight,
the beetle struggling pitifully on its back being eaten by an
army of ants, which she frees from its tormentors only to be
tormented herself by the idea that she has condemned it to
a still slower and more painful death. Again and again her
sympathy for all suffering creatures, for man and beast,
breaks through. It is more sensitive and highly developed in
her than in most people; it is a capacity for realising the pain
of others, for actually feeling it with them, and it stirs her to
the depths. Such feelings have produced the great philan-
thropists of all ages. She was always ready to help, and to
help quickly, but she knew that all she could do was so very
little, and in the misery of the individual she never forgot the
greater misery of the world:

" Do you remember the General Staff Report on the
Trotha Expedition in the Kalahari Desert? ' The groans

of the dying and the hoarse shrieks of parched men broke the majestic stillness of the night.' That majestic stillness in which such a chorus of unheard cries sounds! They re-echo with such force in me that there is no room for the ghetto, and I feel myself at home in the whole world, in the world of clouds, birds, beasts and human tears." [1]

In her introduction to the autobiography of the Russian writer Korolenko [2] Rosa Luxemburg refers in greater detail to the feelings of " solidarity with mass misery " and of " social responsibility " which always moved the great writers of Russia. And she might be writing of herself when she speaks of Russian literature as " shaking with desperate strength at the social and political chains of the age, chafing itself raw, and willingly paying the price of the struggle with its heart's blood ". Perhaps her personal experience is guiding her when she seeks for the cause of Leonid Andreiev's literary decadence in " a super-abundance of social sympathy under which the energy and resistance of the individual must give way ". On her part her determination and energy were co-equal with her human solidarity, and she was urged forward by an imperative need to master the full significance of social phenomena. She never hesitated to accept the final consequences of her own logic, and she became a revolutionary. These were the fundamental elements of her character as a political fighter.

These elements can be descried not only in her origin and in her theories, but also in all her revolutionary acts throughout life. In 1918, in the midst of the revolutionary struggles, she did not forget her promise to her political fellow-prisoners, and she called publicly for the improvement of their prison conditions and for the abolition of the death sentence. She has clearly laid down her guiding rule as a revolutionary fighter:

" Determined revolutionary activity coupled with a deep feeling for humanity, that alone is the real essence of Social-

[1] In a letter to Mathilde Wurm. The Trotha Expedition was a deliberate campaign of extermination against the rebellious Herero tribesmen in German South-West Africa (1904–6). Men, women, and children were driven out into the Kalahari Desert, where they perished miserably of thirst.

[2] Vladimir Korolenko, " *Geschichte meines Zeitgenossen,*" translated from the Russian, and provided with a preface by Rosa Luxemburg in 2 vols., Paul Cassirer Verlag, Berlin, 1919.

ism. A world must be overturned, but every tear that flows and might have been stanched is an accusation; and a man hurrying to a great deed who knocks down a child out of unfeeling carelessness commits a crime."

At the same time she was well aware that the stakes in the political struggle were human life and human happiness, and that the revolutionary struggle would demand severity. She never sought to avoid any necessity imposed by the political struggle if it shortened the way to the final aim and spared still greater suffering. She was always keenly conscious of her responsibility before history, and she never attempted to shelter behind it, to avoid necessary conflicts, to persuade the masses that their yoke was lighter than the sacrifices they would have to make before they could shake it off. Responsibility is the imperative of action, it is the readiness to take necessary decisions, and to weigh up the situation, but also to throw one's own weight and the weight of others into the scales, to let others sacrifice themselves at need, and be prepared to sacrifice oneself gladly at equal need. The calm certainty that the test, if it ever came, would find her ready and willing, was the basis of that firm confidence which inspired admiration in some and disapproval in others.

She knew her own value, and the conviction spurred her on to still greater achievements. It united with the passionate energy she devoted to everything she did. But passionate as was the flame which burned in her, she was above all a woman of thought and will. Her heart was disciplined by her head, and all her political decisions first passed the test of reason and justified themselves in theory before they developed into action. Thought and action were an indissoluble unity. She was never satisfied until she had been able to fit contemporary observations and experiences into the whole picture of social development, and that compelled her again and again to go below the surface of apparently contradictory happenings to find the unifying whole, the inherent contradictions of society expressing themselves in the course of history and ordering all the apparently fortuitous factors of time and place.

It is quite certain that the capacity of man to recognise truth is greatly influenced by his own deepest wishes and desires, and therefore only socialist thinkers can accept the

Marxist conception of history and its methods of investigation in their dialectical realism, because in them a harmony is achieved as the result of scientific perception between the ideal and the real. For Rosa Luxemburg Socialism was not only a hope, but the fixed object of all her endeavours. Like Lenin, she never hesitated to accept any consequences once she recognised them as logical and inevitable; and no thought ever arose that she might let the cup pass, no matter how bitter it might be. There was no room for compromise in her thoughts, and there was no conflict between her thought and her practical action.

This attitude alone, the result of iron self-discipline, was sufficient to make her superior to most of her comrades-in-arms. In addition, she possessed an almost visionary power, and harnessed in the traces of Marxist thought she let it plunge forward. From this came the creative realism she displayed again and again, though on occasion it earned her the reproach of being a dreamer. What she taught seemed often to contradict reality, because it did not tally with the facts of the momentary situation. Her theory of capitalist accumulation was more often attacked because its opponents had not sufficient deductive power to take their minds beyond the contemporary and flourishing period of capitalist imperialism, than because its acceptance would have involved disagreeable political consequences.

Brilliant political strategy is impossible without the gift of looking into the future. Like the greatest strategists of the class struggle, Marx, Engels, Lenin, Trotzky, she was compelled to don the mantle of the prophet again and again, and, like them, her assumptions occasionally proved to be wrong, because no one can possibly know and correctly estimate all the elements of future development. Her revolutionary impatience, too, occasionally got the better of her, but when each case is examined on its merits, it is seen that from the higher ground of her knowledge she overlooked bends and turns in the path of development here and there, and saw the final objective nearer than it actually was. The expected happenings, class conflicts, etc., sometimes failed to mature, perhaps because still newer factors brought about a change in the historical process, but invariably they did break out finally, and more violently than ever; and again and again her fundamental ideas on the motive forces of history were triumphantly justified.

Intellectual effort was both a pleasure and a vital necessity for her, and she found the highest expression of life in conflict, intellectual conflict primarily. Almost everything she wrote was polemical. Even where she is investigating complicated theoretical problems she has always one keen eye on her opponents, ready at a moment's notice to engage them in conflict. " Do it with a will " was a maxim she lived rather than followed, and the joy of battle finds expression in all her polemics. When she had her opponent before her point she was at her best and most brilliant, and every thrust was delivered with vigour and spirit. An opponent worthy of her steel could not but admire her polemical mastery even when he was himself the victim of it. A man like Plechanov, one of the greatest minds of the socialist movement, could not forbear to express his admiration at the brilliance and effectiveness of her attack on his views at the London Congress of the Russian Social Democratic Party, but there were others, the narrow-souled, in whom the point rankled, and they were loud in their condemnation of her " malice " and " quarrelsomeness ". However, her battle was always of intellects, and on the very rare occasions when she attacked the man, it was because only a lively retort in kind seemed fitting.

The strongest elements in her character fused to a harmonious whole in her socialist ideas: deep human sympathy, an earnest desire for truth, an iron will, and a lust for intellectual conflict. In an obituary article Clara Zetkin declared:

" In Rosa Luxemburg the socialist idea was a dominating and powerful passion of both heart and brain, a truly creative passion which burned ceaselessly. The great task and the overpowering ambition of this astonishing woman was to prepare the way for social revolution, to clear the path of history for Socialism. To experience the revolution, to fight in its battles—that was highest happiness for her. With a will, determination, selflessness and devotion for which words are too weak, she consecrated her whole life and her whole being to Socialism. She gave herself completely to the cause of Socialism, not only in her tragic death, but throughout her whole life, daily and hourly, through the struggles of many years. . . . She was the sharp sword, the living flame of revolution."

No sacrifice would have been too great for her, and she confessed that the words Konrad Ferdinand Meyer puts into the mouth of Hutten were applicable to herself:

" *Mich reut die Stunde, die nicht Harnisch trug !*
Mich reut der Tag, der keine Wunde schlug !

Mich reut—ich streu mir Asche auf das Haupt—
Dass ich nicht fester noch an Sieg geglaubt !

Mich reut, dass ich nur einmal ward gebannt !
Mich reut, dass oft ich Menschenfurcht gekannt !

Mich reut—ich beicht es mit zerknirschtem Sinn—
Dass ich night dreifach kuhn gewesen bin ! " [1]

These lines are engraved on the tombstone of her friend Bruno Schönlank, and quoting them once in a letter to her secretary, she expressed the wish that they might be on her own. Perhaps it was her secret wish, but when she saw them again in black and white, their all-too-heroic pathos repelled her, and she sought retreat in self-irony:

" You didn't take me seriously, did you ? No, put on my tombstone two syllables, just ' Tsvee-tsvee '. That's the call of the tom-tit, and I can imitate it so well that they come fluttering around. It's a clear, fine sound, like a steel needle in the frosty air. But do you know that for some days now there's been a little warble in it, a faint undertone ? And that means the first almost imperceptible sign of approaching spring. Snow still covers the ground, and there's frost in the air, but we know, the tom-tits and I, that spring is on the way. And if I shouldn't experience it for impatience, just remember what to put on my tombstone —nothing else."

[1] " I regret the hour in which I wore no armour!
I regret the day that struck no wound!

I regret (strewing ashes on my head)
That my belief in victory was not more fervent!

I regret that I was banished only once!
I regret so often feeling human fear!

I regret (confessing with humiliation)
That I was not thrice more daring! "

The grand lines, their rejection, and the character of it, are all Rosa Luxemburg. To lose herself in the contemplation of Nature, to grasp the whole struggle of humanity on its way forward, to understand the world with her brain, to live life to the full, and to accelerate its rhythm in passionate endeavour—that was the way of her life. And her motto: " Man must live like a candle burning at both ends."

In her uncompromising devotion to scientific truth, in her ceaseless efforts to capture it, in her brilliant intuition, and her determination to conquer, coupled with her deep humanitarian idealism, she is like that other great Pole, Marie Curie. But she is inherently freer, less bound, and without the asceticism of the great scientist. As a revolutionary she had the deep sensitiveness, the artistic nature, the enthusiasm, the passion, the rare fighting spirit, and the great capacity for self-sacrifice of Louise Michel, but her deep knowledge of conditions, the scientific basis of her conception of life, and her sure political instinct raise her above " the Red Virgin ". The great talents of her heart and head and a determined will to action united in her to complete harmony. Our generation will never see her like again.

3. THE WRITER

Poles reading her Polish writings wax enthusiastic at her literary style, at its power and its beauty, and place her amongst the great masters of language in Polish literature. Germans who are even only slightly acquainted with her work in German can well understand that. She disliked writing in Russian, and she felt a faint mistrust even of her German, always fearing that her Polish might affect its style. There was no need for her misgivings; she wrote a clear and masterly German, and, apart from her very earliest writings, there is nothing to indicate that German was not her mother tongue, except perhaps an occasional rigidity in construction. She had mastered the spirit of the language, and its whole vocabulary was at her command; the idioms of the common people gave her no trouble, and she could use them with ease, and did so whenever they added colour and force to her argument.

As a hammer in the hand of the smith becomes an extension of his arm, so language to her was a part of her being. Sometimes she writes long sentences with many subordinate clauses, but she never falls into the trap so fatal to many to the manner born: to lose the thread of ideas in the maze of by-paths. Her sentences, even when they are complicated, are never involved: they are born of her ideas, and in all their clauses and subordinate clauses they run smoothly and resolve themselves clearly. Her great talent as a propagandist expresses itself brilliantly in her prose: she never forces her ideas on unwilling readers; she seeks to convince; she is more teacher than agitator. Her manner of looking at the world and its problems expresses itself in her writing; she sees the complex phenomena of life, and in particular of social life, as a whole, as a great process. And yet her writing is never pedantic. It always reflects reality, and one can always feel the warm and forceful temperament of the author.

The development of her style shows the self-discipline of the artist. In the beginning it is colourful, luxuriant; later it become "as simple as possible and without accessories". Writing to her friend Hans Diefenbach, she declares, with obvious pleasure at the "heresy", that her taste, "whether in scientific work or in art, turns more and more to the simple, the calm and the grand, and therefore I now find the much-praised first volume of Marx's 'Capital', with its superabundance of rococo ornamentation in the Hegelian style, a horror". It is probable that she herself always had to fight against the temptation to floridity of style. Her lively intellect could decorate ornately enough, and word-pictures presented themselves ceaselessly, but they were disciplined always by artistic tact. She often thought in keen antitheses, but she never presented them in the anti-thetic form which turns the style of Hegel and the younger Marx into a display of verbal fireworks, brilliant, but often blinding too.

Like most great stylists, she loved the word-picture, and it dovetailed into the construction of her ideas with the same ease with which it arose in her mind in the development of her thesis. It served her well in polemics, too, because she recognised the weaknesses of her opponents almost at a glance and had both wit and humour at her command to expose them. Her *bourgeois* politician "grasps ecstatically at the stars and finds himself ludicrously holding the tassel of his nightcap ". Her thought-processes are always plastic and graphic; her word-pictures vital, well formed, and complete. Often they culminate in a point which flares up like an exclamation mark, or dies away in a mock sigh which induces laughter. She concludes the description of a political tragi-comedy with the words: " And even the dying gas-jets in the auditorium began to smell foul." The whole atmosphere of the fiasco is there in a sentence. And with wicked mockery she describes Jaurès, her old friend the amiable enemy, still churning out the optimism of the early, hopeful days of socialist ministerialism as though the apple-blossom were still gently falling through the balmy air, instead of cold blasts making the bare boughs creak and howl:

" The melodics Jaurès still sings us remind me of the good old *arias* of Verdi: once in sunny Italy they were on the lips of every happy, dark-eyed urchin like the promise of a people's spring, and now we hear them still, but ground out with horrible monotony on barrel-organs: *Tempi passati!* And the organ-grinder stares into space with an air of detached boredom as he grinds; the same songs, but the spirit has gone."

And her metaphors always have both strong feet on the ground—or almost always. Occasionally an all-too-daring simile may misfire, but nowhere in all her writings is there any pathetic descent from the sublime to the unconscious ridiculous, such as happened occasionally even to a practised hand like Lassalle. And in matters of taste her choice is faultless. She not only has the tact that Lassalle so often lacked, but she hated the least suspicion of pathos out of place. And when the recital of fact after terrible fact renders her style moving and creates pathos despite herself, where the events themselves are tragic and moving, she seeks refuge rather in the dissonance of irony. Her writings during the World War are particularly marked by it. Her famous " *Juniusbroschüre* " begins:

" The frenzy has passed. The patriotic uproar has died

down on the streets. The hunt after foreign gold transports; the stream of lying rumours; the wells poisoned with cholera germs; the Russian students throwing bombs at every railway bridge; the French aeroplanes bombing Nuremberg; the self-righteous excesses of the spy-scared mob; the excited crowds in the cafés where the blare of patriotic music and the chorus of patriotic songs deafened the ears; the whole population turned into a raving mob prepared to denounce, to shriek hurrah, to mishandle women; the atmosphere of ritual murder and Balkan politics in which the policeman on the street-corner remained the only representative of human dignity—already a thing of the past."

She wrote regularly for newspapers, but she was not a journalist, and she never bowed her head to that mechanical yoke: grinding out comments day after day on ministerial speeches, parliamentary bills, diplomatic conflicts. It was almost invariably important political or tactical problems which caused her to write, but those few purely journalistic articles she did write could be taken as masterpieces of how it should be done. Her casual newspaper articles were raised above the flat level of the day because they took the passing events from the rut and put them into their place in the scheme of things, because the isolated phenomenon was explained as a symptom of social processes, because the wound was shown as part of the whole martyrdom of humanity by capitalism. In 1902 Mont Pelée on the island of Martinique burst into eruption, and she compared it to the eruption of world politics which devastated not whole towns but whole countries with brutal and monotonous regularity. After a lull of fifty years, new legislation gave slightly increased protection to child labour, and she ripped the mask of hypocrisy away from the face of society, which in the holy name of the family permitted the domestic industrial worker to exploit the labour of its own child to a greater extent than he might legally have exploited that of another's child. And during the Christmas festivities in 1911 150 homeless men and women, the pariahs of modern society, fell ill in Berlin's casual wards from drinking fusel, and more than half of them died. It inspired her to write an indictment in the hard and polished style of a Swift, but in it her deep sympathy with the utter misery of these unfortunates, and her indignation at the society which cast them out, rose to heights of real pathos. But not one word in the whole is over-emphasised.

4. THE ORATOR

The renunciation of mere brilliance for brilliance's sake is clearest where the temptation to indulge in it is greatest—in public speaking. Rosa Luxemburg was a fascinating speaker, but she never indulged in mere rhetoric. She was economical in the use of grand words and gestures, and she achieved her effect purely by the content of her speeches, though in this she was assisted by a full and melodious voice which was heard and understood without effort in the farthest corners of a great hall. She never spoke from notes, and she preferred to walk up and down the platform, finding her contact with her audience better in this way. It was established in a few sentences, and from then to the end of her speech she held her audience completely. Like all great speakers, it was inspiration which gave her speeches the final touch. She never tried to win an audience by appealing to its momentary mood, and she seldom appealed to its feelings. She aimed always to make it see the things she was describing and to make it realise the truth of her words so that the realisation might lead to action. She held her listeners by the unescapable logic of her remarks and by her ability to express the essence of things in the simplest fashion. She never talked over their heads, and a forceful picture, a striking simile, were often sufficient to enlighten an audience on a previously obscure point, or to fill with new life something that by much repetition had hardened into a mere phrase. What her audience had felt rather than known, became a certainty when she spoke. New aspects were seen and wider horizons opened up. Her listeners felt themselves raised from the every-day round into the world of ideas. And, above all, the speaker faded completely into the speech. The ideas she expressed became the important thing, and her listeners heard only the high, clear voice which expressed them, until some remark that went home with particular force brought them back again suddenly to

H

the frail women standing on the platform before them. Nevertheless, it was the personality behind the speech; the energy and vitality; the harmony of feeling, thought, and will; the clarity, vigour, and aptness of her ideas; and the well-disciplined temperament which fascinated an audience.

This personality came suddenly to the fore, right into the limelight, when Rosa Luxemburg had the good fortune to find an opponent worthy of her. Her polemical ardour aroused, she would mercilessly use all her talents and all her vigour to defeat him utterly, or, rather, to defeat his ideas. She found the weak spots in her opponent's armour at once; saw the point at which his logic deserted him, and sent shaft after ironical shaft until he was quite undone. Max Adler refers to the effect of such fighting speeches in a memoir of Rosa Luxemburg published in " Der Kampf " in February 1919:

> " Passionate revolutionary ardour inspired this frail little woman, and again and again, despite the enemies and mockers she too had to contend with, she brought party congresses under the spell of her powerful temperament, until even her opponents were compelled to join in the rapturous applause that burst out at her speeches. And it was characteristic of her that her intellect never lost control of her temperament, so that although she always spoke with fire and spirit her speeches were tempered with deliberate thought, so that their fire warmed and illuminated rather than consumed."

The effect was, of course, even greater at public meetings than at party congresses, where the opposing camps were already more or less firmly established and the factional spirit strong. Her ready wit, her presence of mind, and her instinctive grasp of the psychological moment were displayed in an incident which took place during the election campaign of 1907. She was speaking on colonialism and foreign politics in one of the great halls in the Hasenheide district of Berlin. A police lieutenant and a veteran constable were present on the platform to watch the proceedings, in accordance with the prevailing laws of public assembly, so that if the officer thought fit he could declare the meeting closed at any time. The lieutenant was young and obviously very nervous, and on several occasions his hand went to his helmet lying on the table before him. The donning of the helmet was the signal to break up. Rosa Luxemburg noticed the gesture, and each time she confused the unfortunate man by rapidly changing the subject. And when he finally seemed on the point of making a determined effort, she addressed him directly, promising that neither the content nor manner of her remarks should exceed permitted limits. Unwillingly the lieutenant leant back in his seat again, and she then proceeded to describe the dull and hopeless life of the lower middle-class strata flung hither and hither in the great struggle between capital and labour, and finally crushed. She described their eternally frustrated hopes, their childlike illusions, and their joyless and cheerless lives. And then she touched on the position of the minor State officials, showing their lack of responsibility and choice, their often unwilling service in the repressive institutions of the State—their tool and their victim at the same time. She explained the well-known saying of Marx that the *bourgeoisie* turned the doctor, the lawyer, the priest, the poet, and the man of science into its hired labourers, and turning to the lieutenant she declared : " And you, too, whether you know it or not, are an instrument in the hands of the *bourgeoisie* to permit its further exploitation of the people." Her daring increased the interest and tension, until finally, at a particularly striking observation, a storm of applause broke out, and it was seen that the old heavily-moustached constable was clapping delightedly with the rest. When the speaker dealt with things which touched him so nearly he forgot everything else, his office and his task ; he belonged to the masses in the hall below him and he clapped with the rest—until he caught sight of the horrified and astounded face of his lieutenant, and then his arms dropped automatically to his side. A moment before he had been a man of the people with the people ; now he was suddenly transformed into an official again.

In the days before the World War—days which passed imperceptibly without any great upheavals, and when the masses on the whole regarded existing conditions as unalterable—Rosa Luxemburg succeeded in implanting an understanding for the coming great struggles when the masses would fight for great things, and socialists would have to stake everything. She aroused enthusiasm for the coming struggles, and she made her listeners believe in the reality of the warning and the exhortation she brought them:

"Be prepared for the day when Socialism will ask not only for your vote, but for your life itself!"

Chapter Eleven : THE WORLD WAR

1. The Fourth of August

On June 28th, 1914, the spark fell into the powder-barrel of Europe. Franz Ferdinand, heir to the throne of Austria-Hungary, was murdered, together with his wife, in Serayevo by Serbian nationalists. However, the tension caused by the outrage gradually lessened, and it seemed as though the European horizon would clear again as it did in 1905–6 after the Morocco incident, in 1909 after the annexation of Bosnia, in 1911 after the Morocco and Tripoli incidents, and in 1912–13 after the Balkan War. The most dangerous knot of imperialist antagonism—that between Great Britain and Germany—seemed about to be unravelled, and the two Powers had reached an agreement covering a whole series of colonial questions when, on July 23rd, the Habsburg monarchy sent an ultimatum to Serbia. The ultimatum had been re-drafted seven times in order to exclude any possibility of its acceptance, and on July 25th Austria-Hungary, supported and encouraged by Germany, declared war on Serbia. On July 29th a partial mobilisation was ordered in Russia.

On July 29th and 30th the Bureau of the International met in Brussels to discuss the war situation, and most of the prominent leaders of the European socialist parties were present: Rosa Luxemburg, Jean Jaurès, Guesde, Axelrod, Victor and Fritz Adler, Keir Hardie, Haase, Kautsky, Grimm, Morgari, Angelica Balabanova, and many others. The proceedings, as far as we know of them, bear witness to the blindness, the utter lack of understanding, the lack of determination, the helplessness, and the complete incapacity of the majority of those present. Their only hope was for a miracle. Victor Adler represented the Austrian Social Democratic Party. On former occasions when war was a purely theoretical matter he had cut a grand figure, and at the Peace Congress in Basle in 1912 he had declared in ringing tones: " We hope that such a crime would be followed automatically—automatically I say—by the end of the rule of these miscreants." But now all he could do was to stammer: " Don't expect any further action from us. There is already a state of war. . . . I have not come here to address a public meeting, but to tell you the truth: at a moment when hundreds of thousands are already marching to the frontiers and martial law exists no action is possible." [1]

What the leaders of the international working-class movement gathered there said to this is not recorded, but six years later Kautsky admitted:

" It is peculiar that not one of us who was there got the idea of asking what was to be done if war really did break out; what attitude the socialist parties should take up in the war? " [2]

All they actually did was to adopt a resolution calling on the workers of all countries " not only to continue their demonstrations against war and for peace and a settlement of the Austro-Serbian conflict by arbitration, but to intensify them ", and put forward the Congress of the International, which was to have taken place at the end of August in Vienna, to August 9th in Paris. The meeting was an unspoken confession of bankruptcy.

We do not even know what Rosa Luxemburg had to say at the session, because down to the present day its proceedings have been kept a secret. However, from a description by Angelica Balabanova of a public meeting held in Brussels after the session, we do know at least that Rosa Luxemburg did not share the hopeless depression of her fellow-delegates. We see Jaurès, a few days before his assassination, a hopeless and beaten man, addressing a deeply depressed audience with

[1] As reported by Fritz Adler in Max Ermers' book, " Victor Adler ", Vienna, 1932.
[2] Karl Kautsky, " Vergangenheit und Zukunft der Internationale " (" The Past and the Future of the International "), Vienna, 1920.

none of his usual oratorical fire, and throwing his arms in the air in despair and hoping for a miracle at the last moment. " Only for a while did the meeting awaken to confidence— when Rosa Luxemburg took the floor." [1]

On July 31st both Austria-Hungary and Russia ordered full mobilisation, whereupon the German Government sent an ultimatum with a twelve-hour time limit to Petersburg. In an atmosphere of uncertainty and anxiety, and hourly expecting the arrest of all prominent party leaders, the Central Committee of the German Social Democratic Party held a session, together with representatives of the party fraction in the Reichstag, to discuss their attitude to the granting of war credits. Haase and Ledebour were in favour of voting against the credits, but all the rest opposed them, though it was believed that in the fraction itself the radicals would get the upper hand. It was decided to send Hermann Müller to Paris to discuss joint action with the leaders of the French Socialist Party.

On July 31st Jean Jaurès was assassinated in Paris, and the following day Hermann Müller met the other party leaders. The struggle against war, or the continuation of the class struggle during the war if it came, was not discussed, but merely the question of war credits. In the name of the German Social Democratic Party, Müller informed his French colleagues that the German socialist deputies would probably vote against the credits; they might abstain, but under no circumstances would they vote in favour. The French socialist leaders declared that the war was a defensive one for France, and they would therefore vote in favour of war credits. Müller answered that the deeper-lying causes of the war were to be found in the policy of imperialist expansion and armaments which had been pursued equally by all the Powers for years. He thus argued along traditional socialist lines, but neither he nor anyone else even mentioned the clear and definite decisions of the International. The Belgian representative, Huysmans, even tried to persuade Müller that the German socialists ought not to vote against war credits, but abstain from voting instead. The discussion clearly showed the embarrassment of the French socialist leaders at the idea that

[1] Angelica Balabanova, " *Erinnerungen und Erlebnisse* " (" Memories and Experiences "), Berlin, 1927.

their German colleagues might adopt a too-radical attitude. They were no longer prepared to think internationally and they were already lining up with their own *bourgeoisie*, but they were still anxious to preserve some appearance of international socialist agreement.

While the discussions were proceding Germany declared war on Russia, and then followed in rapid succession the explosions which set the whole of Europe in flames. On August 3rd the German social-democratic Reichstag's fraction decided to vote in favour of war credits. Out of 111 deputies only fifteen, including Karl Liebknecht, Haase, Ledebour, and Rühle, declared themselves in favour of voting against them. Their request for permission to vote against was rejected, and on August 4th the whole social-democratic Reichstag's fraction voted in favour of the war credits, the minority submitting against their will to fractional discipline.

The action of the social-democratic fraction caused consternation in the international working-class movement, and at first the report was disbelieved. The newspaper of the Roumanian socialist party declared the report to be a monstrous war lie, and even Lenin believed that the issue of the *Vorwärts* containing the report was a forgery issued by the German General Staff to cause confusion. The Left Wing realised clearly that although the failure of other parties in the International would not necessarily spell complete disaster, the failure of the German party would be decisive, and mean the victory of nationalism all along the line and the utter collapse of the International. Such a thing was inconceivable, and the report was disbelieved. But a false report that Karl Liebknecht and Rosa Luxemburg had been court martialled and shot out of hand was believed as thoroughly credible.

2. The Banner of Revolt

The decision of her party was a heavy blow to Rosa Luxemburg, but it is not true that " in the last few years prior to the war she believed that the outbreak of war would be answered by the proletariat with revolution ", as Kautsky has declared. She knew from the experience of the Russo-Japanese War how difficult it was for the working class to take the great step from war to revolution, and her rejection of the proposal before the International that the outbreak of war should be answered with a general strike, demonstrates clearly that her views were much more realistic than Kautsky suggests. However, there is no doubt that when the German working class let itself be led to the slaughter without the slightest attempt at resistance, and when all the long years of propaganda and agitation seemed to have gone for nothing within the space of a few days, she was deeply shocked. The complete capitulation of German Social Democracy, its desertion to the camp of imperialism, and the resultant collapse of the International were blows which temporarily laid her whole world in ruins.

For the first time in her life she gave way to despair. It did not last long, however, and she was soon once again the upright and determined fighter of old, prepared to face any odds. In the evening of August 4th—the day on which the leaders of German Social Democracy concluded their alliance with the Kaiser and his General Staff—a small group of socialists met in Rosa Luxemburg's flat and determined to take up the struggle against imperialist war and against the war policy of their own party. Amongst them were Franz Mehring, already a grey-haired old man, Paul Lenoch, and Julian Karski. That was the beginning of the rebellion which went into history under the banner of Spartakus. From Stuttgart Clara Zetkin declared herself with the group, and it was not long before Karl Liebknecht joined too, having recognised that the party decision in favour of war credits was no mere temporary departure from Socialism, as he had at first thought, and he too was prepared to accept all the consequences of unpopular resistance. Throughout Germany, and particularly in the industrial centres of Berlin, Wurtemberg, Saxony, the Rhineland, the Ruhr, Hamburg, Bremen, etc., there were members of the party who had remained loyal to their old beliefs. Gradually they came together, and then the struggle against imperialist war began both openly and covertly.

The months which followed were difficult ones for Rosa Luxemburg and her companions. Day after day brought news which dejected and disgusted them. Socialism and socialist principles were abandoned and trodden under-foot by men who knew perfectly well that the war was not a war of national defence, that all the Great Powers bore their share of responsibility for it, that the war sprang from deep imperialist antagonisms and served predatory ends. They were men who had solemnly promised a hundred times and more, in word and writing, to fight against war without fear of the consequences. They now poured forth a spate of lies, concluded the famous " Labour Truce ", and handed the women over to the employers as regimented wage-slaves, and the men to the General Staff as cannon-fodder.

And daily came the news of new desertions from the socialist camp. When Scheidemann, vain as a peacock, revelled in patriotic pathos; when Südekum became a propagandist for German imperialism in neutral countries; and when Rosa's old enemies, the trade-union leaders, fraternised at banquets with Stinnes and Thyssen, their actions produced nothing but disgust and contempt, but when Plechanov, who had always preached a revolutionary rising against war, now became the standard-bearer of Tsarism against Prussian barbarism, when Guesde, the rigid Marxist, entered the French War Cabinet, and when even Rosa's old friend, Vaillant, suffered a relapse into his old Blanquist nationalism and saw the France of stock-exchange jobbery and colonial oppression with the aureole of 1793, it was different. She had long parted from her old friend Parvus, who had amassed a considerable fortune by speculation during the Balkan wars, and he now became adviser to the German Foreign Office and organiser of Germany's trade with the Scandinavian countries. At the beginning of the war he visited her, but she felt the visit as an insult, and refused to receive him. Cunow, chief editor of the *Vorwärts*, and one of the " koscher " group with which she took over the editorship in 1905, now competed with the Austrian Renner in prostituting Marxism to the service of imperialism. Paul Lensch, one of Rosa's first pupils and staunchest supporters, also deserted to the camp of the orthodox, and began to praise the organised system of semi-starvation introduced into Germany as a great victory for socialist ideas, and Germany's imperialist war against Great Britain as the revolution. Konrad Haenisch, once an enthusiastic trumpeter of the International, now changed his tune to " *Deutschland, Deutschland über Alles* ", and Karl Kautsky did his best to cover

H 2

the shame of the socialist movement with a threadbare garment of sophistries, banalities, and misrepresentations, declaring it quite impossible to determine the character of the war because it had not broken out according to traditional forms: " Normally States formulate their demands, declare war, and then mobilise. This time mobilisation did not take place because of war, but war broke out because of the mobilisation. . . ." And he airily dismissed the collapse of the International with his now-famous utterance: " The International is not an effective weapon in war-time; it is essentially a weapon of peace." Socialist theory abdicated, and demanded that the working class should cease to exist as a political factor.

Rosa Luxemburg now concentrated all her efforts on organising resistance against the war policy of the official party, and she worked harder than ever in the Berlin organisation, both amongst the rank and file and in its leadership. The first successes came sooner than might have been expected in view of the defection of the majority of party officials. There were seen to be strong oppositional minorities everywhere, and in Niederbarnim a majority of the party members were in opposition. However, against the double oppression of party and military censorship it was difficult for oppositional tendencies to find public expression, and the problem arose of how to encourage the leaderless workers in the province who were opposed to the war, but who were often overwhelmed by the arguments of trained officials and discouraged by the feeling that they were alone. There were fifteen men in the Reichstag who had opposed voting for war credits; if they could be brought to make a public demonstration, the war-resisters would see that they were not alone. In addition, foreign public opinion would see that there were still socialists in Germany and that the socialist struggle against war had begun. Clara Zetkin describes the efforts made in this direction in her preface to a new edition of Rosa Luxemburg's " *Juniusbroschüre* ":

" The public fight was to begin with a protest against the voting of war credits by the social-democratic Reichstag's fraction, but that protest had to be formulated cunningly enough to get past the watchful eye of the military censorship. Further, the more well-known Social Democrats who could be persuaded to sign it the better, so we did our best to formulate it in a way which would find the support of the greatest number of those prominent comrades who were already sharply criticising the policy of the party in private discussions. This consideration cost us many a headache, reams of paper, and scores of letters and telegrams, and in the end all for nothing. Out of all those prominent comrades who were brave enough to criticise the party majority behind the scenes, only Karl Liebknecht joined with Rosa Luxemburg, Franz Mehring and myself in defying the soul-destroying and demoralising totemist idol into which party discipline had developed."

This experience occurred every time the German Government asked the Reichstag for new credits. At first quite a number of social-democratic deputies declared themselves prepared to vote against the credits, but as the division approached, the group gradually dwindled. They all discovered eminently reasonable excuses for their change of mind—except one or two who were frank enough to admit that they had not sufficient stomach for the job—and on the day of the division only one man was left: Karl Liebknecht. Perhaps that was a good thing. One man defied the whole Reichstag, and under the eyes of the world he broke a lance against the general war madness and against the omnipotence of the State. In doing so he demonstrated that the great need of the moment was personal courage, and his name became a symbol, a battle-cry against war, and it was repeated over the whole world, even in the trenches, above the clash of arms, uniting thousands and then tens of thousands against the world slaughter. On that December 2nd, 1914, a revolutionary front against war became visible in Germany, and from that day on, too, the revolutionary alliance of Karl Liebknecht and Rosa Luxemburg became unbreakable, and did not end even with death.

3. " THE INTERNATIONAL "

The political activity of Rosa Luxemburg in the early months of the war was very different from that of Lenin in Switzerland in the same period. The difference was not due to any important divergence in their attitude towards the war and Socialism, but solely to the conditions under which each revolutionary leader worked. Lenin was a political emigrant, now almost completely cut off from the masses of his people. His work was for a small group of men and women well trained in socialist theory, and he was therefore able to go straight to the crux of the problem raised by the war. He rejected the slogan of peace as too indefinite and too passive: it tended to turn the hopes of the masses once again to the good-will of the very people who had plunged the world into the holocaust. Even the slogan of a " democratic peace " was not suitable to the circumstances the war must produce and reproduce. If socialists really wished to act in the spirit of the Stuttgart resolution of the International and " utilise the economic and political crisis brought about by the war to arouse the masses of the people and accelerate the overthrow of capitalist dominance ", then they must, he declared in trenchant antithesis, work now for " the transformation of the imperialist war into a civil war ", and propagate, organise, and prepare civil war. His chief attacks were directed against Kautsky, and it is not difficult to see in this circumstance some measure of his disappointment and chagrin at having once been mistaken in Kautsky and having defended him against Rosa Luxemburg. Writing to Shliapnikov in October 1914, he declares:

" Rosa Luxemburg was right; she realised long ago that Kautsky was a time-serving theorist, serving the majority of the party, serving opportunism in short. There is nothing in the world more deleterious and dangerous for the intellectual independence of the proletariat than the repulsive self-satisfaction and disgusting hypocrisy of Kautsky, who glosses over everything and attempts to lull the awakening conscience of the workers with sophistry and pseudo-scientific verbosity."

Rosa Luxemburg's task, on the other hand, was to produce a direct effect on the masses of the workers, to secure some action, no matter how modest in the beginning. To do this she had to reckon with the opportunities and the psychological conditions that offered themselves. What she said and wrote in these first months of the war, and what she explained in innumerable discussions and internal party meetings, were chiefly confined to the simplest analysis of the causes of the war and its character, and to internal party questions, particularly the question of discipline:

" The discipline owed to the party as a whole, i.e., to its recognised programme, by its members is more important than the direct discipline to a particular organisation of the party. In fact it is this larger discipline alone which justifies the subordinate one and at the same time describes its natural limits."

Liebknecht was therefore the one truly disciplined member of the Reichstag fraction when he voted against the war credits in accordance with the recognised principles of the party.

It was not long before this enlightenment work based solely on the needs of the moment proved insufficient. The problem had to be taken by the roots and brought before a larger public. Some sort of mouthpiece was necessary for this purpose, and, after great efforts and many disappointments, the party publishing house in Düsseldorf was persuaded to take the risk of publishing the organ of the opposition. In the spring of 1915 the *Internationale* appeared under the joint editorship of Rosa Luxemburg and Franz Mehring. Amongst its contributors were Clara Zetkin, August Thalheimer, Käthe Duncker, Paul Lange, and Heinrich Ströbel. Its literary and intellectual level was very high, and its contributors represented a galaxy of talent. Mehring analysed the attitude of Marx and Engels to the problem of war and applied their principles to the imperialist war raging throughout Europe. Clara Zetkin dealt with the position of women in war. Lange attacked the " Labour Truce " policy of the trade unions. And Rosa Luxemburg wrote an article under her own name entitled " The Reconstruction of the International ", and a second one under the pseudonym Mortimer entitled " Future Prospects and Projects ", which was a criticism of a book by Kautsky.[1]

In her first article she made no attempt to beat about the bush, but declared forthrightly that German Social Democracy had abdicated politically on August 4th, and that the Inter-

---

[1] Karl Kautsky, " *Nationalstaat, imperialistischer Staat und Staatenbund* ", (" The National State, the Imperialist State and the League of States "), Nuremburg, 1914.

national had collapsed in a fashion unparalleled in history. The alternatives Socialism and Imperialism had adequately summed up the political attitude of the working class, but the moment the alternatives had developed from theory to practice, Social Democracy had lowered its flag and abandoned the field to imperialism without a shot. Kautsky, the representative of the so-called Marxist Centre, had contributed greatly to the final collapse. The inspiring appeal of the Communist Manifesto, " Workers of the World Unite ! " had been re-phrased by Kautsky into " Workers of the World Unite in peace, but slit each other's throats in war ! "

Her deep embitterment found expression in a new and sharper note in her writings, and it marks everything she wrote during the war. However, her writings remained constructive : it was absurd to pretend that after the war the International could be resuscitated as an organisation of the class struggle unless a determined effort were made during the war to re-build it on that basis. The International must either completely revise its old tactics, proclaim class collaboration instead of class war, and work for the imperialist interests of each national *bourgeoisie*, or it must completely abandon the policy inaugurated on August 4th. The first step in the right direction was a struggle for peace, but it would have to be a real struggle, not solemn proclamations in parliament against " a policy of conquest " and in favour of such fine future programmes as disarmament, the abolition of secret diplomacy, the open door for all in the colonies, and a League of Nations, whilst at the same time supporting the prosecution of the war :

> " If the collapse of August 4th has proved anything it is the great historic lesson that the only effective guarantee of peace and the only bulwark against war is the determined will of the proletariat pursuing an unwavering class policy and loyally upholding its international solidarity throughout all imperialist storms ; and not pious wishes, cleverly concocted solutions and Utopian demands addressed to the ruling classes. . . . In this matter too there are clear alternatives : Bethmann-Hollweg or Liebknecht, imperialism or Socialism, Socialism as Marx understood it."

And in conclusion she showed the real reason for the failure of Social Democracy, and at the same time the one hope for the rebuilding of the International. Pointing out that in Marx " the keen historical analyst and the daring revolutionary, the man of ideas and the man of action were indissolubly united ", she declared :

> " When the great historic testing time arrived, a time which it had foreseen and prophesied in all important points with the certainty of exact science, Social Democracy proved to have nothing of the second vital element of the working-class movement; the vigorous will not only to understand and interpret history, but to play a part in shaping it. Despite its clear recognition of coming events and despite its organisational power, Social Democracy was seized help-lessly in the current of events, whirled around like a rudder-less hulk and driven before the storm of imperialism instead of setting course through the storm to the saving island of Socialism. The international can be born again and a peace in the interests of the proletariat obtained only from the self-criticism of the proletariat remembering its own power. . . . The way to this power is at the same time the way to peace and the rebuilding of the International."

This article is of great importance for an estimation of Rosa Luxemburg's tactical attitude during the war. Each argument is obviously carefully weighed with a view first of all to testing the margin of expression still left by the military censorship, and secondly to saying as much as the radical elements in the German working-class movement were still open to receive. It is clear, therefore, that it is not a full expression of her ideas. She registers the collapse of the International, dismisses the majority of the party leaders, the social imperialists, with a few telling blows, and then concen-trates the major fire against Kautsky. It is quite clear that she regards the final parting from the war socialists as inevit-able both nationally and internationally, but the exact line of demarcation is not yet clear to her. Kautsky's lack of in-tegrity in his " opposition " to the party majority convinced her that he was irrevocably lost for any future revolutionary party, but apart from the masses, now either swept away by war-fever or hesitant and uncertain of their attitude, there were still many amongst the officials of the party who were by no means wholeheartedly with the party leaders, though they might for the moment still follow them. These people had to be won back to Socialism. For this reason, therefore, and despite the limitations it imposed on them, Rosa Luxemburg and her friends remained in close contact with the Ledebour, Hoffmann, Haase group, though they constantly criticised its weaknesses. In this respect Rosa Luxemburg was in full agreement with Lenin, who also declared that many of these people could still be saved for Socialism, but only on condition that a decisive break with the Right-Wingers took place.[1] But, Lenin strictly rejected the simple slogan of " Peace ", whereas Rosa Luxemburg made it the centre of her political agitation. However, she made it quite clear that the peace she meant was not the sort of peace that some hoped could be obtained by an appeal to the better nature of the ruling classes, and it was in this respect that Lenin had misgivings concerning a general slogan in favour of peace. Rosa Luxemburg spoke only of the class struggle, and not of revolution and civil war, whereas Lenin firmly insisted on civil war and revolution in all his utterances, but there was never any doubt that the peace she wanted—" a peace in the interests of the proletariat "—could be obtained only by the seizure of power.

In the Mortimer article she tore Kautsky to pieces, trouncing his pronouncements on imperialism, and sharply rejecting his identification of " modern democracy " as the aim of Socialism with the parliamentary régime :

" Has not Social Democracy always contended that ' full democracy, not formal democracy, but real and effective democracy ' can exist only when economic and social equality has been established, i.e., when a socialist economic order has been introduced, and that, on the other hand, the ' democracy ' which prevails in a *bourgeois* national State is, in the last resort, more or less humbug ? "

The aim of the first number of the *Internationale* was to open up a systematic examination of all the problems of working-class policy raised by the war, and it was a resolute beginning. Unfortunately the military censorship thoroughly appreciated its significance, and promptly suppressed it. The Public Prosecutor then indicted Rosa Luxemburg, Franz

[1] Nikolai Lenin and Gregori Zinoviev, " *Gegen den Strom* " (" Against the Stream "), Hamburg, 1921, p. 24.

Mehring, and Clara Zetkin as editors, Bertens as publisher, and Pfeiffer as printer on charges of high treason.

4. A YEAR IN PRISON

When the first number of the *Internationale* appeared in April 1915, Rosa Luxemburg had already served two months of the sentence passed on her in Frankfort the previous year. Before the outbreak of the war she had been in very poor health, and the effect of the war and the collapse of the International made her so ill that she had to go into hospital. Owing to her illness the date on which she was to go to prison was postponed until March 31st, 1915. On February 19th she was about to leave for Holland with Clara Zetkin to attend an international socialist conference of women when she was suddenly arrested and taken to serve her sentence in the women's prison in the Barnim Strasse in Berlin. As a dangerous revolutionary she was to be put out of harm's way for the duration of the war, and in fact her imprisonment lasted with short interruptions until she was released by the 1918 Revolution. She describes the first day in prison in a letter to a friend:

" They took me in the ' Black Maria ', but that didn't disturb me unduly: I had already experienced it once in Warsaw. The situation was so strikingly similar that it started a train of humorous thoughts. There was one difference, though: the Russian gendarmes treated me with great respect as ' a political ', whereas the Berlin police said they didn't care a snap of the fingers what I was, and thrust me in with the rest of my new ' colleagues ' without further ceremony. Ah well, that's a matter of minor importance, and life has to be taken with serenity and a grain of humour. You mustn't get exaggerated ideas about my heroism, though, and I'll admit that when I had to undress and submit to a bodily examination for the second time that day the humiliation almost reduced me to tears. Of course, I was furious with myself at such weakness, and I still am when I think of it. But the first night the thing that made a deeper impression on me than the fact that I was once again in a prison cell, snatched from the land of the free, was—— Guess what it was? That I had to go to sleep without a night-dress and without being able to comb my hair. And to display my classical education: do you remember the first scene in Schiller's ' Mary Stuart ' ? Mary's trinkets are taken from her, and Lady Kennedy observes sadly : ' To lose life's little gauds is harder than to brave great trials.' Look it up ; Schiller puts it rather better than I do. But heavens ! where are my errant thoughts leading me ? *Gott strafe England !* And forgive me that I compare myself to an English queen."

This time Rosa Luxemburg went to prison very unwillingly, and in November she wrote to Diefenbach : " Six months ago I was quite enthusiastic about it, but now the honour falls as heavily on me as the Iron Cross on you." She knew how badly she was needed outside. At first she seems to have been treated with a certain amount of laxity, for she was able to write her " *Juniusbroschüre* ", and by April she had smuggled the manuscript out of prison. After that it was six months before she managed to write and smuggle anything else out. Perhaps her treatment became more severe as the result of an encounter she had with an insolent detective who came to examine her. What actually happened is not quite clear, but Rosa Luxemburg put an end to the interview by throwing a book at his head, and for this she received further punishment.

The enforced inactivity of prison life weighed heavily on her, particularly because of what was happening outside. The war dragged on, claiming hecatombs of victims, privations increased, hunger became a normal phenomenon, and there seemed no break in the moral degradation of the masses. At first she had hoped that peace would soon come and give her freedom, but the news of one German victory after the other arrived, and every battle led only to new battles. The leaders of the Social Democratic Party had now completely overcome their original scruples, and the crassest form of nationalism was rampant. Hopes of a knock-out German victory were high in 1915, and it was a black year for socialist ideas. The opposition put up by Rosa Luxemburg's followers, together with some representatives of the " Marxist Centre ", made no intellectual progress, and when Rosa Luxemburg read their pronouncements in prison she was deeply disappointed at their feebleness and at the paucity of their ideas. In June a ray of hope broke through when a protest petition signed by about a thousand officials of the party was presented to the Central Committee, but it was not an inspiring document, and it lacked fire, whilst its well-meaning originators showed no inclination to follow up their protest by action. An international women's conference organised by Clara Zetkin took place in Berne in March 1915, but it met with no very great response, and it was September 1915 before the famous international socialist conference in Zimmerwald gave new impetus to the opposition. In October housewives demonstrated spontaneously in Berlin and other big towns against the rising cost of living, and it became clear that the prospect of another war winter was causing deep resentment amongst the masses.

The opposition lacked leaders with fire and energy, and, above all, it lacked Rosa Luxemburg. Her nearest collaborators had almost all been conscripted, and even Karl Liebknecht, Reichstag's deputy though he was, was forced into uniform and sent to the war area, from which he managed to escape only to attend the now rare sessions of the Reichstag, at which he discharged a blast of " Interpellations " at the Government, using the only weapon open to him to expose the imperialist aims and methods of the war-lords. He also published a number of leaflets which created a sensation by their vigour and clarity, particularly the most famous of them, which began: " The worst enemy is at home! " Clara Zetkin was arrested in July 1915, and when she was released in October she was already seriously ill. In Berlin Wilhelm Pieck, Ernst Meyer, and Hugo Eberlein and in Stuttgart Friedrich Westermeyer, were arrested and held for many months.

Encouraging reports from outside were rare, and discouraging ones very, very frequent, and Rosa Luxemburg writes: " I have trained myself to stand everything with the same stoicism, and to swallow it all without even a grimace." She sought consolation in hard work. She wrote her " Anti-Critique " in answer to the critics of her " Accumulation of Capital", worked on her "Introduction to Political Economy", and began to translate Korolenko's autobiography. Towards the end of 1915 she seems to have found some way of communicating more directly with the world outside, and from this period dates her secret correspondence with Karl Liebknecht, of which some fragments are still extant. She immediately took the political initiative, and persuaded him that the alliance with the " chronic wobblers " of the Marxist "Centre" had now developed into a hindrance to revolutionary progress and action. At her instance a national conference of Left-Wing elements took place in Berlin on New Year's Day, 1916. It was decided to form a more definite organisation, and the name Spartakus, which had been taken for the issue of their publications, now became the name by which the new body was generally known. Rosa Luxemburg drew up a list of " guiding principles " to be discussed by the conference, and the manuscript succeeded in evading the suspicious eye of the prison authorities and finding its way to the proper destination, where it became the programme of the new Spartakus League.

At the end of the month Rosa Luxemburg's sentence was up and she was restored to what freedom the military dictatorship had left in Prussia. The experience of breathing free air again and being amongst friends after a year of imprisonment, in which she had no one to whom she could turn for support and sympathy, proved almost too much for her at first, and her nerves threatened to give way. She, the consummate master of masses, had developed a shyness and a fear of people, but they surrounded her impulsively from the very first day. The majority of the women amongst whom she had worked had remained loyal to her, and they prepared her a great reception to demonstrate their happiness at her release, their sympathy with her in her sufferings, and their heartfelt thanks for her efforts on their behalf. And then friend after friend, comrade after comrade, came to her, and she was plunged at once into the midst of political discussions and political work. Her first day of freedom was something very much like torture, and from then on there was no rest for her and no peace. At once she was swept up in the whirl of active political life under extraordinarily difficult circumstances, and she had to summon up all her remaining strength to keep herself going and give to the utmost what was wanted of her. She continued this life of intense mental and physical activity until the prison doors once again closed behind her.

5. THE "*JUNIUBROSCHURE*"

On her release from prison she found the manuscript of her book "The Crisis of Social Democracy" untouched on her desk. The technical difficulties of issuing illegal material, and the arrest or conscription of most Left-Wing officials, had prevented its printing. She determined to overcome these obstacles, and she succeeded: in April 1916, a year after it had been written, the book was printed and published. Although it was published illegally and great difficulties attended its distribution, one edition after the other was exhausted, and it became the intellectual arsenal of thousands of illegal workers.

Rosa Luxemburg wished to publish it under her own name, but she was dissuaded by her friends, who knew that it would mean her immediate arrest and re-imprisonment, so she chose a pseudonym: Junius,[1] the pseudonym of an earlier champion of liberty against absolutist abuses, and her pen added new lustre to it: there was the same intimate knowledge of political facts, the same polemical vigour, the same overwhelming weight of argument, and the same powerful and elegant language, though this time it was even more impetuous and passionate, just as the abuses attacked were even more horrible.

The book opens powerfully, and Rosa Luxemburg's indignation expresses itself in bitter and ice-cold sarcasm. She describes a world in which the mass slaughter of human beings had degenerated into a monotonous daily task, in which business flourished on mass ruin, and in which the mad hunt for war profits was praised as an expression of the same patriotism which led others to lay down their lives on the battlefield. She shows the devastation of whole countries and the incidental destruction of all the much-vaunted cultural idols of the *bourgeoisie*, painting a picture of *bourgeois* society in the raw, naked and snarling: "not neat and laundered and pretending to culture and philosophy, to ethics and

---

[1] The "Letters of Junius" were published in the *Public Advertiser* from January 1769 onwards for a number of years. They attacked George III and his Ministers, and displayed an extraordinary knowledge of governmental affairs. They have been attributed to Edmund Burke, to Richard Burke, to Lord Temple, to Lord George Sackville, to Lord Shelborne, to Barré, to Wilkes, to Horne Tooke, to Glover, to Wedderburn, to Gerard Hamilton, to Sir Philip Francis, and to a number of lesser-known people. —TR.

humanity, to law and justice, but as it is now, a ravenous beast, a riot of brutal anarchy, the searing breath of destruction for culture and humanity ". She scourges the treachery of socialist leaders to the cause of Socialism, and she does not spare the socialist workers who abandoned all their ideals to follow the roll of the capitalist war-drum at the behest of false leaders. Like that of Junius before her, her style is antithetic; every sentence sounds like the crack of a whip, every word sinks in like acid.

But the work is not a mere pamphlet; like all her writings, it is disciplined, and her feelings are not allowed to carry her away. Her fierce indignation is schooled to her aim: to teach, to convince, to solve the problems raised by the war. In her hands the pamphlet becomes a guide to modern history and proletarian strategy. The imperialist drive of the Great Powers which she had already described in the historical chapters of her " Accumulation of Capital " she now traced back through the foreign-political entanglements of decades, showing how the antagonistic interests of the two great imperialist camps became more and more involved, until finally the knot had to be cut with the sword, and in so doing she laid bare the real and universal character of the war:

" The war which began on August 4th was the war which socialist deputies, newspapers and pamphlets had been condemning for many, many years as a monstrous imperialist crime unrelated to the real interests of human culture or the real interests of the peoples, and diametrically opposed to both. . . . Only small countries like Belgium and Serbia are formally waging a war of defence, and even they are only pawns in the game of world politics. Thrust ruthlessly into war they immediately become the tools of the belligerent world powers, and their situation cannot be judged by formal considerations or apart from the situation as a whole. . . . The historic ambient of imperialism will always determine the character of war whatever individual countries may be involved in it."

It is interesting to note that she resolutely condemns the suggestion that socialists could copy the attitude of democratic parties in former, nationalist wars, and she points out that even the criterion which was decisive for Marx and Engels

until late in the nineteenth century was no longer applicable.
Marx and Engels demanded in all the great conflicts of their
day that the proletariat should side with the power whose
victory would best serve the cultural progress of humanity and
the interests of the international proletariat as a whole. Rosa
Luxemburg showed that both groups of powers were fighting
for conquest, and that the victory of either of them would
result in new oppression, and fresh damage to the interests of
the international working class. The workers of the world
should therefore side with neither group, but stand united
internationally in the struggle against imperialism as a whole.
She even declared that in the epoch of imperialism there
could no longer be any national wars in the old sense, and
Lenin sharply attacked this statement,[1] pointing out that wars
of national liberation fought by subject peoples against imperialist Powers were still destined to play a great rôle in the
epoch of proletarian world revolution. There is no doubt
that Rosa Luxemburg would have accepted Lenin's viewpoint
in this matter without demur, because what she meant was
that nationalist wars between imperialist Powers were no longer
possible. In this she was right, and in his criticism Lenin
even indicates the possibility that this was her real meaning,
and not that nationalist wars were impossible altogether.

However, it is another idea which causes more surprise.
She is dealing with the problem of national defence and,
apparently in diametrical opposition to her usual argumentation, she declares it the duty of Social Democracy to defend
the country in a great crisis, and she accuses the German
Social Democratic Party of " leaving the Fatherland in the
lurch in the hour of danger "—the very thing its leaders
prided themselves on not having done. The apparent contradiction is easily resolved. She is referring to the Jakobin
wars, to the Paris Commune, and to a hypothetical war, not
an imperialist war, of France and Russia against Germany in
1892 as described by Friedrich Engels, and she points out
that when Engels speaks of national defence in the spirit of
social-democratic policy he does not mean the support of a
Prussian Junker militarist government and its General Staff,
but a revolutionary action akin to the example of the French

[1] Nikolai Lenin and Gregori Zinoviev, " *Gegen den Strom* " (" Against
the Stream "), Hamburg, 1921, pp. 415 *et seq.*

Jakobins. It is quite clear that she is referring to the defence of the Fatherland after the seizure of power by the working class, and she is accusing Social Democracy of abandoning the class struggle, the only means by which the working class can seize power. As elsewhere in this work, she is not speaking with her accustomed forthrightness of the revolutionary seizure of power, but the whole context shows clearly what she means. It is possible that during the writing she still reckoned with the possibility of legal publication, which caused her to be more than usually circumspect in the expression of her ideas. But for this reason her readers found it rather difficult to follow her ideas, particularly when she connected them with a programme of action which culminated in the slogan, " A single great German Republic! " She is returning here to the idea she propounded in 1910 as a possible lever of revolution. In 1910 it was undoubtedly correct, but under war-time conditions there was a danger of its exploitation to justify the war policy of the democratic countries. A German *bourgeois* republic would inevitably pursue an imperialist policy too, so that the slogan did not contain a proletarian solution of the war problem.

Rosa Luxemburg did her utmost to prevent any confusion arising from her slogan by mercilessly exposing the liberator legend with which both imperialist camps tried to win the support of the masses. Was not the aim of the *Entente* to liberate the German people from Kaiserdom? And was it not the task of Hindenburg to carry the revolution into Russia at the point of German bayonets? She very effectively knocked the standard of democracy out of the hands of the imperialist Powers, and tore to pieces the liberator legend of the German social-democratic leaders. She also pointed out the change in the foreign-political rôle of Tsarism, and showed the fatal effect of the war on the revolution in Russia :

" German bayonets have not destroyed Tsarism; they have destroyed Tsarism's enemies; they gave Tsarism the most popular war the country had experienced for a century. Everything tended to give the Tsarist government the nimbus of moral justification: the war provocation of Berlin and Vienna, clearly visible to everyone outside Germany; the ' civil truce ' in Germany and the nationalist delirium it let loose; the fate of Belgium; and the necessity of going to the aid of the French Republic—no absolutist government ever had such a favourable case. The fluttering standard of the Russian revolution went under in the wild turmoil of war—but it went under honourably, and it will rise again above the slaughter, despite German bayonets, despite victory or defeat for Tsarism."

And then, despite the daily reports of German victories, she calmly prophesied the collapse of Austria and Turkey together with Tsarist Russia. And despite their " brotherhood of arms ", she prophesied rivalry between Japan on the one side and Great Britain and the U.S.A. on the other in China. Peace would be equally oppressive for the workers whether their governments were victorious or defeated, unless it was a peace obtained " by the revolutionary intervention of the proletariat ". There was only one way to bring this about: to continue and intensify the class struggle even in war-time— in fact, more than ever in war-time.

And she concludes with a passage of almost visionary power:

" Imperialist bestiality has been let loose to devastate the fields of Europe, and there is one incidental accompaniment for which the ' cultured world ' has neither heart nor conscience—the mass slaughter of the European proletariat. . . . It is our hope, our flesh and blood, which is falling in swathes like corn under the sickle. The finest, the most intelligent, the best trained forces of international Socialism, the bearers of the heroic traditions of the modern working-class movement, the advanced guard of the world proletariat, the workers of Great Britain, France, Germany and Russia, are being slaughtered in masses. . . . That is a greater crime by far than the brutish sack of Louvain or the destruction of Rheims Cathedral. It is a deadly blow against the power which holds the whole future of humanity, the only power which can save the values of the past and carry them on into a newer and better human society. Capitalism has revealed its true features; it betrays to the world that it has lost its historical justification, that its continued existence can no longer be reconciled with the progress of mankind. . . .

" *Deutschland, Deutschland über Alles!* Long live Democracy! Long live the Tsar and Slavdom! Ten thousand blankets, guaranteed in perfect condition! A hundred thousand kilos of bacon, coffee substitutes—immediate delivery! Profits are rising as workingmen fall. And with each one sinks a fighter for the future, a soldier of the Revolution, a liberator of humanity from the yoke of capitalism, and finds a nameless grave.

"The madness will cease and the bloody product of hell come to an end only when the workers of Germany and France, of Great Britain and Russia awaken from their frenzy, extend to each other the hand of friendship, and drown the bestial chorus of imperialist hyaenas with the thunderous battle cry of the modern working-class movement: 'Workers of the World Unite!'"

6. SPARTAKUS

The "*Juniusbroschüre*" is the most powerful and moving document the war produced. Its trenchant logic and its stirring appeal are unique. It was written for mass propaganda, and despite the extraordinarily difficult conditions of distribution which existed during the war, it accomplished a tremendous amount. To-day it is still more than a historical document: it is the thread of Ariadne in the labyrinth of our times. However, a year passed between the day it was concluded and the day it was published, and that year had done much to give a powerful impetus to the movement against war, so that practical instructions for revolutionary action became necessary. They were given in the "Guiding Principles for International Social Democracy" drawn up by Rosa Luxemburg whilst she was in prison and published together with the "*Juniusbroschüre*".

Their deliberate aim was to detach the supporters of Liebknecht and Luxemburg from the hesitant and uncertain elements in the opposition. The tactical conclusions of the "Guiding Principles" therefore firmly rejected "Utopian and in the last resort reactionary plans" of a purely pacifist nature (international arbitration courts, disarmament, the freedom of the seas, the League of Nations, etc.) on which the supporters of Kautsky and Hugo Haase set their hopes, and proclaimed clearly:

"Imperialism, the last phase and highest development of the political rule of capitalism, is the deadly enemy of the workers of all countries. . . . The struggle against imperialism is at the same time the struggle of the proletariat for political power, the decisive conflict between capitalism and Socialism. The final aim of Socialism can be achieved only if the international proletariat fights uncompromisingly against imperialism as a whole, and takes the slogan ' war against war ' as a practical guide to action, summoning up all its strength and all its capacity for self-sacrifice."

Organisational principles were also very clearly laid down, and the revolutionary movement was to be completely separated from those elements which had surrendered to imperialism. A new international was to be founded, an organisation of a higher type than the one it was to replace : an organisation " with a uniform conception of proletarian interests and proletarian tasks, and with uniform tactics in war and peace ". Great stress was laid on the necessity for international discipline :

" The central weight of the class organisations of the proletariat lies in the International. In peace time the International must decide the tactics of all its national sections towards militarism, colonialism, commercialism and the May-day celebrations, and it must also decide on the general tactics to be adopted in time of war. . . . The obligation to carry out the decisions of the International must transcend all other organisational obligations. . . . The only means of defending real national freedom to-day lies in the international class struggle against imperialism. The Fatherland of the workers of all countries is the Socialist International, and everything else must be subordinated to its defence."

These " Guiding Principles " caused violent discussions in the ranks of the German opposition. They were completely unacceptable to the Right-Wing elements behind Kautsky, whilst the more radical elements behind Georg Ledebour were unwilling to accept the strict international discipline they proposed. Rosa Luxemburg remained firm with regard to international discipline, pointing out that the old International had collapsed just because it was not really united internationally either in spirit or in action. Amongst all the great leaders of the working class she was the most decided internationalist both in thought and feeling, and it was not mere propaganda, but a solemn proclamation of her fundamental ideals when she declared in the discussion:

" The international fraternisation of the workers of the world is the highest and greatest thing on earth; it is my guiding principle, my highest ideal and my real Fatherland. I would sooner lose life itself than be disloyal to this ideal."

She was often bitterly reproached for interfering in the affairs of other parties, but she refused to admit the justification of such accusations. She regarded the international proletariat as one, as a unitedly-acting body; and it was her greatest aim to achieve this unity in reality. Whoever refused to work for this proved to her that he stood on altogether different ground.

The line of demarcation was drawn within the opposition, and the Left Wing rallied around Liebknecht and Luxemburg. A conference was held in the middle of March 1916, and it showed that a powerful movement had already arisen from amongst those few who had raised the standard of rebellion in the summer of 1914. Delegations were present from most industrial areas. The Socialist Youth, which had held a secret conference at Easter 1916 in Jena, was overwhelmingly behind Spartakus. The growth of the movement increased the weight of work on Rosa Luxemburg's shoulders, but she bore it gladly: extensive correspondence had to be carried on; discussions, even the most necessary ones, seemed endless; and she had to travel constantly into the provinces to encourge and assist the work of organisation.

In addition—an unusual task for her—the impatient ones had to be curbed. Many of them found it intolerable to remain members of a party which had now become an auxiliary organisation of the General Staff, and whose leaders were progressively destroying the democratic rights of the members: the local organisations had been deprived of their control over the local newspapers, and oppositional members were being expelled from the Reichstag's fraction. Many members of the opposition therefore wanted the formation of a new and completely independent party, but Rosa Luxemburg was determinedly opposed to this. A revolutionary party would have to be formed sooner or later, she admitted, but as long as it was still possible for members of the opposition to work in the old party without abandoning their own principles, then they must do so, and not leave the party and the masses of its members completely in the hands of treacherous leaders, whilst forming a new organisation which could, for the moment at least, be little more than a sect.

Liebknecht was eager for action, and she agreed that everything possible should be done to rouse the masses against the war. May Day 1916 was chosen for the first trial of strength, and Spartakus agitated in the factories of Berlin and its suburbs for a demonstration on the Potsdamer Platz. It was a great success despite the fact that the police had got wind of it and were in the square in force from the early morning hours. At eight o'clock in the morning many thousands of workers—almost ten thousand—assembled on the Potsdamer Platz. Karl Liebknecht, in uniform, and Rosa Luxemburg were amongst the demonstrators. They were immediately recognised, and cheers rose on all sides. Liebknecht's voice then sounded: " Down with war ! Down with the Government ! " It was the signal for a police rush. Rosa Luxemburg placed herself in the way and was roughly thrust to one side. Indignation rose amongst the masses and an attempt was made to free Liebknecht, but it was ridden down by mounted police. For two hours after Liebknecht's arrest masses of people swirled slowly around Potsdamer Platz and the neighbouring streets in constant conflict with the police. For the first time since the beginning of the war masses of workers had demonstrated on the streets against the Government. The ice was broken.

Liebknecht's fate again demonstrated the great significance of personal example. At a time of tremendous difficulties, when the Social Democratic Party was demoralised (which meant the demoralisation of the working class) and the masses had lost all confidence in their leaders, individuals had to come forward and prove by their self-sacrifice that with them, at least, words and deeds were identical, and that deeds were still possible even in such a situation. Karl Liebknecht and Rosa Luxemburg came out on to the streets and risked danger in order to give the masses a personal example.

After Liebknecht's arrest the Spartakus League, as it was

now already called, became very active, and many leaflets were illegally distributed throughout the country. Rosa Luxemburg herself wrote a series of them, explaining Liebknecht's action to the workers and urging them to follow his example. Liebknecht himself did his utmost to support the campaign by using the only means open to him: he bombarded the military judicial authorities with declarations which all began " Re the investigation which has been opened against me . . . ", and which invariably turned out to be appeals to the masses for use as propaganda. In reality he made no attempt to defend himself, and turned the proceedings into an indictment of Germany's war policy. Each of these documents found its way out into the open somehow, and was printed by the Spartakus League and distributed in masses throughout the country, and as a result many thousands of new recruits were won for the struggle against the war.

On June 28th, 1916, Karl Liebknecht was sentenced to two years and six months hard labour. On the day of the trial big demonstrations took place in Berlin, and on the day the sentence was announced 55,000 workers went on strike in Berlin munition factories. Demonstrations also took place in Stuttgart, and strikes in Brunswick and Bremen. The political strike, allegedly impossible in peace-time with a strong and united organisation, and decried as anarcho-syndicalism and revolutionary romanticism, became a reality in war-time when the striking workers were threatened with hard labour or the trenches. In so far as the spontaneous will and initiative of the masses were given a direction and an objective, the strikes were the work of Spartakus, and it was seen that although the organised Spartakists were few in number, there were hundreds of thousands of workers all over the country prepared to follow Spartakist slogans. Spartakus was the expression of the masses. The " civil truce " had lost its validity. The nationalist frenzy was at an end. The German working class was returning to its senses.

But German militarism revenged itself as well as it could, and hundreds of Spartakists were arrested. The factories were " combed out ", and thousands of those who had taken part in the strikes were called up and sent to the front, but the result of this move was that thousands of carriers of revolutionary ideas were carefully sent to regiments at all parts of the front. Increasingly severe sentences were passed, and mass trials took place. For a time militarism seemed to have won back much of the ground it had lost. Owing to the arrests and the " comb-out ", the political movement in the factories lost its leaders for a while, and when on appeal Liebknecht was sentenced to four years hard labour, there were no protest actions. For the moment the oppositional movement had been paralysed, but Liebknecht's undaunted words on receiving his sentence—" No general ever wore his uniform as proudly as I shall wear the broad arrow "—made a deep impression on public opinion. The lonely man in Luckau gaol, set to cobbling shoes, had become a symbol for great masses of people.

7. THE BARNIM STRASSE, WRONKE, BRESLAU

On July 10th, 1916, Rosa Luxemburg was re-arrested. In later years, when giving evidence at a political trial, General von Wrisberg declared that her arrest was carried out by the authorities at the direct request of a social-democratic deputy. Shortly afterwards the seventy-year-old Franz Mehring was also arrested. Ernst Meyer remained free for a little while longer, and then he too was sent to prison. Julian Karski was interned in a concentration camp. But Spartakus was not without a capable leader. Leo Jogiches took command. His political judgement, conspiratorial experience, energy, and strict discipline, and, above all, his gift for managing men and women, stood the movement in good stead. Under his leadership the movement made rapid progress, and the " *Spartakus-briefe* " [1] appeared with unfailing regularity, and no longer cyclostyled, but regularly printed for wholesale circulation. They were no longer the information bulletin of a small group intended for internal use, but a political organ in which world happenings were analysed and a whole arsenal of

[1] " Spartakus Letters." The " Letters " were issued by the " *Gruppe Internationale* " (" International Group "). They appeared from December 1914 to August 1915 under the title " *Zur Information* " (" Information Bulletin "), and then from August 1915 to October 1918 under the title " *Politische Briefe (Spartakus)* " (" Political Letters "). The chief contributors were Rosa Luxemburg, Karl Liebknecht, Franz Mehring, Julian Karski, and Ernst Meyer. The " Spartakus Letters " were collected and issued in 1921 in two volumes by Frankes Verlag, Leipzig.—TR.

intellectual weapons presented. Although she was in prison, Rosa Luxemburg wrote regularly for the paper; her writings found their way outside, and prison walls were unable to stifle her voice.

This time Rosa Luxemburg was not tried and duly sentenced, but held indefinitely in " preventive arrest ", which was the name under which the traditions of the Bastille were revived in Germany. No prisoner could be held for more than three months under a preventive arrest warrant, but a new arrest warrant, the modern *lettre de cachet*, arrived with Prussian punctuality every three months. It was not penal detention, but in many respects it was worse. The first stage was the women's prison in the Barnim Strasse, where she was in familiar surroundings. However, the military authorities were anxious to prevent all communication between her and the outside world, and they therefore ordered special measures of isolation. Until they could find a more secure place for her she was sent from the Barnim Strasse to the Police Presidium, where there was no proper accommodation for prisoners, and where, in fact, prisoners were never held except for a night or two awaiting transfer to regular prisons. The cells there are without artificial light, and in autumn they are dark at five or six o'clock in the afternoon. In addition, there is no proper sleep for the prisoners because the whole night through the sound of heavy footsteps echoes through the corridors, keys rattle, cell doors open and close with a slam as new prisoners are delivered at all hours of the night. On top of that is the thunderous noise of trains passing close by and shaking the whole building. " The six weeks I spent there left grey hairs on my head and wore away my nerves," writes Rosa Luxemburg.

At the end of October 1916 she was transferred to the fortress prison of Wronke, situated in a far-off corner of the province of Posen. At least there was peace and quiet in Wronke and the cell door was left open all day, and in the grounds Rosa Luxemburg had flower-beds to which she attended, and birds to whose song she could listen. The months spent in Wronke were idyllic in comparison, but in July 1917 she was again transferred, this time to Breslau. Breslau Central Prison is a gloomy building—no flowers there, no birds singing, and no freedom. She was locked in her cell all day except for short periods of exercise. In the bare prison yard she would walk around, keeping close to the walls, where a little sun came in, and gazing at the shoots of green grass which forced their way between the flagstones even there. That was, all in all, the life which Rosa Luxemburg led for three years and four months of the war, until the Revolution of November 9th, 1918, set her free.

Outside, the world was in flames, and in her mind and heart was a passionate urge to work, to learn, and to act, to lay the basis for a new socialist order of society in this welter of insanity into which capitalism had plunged the world. Instead she was kept cooped up and helpless, as though in a glass case, in rarefied air, oppressive loneliness, and leaden silence, in which for weeks on end she hardly heard the sound of her own voice. With horrifying clearness she saw the mutilated bodies in the trenches, the privations of the masses, the deaths of children, the decline of a whole generation, the brutalisation and the destruction of all the best things in human culture. But no privation, no force, no suffering could break her will. With quiet dignity she led the life imposed on her and sought consolation in the occasional far twittering of a bird, in every flower she could see, in the busy comings and goings of the ants between the stones, in the humble-bee that once found its way into her cell, in the almost frozen butterfly which she took and put in the sun to restore it to life, in the great cumulous clouds billowing upwards in the narrow stretch of blue visible to her. She lived in fancy with her friends outside, worried about them, busied herself for them. She read each rare letter over and over again, reading between the lines, sensing the real feelings of the writers and their troubles. And she could still encourage and support others: " Be calm. I will stand by you; nothing will upset me. There is no element of vacillation in me," she writes to Mathilde Wurm. And to Sonia Liebknecht: " Dearest Soniushka, you must be calm and serene. We must take life as it comes, courageously, un-dismayed and smilingly—Despite everything! " She is able to put herself in the position of others, to feel the needs of each one, and for each one she falls naturally into a suitable vein. To Sonia Liebknecht she is motherly, protective, encouraging, and consoling. To Luise Kautsky she is comradely with a slight trace of friendly irony. To Clara Zetkin she writes in a tone of calm certainty as to a trusted friend. To Diefenbach she chatters cheerfully, often almost frivolously—to a man she knows to be in danger and wants to make cheerful. And in her letters there are suddenly brilliant sketches of her life and experiences.

In the loneliness and monotony of her prison life books were a solace and a refuge. In this one point at least she was privileged beyond the ordinary penal prisoner: she might read—whatever the censor permits. She fed her hunger for beautiful things on the classics and the best modern literature of Germany, France, Russia, and England. She plunged into the natural sciences. But that was all recreation only, and the great thing was her work. In prison again she continued to work on her " Introduction to Political Economy ", on her translation of Korolenko, on a history of Poland, and later a history of the Russian Revolution. At the same time she carefully followed the course of events in the international working-class movement. On every " post day " her articles were ready for print, and they left the prison as " contraband " under the suspicious eyes of the control authorities. In prison she found the right perspective, the right distance to things, and time to study problems thoroughly and formulate her own ideas. Her articles became little masterpieces, whether they dealt with the latest manœuvre of the Scheidemanns, the botching up of an " independent Poland " as a new reservoir of man-power, or the peace bluff of President Wilson. And always the main theme around which her thoughts centred was the necessity of independent revolutionary action by the masses of the people.

Her hopes were fixed on a rising of the people, and she waited for it with burning impatience, and while she waited she showed the workers the terrible consequences their failure to act would have for the whole of humanity. But she was never pessimistic, and she relied confidently on the inevitable course of history, knowing that the German workers in uniform, " the most intelligent, most disciplined, most social-democratic, best organised and trained cannon-fodder ", would one day rise.

She was cheerful, and hardly knew why; looked for the reason in life itself. " There is a song of life in the harsh grinding of the wet sand under the heavy tread of the sentry—if one knows how to hear it." But she had to pay her toll to life: the slaughter and destruction outside, the triumph of barbarism, the brutalisation of life, the individual cowardice of men, and their mass bravery under the whip of militarism, the treading under-foot of all things valued by her, and then her own helplessness and loneliness. Gradually the burden increased until finally her nerves gave way. For seven months she remained physically upright, and in the eighth her nerves sagged. She became a victim of depression; a shadow falling on her would make her shudder; and every little excitement, even a pleasurable one, shook her deeply. And when she had gradually obtained the mastery again, a new and terrible blow descended on her—a very personal one this time: Hans Diefenbach was killed in action, and her letters were returned. The news affected her deeply, and she never completely recovered from it, but when she overcame the first terrible sorrow, she found consolation in words she had written to him at the beginning of the war, and which she now repeated to Sonia Liebknecht:

"You know, Soniushka, the longer it lasts, and the more the baseness and monstrousness of it exceeds all measure, the calmer and firmer I become: one cannot measure the elements, flood, fire, storm, or an eclipse of the sun with moral standards; one can only register them as something real and regard them as an object of investigation and analysis."

A year previously in a letter to Luise Kautsky she had revealed the principle which held her upright in the collapse of her whole world:

"Everyone who writes to me sighs and complains. That is too stupid. Don't you realise that the general smash-up is much too great to moan about? When the whole world goes out of joint one can only try to understand why it happened; and when I have done my duty, at least I feel calm and cheerful again. *Ultra posse nemo obligatur.* . . . To abandon oneself completely to the calamities of the day is intolerable and incomprehensible. Think with what calm composure Goethe looked at things. And remember what he experienced: the Great French Revolution—and seen up close it must have looked like nothing more than a

bloody and utterly useless farce. And then from 1793 to
1815 an uninterrupted chain of wars until the world once
again looked like a mad-house. And with what calmness
and intellectual serenity he continued his studies on the
metamorphosis of plants, on chromatology, and on a
thousand and one other things! I don't expect you to write
poetry like Goethe's, but you can adopt his attitude to life,
his universality of interests, and his inner-harmony—at least
you can strive to attain it. And if you say: but Goethe was
not politically active, then I say that a political fighter needs
to be able to place himself above things even more urgently,
or he will sink into the trivialities of every-day life up to his
ears—of course, I mean a really worth-while political
fighter. . . ."

Chapter Twelve : THE RUSSIAN REVOLUTION

1. The First Triumph

THE OUTBREAK of the war had cut off Rosa Luxemburg
from the Polish and Russian working-class movements,
though she probably had the deep satisfaction of knowing
that her own party in Poland did not fall victim to the general
demoralisation, but remained loyal to her ideas. Josef
Pilsudski and Dashinski immediately attempted to harness
the Polish people to the war-chariot of the Austro-Hungarian
Empire, in the hope of receiving Polish " independence " in
fief from the Habsburgs, but on August 2nd, 1914, the Polish
Social Democratic Party, the Left Wing of the Polish Socialist
Party, and the Jewish Workers' League issued a joint
manifesto :

" The proletariat declares war on its governments and
oppressors. . . . In a struggle for national rights the
Polish proletariat will derive its demands from its class
policy as a whole. . . . In order to carry them through the
Polish proletariat must seize political power."

Rosa Luxemburg's old party remained loyal to this declaration throughout the war, both against Russian Absolutism and the German Generals, and under the régime of the one as under the régime of the other, Pavilion X of the Warsaw Citadel, where she had been imprisoned, was usually the headquarters of Poland's social-democratic leaders.

In Russia and abroad the Bolshevists proved to be the firm backbone of the Russian revolutionary movement. In the beginning there was a certain amount of vacillation, but it did not affect the core of the party. The Bolshevist members of the Duma were banished in 1914 on account of their revolutionary activity. Amongst the Menshevists all shades of opinion were to be found, from those who remained loyal to internationalism to those who now zealously defended their Tsarist Fatherland. After the difficult period which followed on the Russian Revolution of 1905–6 the revolutionary movement had made steady progress in Russia down to the beginning of the war, and in July 1914 barricades were again erected on the streets of Petersburg. The World War flung back the revolution for the moment. The *bourgeoisie* was elated at the idea of foreign conquest; the peasants believed that it meant new land under the plough, and in consequence they were anxious for conquest too; and the working masses were made confused and uncertain by events. However, at the beginning of 1915 there were new strikes and demonstrations, and a process of inner decay set in for Absolutism. The terrible military defeats revealed the incompetence and inefficiency of the Russian war-machine and the demoralisation of the State apparatus. The Court was eaten up by intrigue. Privation increased throughout the country. As the working class became more active, the *bourgeoisie* took courage, thinking it could make certain of victory if it took power into its own hands. Its representatives aimed at securing measures of reform, and unwittingly they assisted at the birth of a social revolution. On March 9th, 1917 (February 25th old Russian time), the workers of Petersburg revolted successfully in alliance with the soldiers, and the Council of Workers' and Soldiers' Deputies was formed. It was actually already in possession of political power, but it still lacked confidence in its own strength, and therefore, carried away by the general wave of democratic hopes, it handed power over to a *bourgeois* government headed by Prince Lvov.

The March Revolution represented the first triumph of Rosa Luxemburg's war policy; the realisation of something for which she had fought all her life; a guarantee that the German Revolution would follow. But imprisonment and isolation weighed doubly heavy on her now, and she wrote to Diefenbach:

> " You can imagine how deeply the news from Russia has stirred me. So many of my old friends who have been in prison for years in Moscow, Petersburg, Orel and Riga are now walking the streets as free men. That is some consolation to me. . . . Although it makes my own chances of release smaller, I am overjoyed at the freedom of the others."

At one time she thought of demanding her deportation to Russia, but whether she finally abandoned the idea, or whether she made the demand and it was rejected, we do not know.

The Russian Revolution now took first place in her mind, and she was seized by a fever of impatience. Tormented by the anxiety that the Russians might succumb in their isolation to their own internal difficulties and to the power of the foreign counter-revolution, she called for an insurrection of the German working class to save the Russian Revolution. The first obvious effect of the Russian Revolution in Germany was very promising: in April 1917 a wave of huge munition-workers' strikes spread rapidly throughout the country and 300,000 workers went on strike in Berlin alone. The General Staff was greatly alarmed, and their liaison officer to the Central Committee of the Social Democratic Party, the Liberal General Groener, publicly declared that all the strikers were cowardly curs. Apart from increasing the general embitterment, his insults had no effect. Once again the factories were " combed-out " and all the men suspected of radical leanings were sent to the front. This paralysed the movement for a while, and the orthodox social-democratic officials regained the upper hand. Even the leaders of the newly-formed Independent Social Democratic Party declared themselves against what they termed " a revolutionary experiment ": Germany was not Russia, and in Germany freedom must be won on a democratic parliamentary basis. Rosa Luxemburg answered them with arguments that stung like whip-lashes, and the longer the depression and passivity of the workers lasted the more urgent her appeals for action became: "Forward! Save the Russian Revolution by ending the war and emancipating yourselves!"

She did her utmost to study the position in Russia, but the material at her disposal was sparse. Naturally, the German newspapers gave a completely distorted version of events, and it was not possible to correct it very effectively from the columns of *The Times* and the *Temps*, copies of which she received occasionally. She made mistakes in minor questions, but in her general interpretation of the character and aims of the revolution she agreed with the Bolshevists. She over-estimated the political strength of the Russian *bourgeoisie*, and just as Lenin once had confidence in Kautsky, now she had confidence in the Menshevists and hoped that they would grow to greater stature with the revolution, just as many minor men had developed to greatness in the French Revolution, but her hopes were disappointed. In her first article on the Russian Revolution, published in the *Spartakusbriefe* of April 1917, she wrote:

"The revolution in Russia has been victorious over Absolutism at the first onset, but this victory is not the end of the struggle; it is only a beginning. On the one hand the *bourgeoisie* will inevitably sooner or later retreat from the advanced Liberal attitude it has now adopted; that follows logically from its own general reactionary character and from its class antagonism to the proletariat. And on the other hand, the revolutionary energy of the Russian proletariat must, now that it has been awakened, develop with the same inevitable logic towards extreme democratic and social action, and resuscitate the programme of 1905: the establishment of a democratic republic, the legal 8-hour day, the expropriation of landed property, etc. And above all, the most urgent task of the socialist proletariat of Russia, a task indissolubly bound up with all its other tasks, is to bring the imperialist war to an end.

"At this point the aim of the Russian revolutionary

proletariat diametrically opposes the desire of the Russian imperialist *bourgeoisie*, which still dreams of Constantinople, and revels in war profits. The action for peace in Russia, just as in all other countries, can develop only along the lines of a revolutionary class struggle against the *bourgeoisie*, a struggle for political power. These are the unavoidable developments of the Russian Revolution."

She had complete confidence in the inexorable development of the historical logic of events, and she was not misled by the fact that Social Revolutionaries and Menshevists entered the Government:

" The coalition government is a half-measure; it burdens Socialism with full responsibility, but it does not even approximately give it the necessary freedom to develop its programme. It is a compromise which, like all such political compromises, is doomed to fiasco. The dictatorship of the proletariat is inevitable."

This fact made the Russian Revolution a burning international problem:

" Unless it receives support from an international proletarian revolution in time a proletarian dictatorship in Russia is doomed to suffer crushing defeat, compared with which the fate of the Paris Commune will seem like child's play."

However, she did not regard this prospect as a reason for hanging back. The law of revolution is ceaseless progress. Any hesitation, any stagnation makes the victory of the counter-revolution certain, and opens up a period of bloody vengeance wreaked by the alarmed ruling classes. The revolution could be saved only if the international proletariat took a hand in the game and supported the Russians, but until then they must continue their struggle for power irrespective of the final upshot.

In a long article, entitled " Burning Questions of the Day ", published in *Spartakusbriefe* in August 1917, she showed the desperate contradictions which resulted from the July offensive of Kerensky:

" The active prosecution of the war by military offensive

or otherwise does not in the given situation serve the interests of the Russian Revolution in any way. It serves the interests of Entente imperialism, and no amount of radical and democratic peace formulas can disguise the salient fact that every military action undertaken by Russia benefits British, French, and Italian imperialisms, i.e., although the Russian Republic professes to be fighting a purely defensive war it is in reality continuing to participate in an imperialist war.

" But supposing Russia refuses to undertake any offensive . . . and limits herself to a passive, waiting attitude? By this passivity, which is in any case only a half-measure, a way of avoiding the problem and not of ending the war, she renders incalculable services to German imperialism by permitting it to concentrate its main forces against the Western front whilst enjoying a more or less secure rear. Thus the Russian Republic is between the devil and the deep sea.

" By reason of its historical character and its objective causes, the World War is an international settlement of accounts between the imperialist powers, and the best will in the world cannot turn it into its opposite in one corner of the world: a democratic war of national defence. Caught in the toils of the world imperialist catastrophe, the Russian Republic cannot extricate itself on its own; and it cannot end the catastrophe on its own. Only the international proletariat is in a position to put an end to it. Only a proletarian world revolution can liquidate imperialist war. The contradictions in which the Russian Revolution is inextricably involved are nothing but the practical ex-pression of the fundamental antithesis between the revo-lutionary policy of the Russian proletariat and the slavish obedience of the European proletariat to its masters: between the class-conscious action of the masses of the people in Russia, and the treachery of the British, French and German workers to their own class interests and to Socialism."

It is clear, therefore, that Rosa Luxemburg did not regard the Russian Revolution with any self-complacent enthusiasm. She analysed the situation with merciless clarity, took careful note of all threatening dangers, and never for one moment gave way to the fatuous hope that a miracle might solve the cruel contradictions. She saw clearly that only the action of the masses in the rest of Europe could sever the knot, and her keenest anxiety was that the insurrection in other countries might come too late to be effective.

She regarded all the hypocritical peace speeches and peace resolutions, intended to persuade the workers to continue the slaughter in the interests of their masters, as one of the greatest obstacles to the development of the political forces of the proletariat, and it appeared to her that even the international peace conference called in the summer of 1917 by the Petersburg Council of Workers' and Soldiers' Deputies in Stockholm, was developing into another attempt to deceive the masses into continuing the war. She felt that if this conference took place between German war-mongers, supporters of unrestricted submarine warfare, the representatives of the Haase–Ledebour opposition, socialist Ministers in imperialist governments, and the representatives of the Russian Soviets, the last vestige of clarity must disappear in the resultant confusion of political ideas and aims.

" What is really being prepared in all this muddle is not peace between the peoples, but mutual reconciliation between the ' neutral ' and the ' belligerent ' socialists, mutual absolution and a general amnesty for past sins, and the reconstruction of the old International as a *maison tolerée* for socialist treachery."

The Stockholm farce would prove to be preliminary spadework for future diplomatic congresses of the belligerent governments. Socialists were preparing the way for an understanding between the belligerent capitalist governments in complete obliviousness of the obvious fact that any understanding between such governments could come about only at the expense of the proletariat. The official programme of the conference—peace without annexations and indemnities—was the formula of an undecided struggle between imperialist Powers, the formula for a breathing-space whilst they prepared themselves for the next round. It was chiefly in accordance with the interests of German imperialism, whereas *Entente* imperialism still had hopes of a decisive military victory. It was the formula for the restoration of the *status quo ante*,

"and this *status quo* includes all the old frontiers and all the old power relations externally, and naturally internally as well: *bourgeois* class dominance, the capitalist State, and imperialism as the dominant power. Thus the Stockholm 'peace preparations' are nothing but a continuation of the August 4th policy, the political abdication of the proletariat as a class, the continuation of its lackey services to the ruling classes and to imperialism. Since August 4th the socialist parties have been the most effective means of paralysing the masses; they have been a counter-revolutionary factor, and they are merely continuing their services in this respect when they now come forward in favour of an understanding between the belligerent governments and of the re-establishment of imperialism in its pre-war positions."

In this case also her prophecy was followed by speedy confirmation. The German junker Government encouraged the attempt to explore peace possibilities in Stockholm and it gave the social-democratic delegation every possible facility, but the *Entente* governments forbade their socialists to attend the Congress, and the idea then collapsed. This article on "Burning Questions of the Day" demonstrates the essential uniformity of Rosa Luxemburg's policy against war and her unwavering determination to recognise truth no matter what it might be. She proves herself here, as on so many other occasions, to be one of those rare revolutionaries with sufficient moral character and courage to reject any jugglery with her own ideas, any attempt to outwit history, and all hopes of a miracle.

2. THE BOLSHEVIST REVOLUTION

There is nothing from Rosa Luxemburg's pen to show us what effect the first news of the successful Bolshevist Revolution had on her. She received the news of the Bolshevist seizure of power at the same time as that of Hans Diefenbach's death, and the latter dealt her a numbing blow. She probably pulled herself together sufficiently to write about the great event in the *Spartakusbriefe*, but just at that time the paper was appearing irregularly and less frequently, owing to technical difficulties and many new arrests, and when it finally did appear again, new great problems (resulting from the November Revolution) had arisen and had to be dealt with. It is quite certain, of course, that she welcomed the Bolshevist seizure of power with enthusiasm; she felt herself raised above the humiliation and demoralisation of the day in Germany by the daring and determination with which the Bolshevists had intervened in world history. However, she immediately recognised the dangers threatening the dictatorship as a result of its isolation, and in a letter written on November 24th to Luise Kautsky she declares:

> " Aren't you delighted at the Russians? Of course, they won't be able to maintain themselves in this witches' sabbath —but not because statistics show us that their economic development is too backward, as your sagacious husband has reckoned out so carefully, but because Social Democracy in the highly developed West is represented by a pack of pitiful cowards who are prepared to look on inactively whilst the Russians shed their heart's blood. Such a disaster is better than ' living for the Fatherland '. It is a world historic event and its traces will persist for centuries."

The first difficult problem facing the Bolshevists was the urgent necessity of concluding peace with imperialist Germany. Their hope that the great example of the Russian Revolution would bring the whole of the international proletariat into movement and enforce a general peace had been disappointed, and the utter demoralisation of the Russian Army made further resistance impossible. Germany's military power threatened to destroy the revolution, but a peace, even if it lasted only for a short time, would grant it a much-needed breathing space. For the Russians the alternatives were: Brest-Litovsk or defeat.

Rosa Luxemburg was well aware of the objective compulsion under which the Bolshevists acted, but she obviously had the impression that they gave way too easily to pressure; and if she was right, the morale of the revolution was threatened: its leaders would lose their grip, and the revolution itself would sink back into opportunism. Her fears in this respect were so lively that in the summer of 1918, on the basis of false reports, she even believed in the possibility of a Russo-German alliance. She could not know how seriously the Bolshevists were wrestling with the thorny problem and with what determination they were preparing for a new revolutionary drive, whilst giving way before the overwhelming pressure of the moment. Above all, she feared that the Bolshevists might play the German diplomatic game and recognise a peace imposed by violence as " a democratic peace without annexations and indemnities ", in order to curry favour with German imperialism. Revolutionaries would then have degenerated into mere politicians, and the dissolving acid of mistrust would spread throughout the movement. However, it was not long before she recognised her error, and then she recorded with satisfaction: " Lenin and his friends made no attempt to deceive either themselves or others about the facts; they admitted the capitulation quite openly."

She publicly declared her approval of Lenin's peace policy, though not without inner misgivings, because the consequences of Brest-Litovsk appeared terrible. Since the end of 1915 she had been certain of Germany's defeat, though that was, of course, not her solution for the imperialist war; she wanted the destruction of imperialism as a whole by the international proletariat. However, she realised that in the event of the workers being unable to summon up enough strength to end the war by revolution, the defeat of Germany was the next best solution. A military victory for rabid German imperialism under the barbarous régime of the Borussian junkers could only lead to terrible excesses. It would cast the whole of Europe and the greater part of the world into chains, and throw humanity far back in its progress towards a higher ideal of human society. At the same time, Germany's victory would be the victory of the imperialist idea in the international working-class movement. It would render the demoralisation of the working class irreparable and crush the Russian Revolution. It now seemed to Rosa Luxemburg that the peace of Brest-Litovsk made such a victory possible once again, and the thought weighed on her like a nightmare. She scourged the leaders of the German working class more bitterly than ever as the real culprits, and she increased her efforts to drive the German working class forward on the road to revolution:

" Only the slavish attitude of the German proletariat
compelled the Russian revolutionary leaders to make peace
with German imperialism as the only power at present in
existence in Germany. And only this slavish attitude made
it possible for German imperialism to exploit the Russian
Revolution. . . . General peace cannot be obtained without the overthrow of the ruling powers in Germany. The
threatening aggravation of the vast slaughter, and the
triumph of the German annexionists in the East and in the
West can be prevented only by lighting the torch of revolution in Germany, only by launching an open mass struggle
for the seizure of political power, and for the establishment
of a German People's Republic. The German workers
are now called upon by history to take the news of revolution from East to West. Hesitation is fatal; action imperative." [1]

Other things besides the decision of the Bolshevists to sign
the Brest-Litovsk Treaty caused Rosa Luxemburg anxiety
about the fate of the Russian Revolution. Her opinions
often differed from those of her nearest friends—for instance,
Paul Levi, who had taken the place left vacant in the Spartakus
League by the arrest of Leo Jogiches in the spring of 1918.
She often dealt with the points at issue in the *Spartakusbriefe*,
but in the autumn of 1918 she wrote a thorough review of
bolshevist policy in order to convince her friends and political
associates, and to come to a thorough understanding of the
problems involved herself. The outbreak of the German
Revolution prevented the completion of the work, and it
remained unpublished until 1922, when Paul Levi issued as
much of it as had been completed. [2]

This work has been much discussed, and in his preface Paul
Levi mentions that suggestions had even been made that
it should be destroyed, meaning that the suggestion came from
Leo Jogiches, but Clara Zetkin has given very good reasons in
her work " Rosa Luxemburg and the Russian Revolution "
(Hamburg, 1922) for discounting Levi's statement. Leo
Jogiches was against the publication of the book because he

[1] " *Spartakusbriefe* ", January, 1918.
[2] Rosa Luxemburg, " *Die Russische Revolution* " (" The Russian Revolution "), a Critical Estimation, Edited and provided with a Preface by
Paul Levi, from Rosa Luxemburg's Literary Remains, Berlin, 1922.

knew that in a number of important points Rosa Luxemburg had subsequently changed her views, and that she intended to write a new book on the subject. However, he was certainly in favour of including the first work in a collected edition, if only for the sake of completeness. In addition, it would have been difficult to destroy the manuscript, because no one knew where it was. In the end Levi published his version of it from a draft, and not from the original. The original manuscript was taken by a comrade for safety in the January days of 1919 and then forgotten. It was unearthed only many years later, and Felix Weil then published the necessary corrections to the Levi edition, and also very important additions to the Levi text in the " *Archiv für die Geschichte des Socialismus und der Arbeiterbewegung* " [1] in 1928.

Revolutionaries in Germany were naturally carried away by the tremendous happenings in Russia, and (particularly on account of the fierce incitement which began against the Bolshevists) they were inclined to accept without criticism everything the Bolshevists did. Rosa Luxemburg never accepted anything uncritically, and she therefore regarded the Bolshevist Revolution with the same analytical and critical eye with which she was accustomed to examine all other historical phenomena. She insisted always that the intelligent and enlightened workers should accept nothing at its face value, but always maintain their critical faculties fully alive and study the experiences of history for whatever lessons they might contain. She feared (prophetically) that in their enthusiasm the German workers would blindly accept the Russian Revolution as an " infallible authority ", and she impatiently dismissed the suggestion that a critical examination of bolshevist policy would " undermine the prestige of the Russian proletariat and destroy the effect of its example : the only thing which can overcome the fatal passivity of the German masses " and declared :

" The German working class can be brought to take action only by a clear recognition of the terrible seriousness of the situation and the difficulty of the tasks facing it ; only by political maturity, intellectual independence and

[1] " Archives for the History of Socialism and of the Working-class Movement ", issued by Professor Dr. Carl Grünberg in Frankfort-on-Main and published by C. L. Hirschfeld in Leipzig.

critical judgement, all qualities which, under various pretexts, German Social Democracy has systematically striven to crush for decades. The German working class can certainly not be brought to take effective action by the whipping up of a revolutionary hurrah atmosphere."

Never at any time did she campaign against the Bolshevists, and she never had the faintest intention of doing so. She was always sparing with her praise, and she has never praised a party with such enthusiasm as she praises the Bolshevists in this work. It is a misrepresentation, and one which has been sedulously spread by the reformists, to say that she condemned the whole bolshevist policy, including the November Revolution, and that she rejected the idea of the proletarian dictatorship, and thereby justified the policy of the Menshevists. Her book leaves no room for doubt, and in the very beginning she asks whether Kautsky and the Menshevists were right in declaring that Russia was ready for a *bourgeois* revolution only, and too immature for anything else, and she answers by pointing out that a struggle immediately began in the revolutionary camp around the two cardinal questions of peace and land, and that the *bourgeoisie* went over to the counter-revolution in both these questions; if the *bourgeoisie* had been successful their victory would have sealed the fate of democracy and the republic :

" A military dictatorship with a reign of terror against the proletariat followed by a return to the monarchical system would have been the inevitable consequences. From this one can see clearly how Utopian, and fundamentally reactionary too, was the tactic proposed by the Russian Socialists of the Kautsky group, the Menshevists. Insisting obstinately on the purely *bourgeois* character of the Revolution they clung desperately to their coalition with the Liberals. . . .

" In this situation the historic service of the Bolshevists was that from the very beginning they adopted the only tactic which could save democracy and advance the cause of the Revolution, and they maintained it with iron consistency. All power to the Soviets and to the Soviets alone was indeed the only solution to the difficulties in which the Revolution was involved; it was the sword which cut the

Gordian knot and led the Revolution out of the *impasse* into the open where it could develop freely.

"Lenin's party was thus the only party in Russia which understood the real interests of the Revolution from the very beginning; it was the party which lent drive to the Revolution—in short, in this sense, it was the only party in Russia which pursued a really socialist policy. . . . The real situation of the Russian Revolution was reduced within a few months to the alternatives: victory of the counter-revolution or dictatorship of the proletariat; Kaledin or Lenin. . . .

"The determination with which Lenin and his comrades came forward at the decisive moment with the only slogan calculated to lend drive to the Revolution transformed them almost overnight from leaders of a persecuted, slandered 'illegal' minority forced to hide in cellars like Marat, into masters of the situation. . . . Lenin and Trotzky and their comrades displayed the utmost courage, energy, revolutionary foresight, and revolutionary logic any party could possibly have displayed. The honour of the Revolution, betrayed by Social Democracy in the West, was saved by the Bolshevists. The November insurrection not only saved the Russian Revolution, it also saved the honour of international Socialism." [1]

3. CRITICISM OF THE BOLSHEVIST POLICY

Thus Rosa Luxemburg praised the November Revolution and its basic principles in the highest terms, but at the same time she criticised Bolshevist policy in the agrarian question, in the question of self-determination, and in the questions of democracy and terrorism.

The agrarian programme of the Bolshevists provided for the nationalisation of landed estates as one of the first measures of Socialism. The social revolutionaries were in favour of distributing the confiscated land amongst the peasants, but Lenin had declared as early as 1905 that this would lead to the establishment of a new village *bourgeoisie*. However, when the problem demanded an immediate solution, the Bolshevists abandoned their own solution and adopted that of the social

[1] Rosa Luxemburg, " *Die Russische Revolution* ", pp. 77, 81.

revolutionaries. Rosa Luxemburg recognised the enormous difficulties facing the Bolshevists, and she was convinced that even in the West the proletariat would experience a tremendous amount of trouble if ever it was called upon to solve the problem. However, she felt that the Bolshevists should at least have tried to keep the highly developed large-scale estates intact as a basis for the socialisation of agriculture and its amalgamation with industry. The distribution of the land was not a step forward, but a measure which would bar the way to Socialism, intensify property differentiation in the rural areas, unduly favour the Kulak element, and establish a new propertied peasantry which would defend its new-won property rights tooth and nail against any subsequent attempts at socialisation. Although the Bolshevists could not be expected to solve the tremendous problem in such a short space of time, at least they should have worked in the direction of Socialism, or done their best to avoid any measures which subsequently tended to make the achievement of Socialism more difficult.

She believed that the Bolshevists had propagated the seizure of the land in order to win peasant support, and she felt that they would be unsuccessful, and that the peasants would refuse to defend the revolution. She was quite wrong. In the civil war it was the peasants, stiffened by contingents of industrial workers, who saved the revolution. And the Bolshevists acted as they did not with cunning forethought, but under compulsion. The peasants seized the land and distributed it amongst themselves without waiting to be asked. If the Bolshevists had tried to oppose this action instead of sanctioning it as they did, they would have had to wage civil war against the peasantry, and that would have been the end of the revolution.

Of course, it must not be overlooked that Rosa Luxemburg's criticism of the bolshevist agrarian policy was made from a prison cell, and in consequence she was not very well informed. Purely on a theoretical basis it is very difficult to understand the real significance of rapidly changing conditions, and this is more or less what Rosa Luxemburg had to do. Once she was free, and in the thick of affairs herself, she invariably displayed a consummate skill in grasping the real significance of a situation.

Her criticism of the Bolshevists in the question of self-determination was also unfounded. She had always opposed this slogan with the irrefutable theoretical argument that real self-determination was possible only under Socialism and never under capitalist conditions, but Lenin was right in practice when he declared that a revolutionary party in a country whose ruling classes oppressed other nations, must put forward the slogan of self-determination if it wanted to obtain the revolutionary unity of all the peoples involved. When the Russian working class seized power it had to put forward this slogan within the framework of the revolution, because it was the only means of preventing the falling away of Soviet areas, and of winning back at least a part of the territory lost in the war—Ukrainia, for instance. It was precisely the national policy of the Bolshevists under Lenin's leadership which won millions and millions of people for the revolution.

Rosa Luxemburg's weightiest criticism of the bolshevist policy referred to democracy and the Constituent Assembly. As in the agrarian question, she argued from the old standpoint of the Bolshevists, who issued the slogan " All power to the Soviets! " and at the same time demanded the convening of a Constituent Assembly. She was unable to understand why the Bolshevists suddenly dissolved parliament. She refused to accept the argument that this body no longer represented the revolutionary feelings of the masses, and pointed out that it could have been dissolved and re-elected on a new basis. It would seem, in fact, to judge at least from one or two remarks made by Trotzky, that even the Bolshevists themselves were not quite clear at the time about the fundamental nature of the step they had taken. The idea which determined their policy prior to the seizure of power, and the idea to which Rosa Luxemburg still held—Soviets and parliament as well—would have led to dangerous dualism in practice, and the Soviet power would probably have fallen between two stools. A choice had to be made: one thing or the other. And there is no doubt that here a fundamental historical law expressed itself spontaneously in the proletarian revolution in Russia. Just as the corporative assembly represented the dominance of feudalism, and parliament represented the dominance of the *bourgeoisie*, so Soviets represented a new system not based on any particular form of private property, but on labour.   In the German Revolution Rosa Luxemburg radically altered her standpoint and vigorously opposed the slogan of the Independent Social Democratic Party: Workers' Councils *and* a National Assembly.

It is more than likely that even when Rosa Luxemburg wrote her criticism she did not attach such importance to the institution of parliament as was subsequently suggested, and certain reservations indicate this.   Her aim was not the preservation of parliament so much as the preservation of democracy: " not a democracy measured by this or that abstract scheme of justice ", but a democracy which is the living source " from which alone all the inherent inadequacies of social institutions can be corrected: the active, untrammelled and vital political life of the masses of the people ".   She was in favour of the sternest measures against all resistance to revolutionary measures, but she was unwilling to see freedom of criticism suppressed, whether the criticism came from friends or enemies of the Soviet régime.   She regarded this freedom as the only real guarantee against a degeneration of the new State apparatus into hidebound bureaucracy.   Unlike *bourgeois* class rule, the proletarian dictatorship required the political training and education of the masses of the people as a whole, and this political training and education could be obtained by the masses only in independent thought, criticism, and initiative.   Permanent public control, the freedom of the Press, and the freedom of assembly were therefore necessary:

" Freedom for supporters of the government only, for the members of one party only—no matter how big its membership may be—is no freedom at all.   Freedom is always freedom for the man who thinks differently.   This contention does not spring from a fanatical love of abstract ' justice ', but from the fact that everything which is enlightening, healthy and purifying in political freedom derives from its independent character, and from the fact that freedom loses all its virtue when it becomes a privilege. . . .

" The suppression of political life throughout the country must gradually cause the vitality of the Soviets themselves to decline.   Without general elections, freedom of the Press, freedom of assembly, and freedom of speech, life in every public institution slows down, becomes a caricature of itself, and bureaucracy rises as the only deciding factor. No one can escape the workings of this law. Public life gradually dies, and a few dozen party leaders with inexhaustible energy and limitless idealism direct and rule. . . . In the last resort cliquism develops a dictatorship, but not the dictatorship of the proletariat: the dictatorship of a handful of politicians, i.e., a dictatorship in the *bourgeois* sense, in the Jakobin sense. . . ." [1]

Rosa Luxemburg was not in favour of *bourgeois* democracy, which is a formal cloak of equality and freedom concealing social inequality and injustice; she was in favour of proletarian dictatorship:

" But this dictatorship consists in a particular application of democracy, not in its abolition; it implies energetic action against the acquired rights and general economic relations of *bourgeois* society, and without this intervention a socialist transformation of society is impossible."

At the same time this dictatorship was to be subject to the direct influence of the masses, subject to the control of public opinion as a whole; it was to be really the dictatorship of a class, and not the dictatorship of a small minority in the name of a class.

This attitude towards dictatorship is the core of Rosa Luxemburg's criticism of bolshevist policy, and it is here she expresses the essence and aim of her criticism. All those who have tried to make her out to be the protagonist of a reformist, anti-bolshevist policy have consciously or unconsciously overlooked her real point. Immediately after enunciating the principle quoted above she writes:

" I am sure that the Bolshevists would have acted in just this way if they had not been subject to the terrible pressure of the World War, the German occupation and all its attendant difficulties, a pressure which must necessarily distort even a socialist policy pursued with the best intentions and based on the most admirable principles." [2]

She recognised, too, that " the widespread use of terrorism ", although it pained her deeply, was the result of this same terrible pressure, and she does not condemn the Bolshevists:

[1] Rosa Luxemburg, " *Die Russische Revolution*," p. 113.
[2] Rosa Luxemburg, *ibid*., p. 117.

" Everything which is happening in Russia is under-
standable as an inevitable chain of cause and effect, beginning and ending with the failure of the German proletariat
to rise to the occasion, and with the occupation of Russia
by German imperialism. . . . Thanks to their determined
revolutionary attitude, their exemplary energy and their
unswerving loyalty to international Socialism the Bolshevists
have indeed done everything possible under extraordinarily
difficult circumstances."

Rosa Luxemburg's aim in all her criticisms is to warn the
workers and the Bolshevists against making a virtue of necessity, against presenting tactics forced on them by terrible
circumstances as tactics inevitable and desirable in themselves
and worthy of emulation by the international proletariat.
The point at issue at the moment was not this or that tactical
detail, but the will to power of the proletariat and its capacity
for action:

" This is the essence and the whole character of bolshevist policy, and in this sense the permanent historic
service of the Bolshevists is that they have gone ahead
with the conquest of political power and pushed forward the
problem of winning Socialism into the world of practical
reality. . . . The problem could be formulated in Russia,
but it could not be solved there. In this sense the future
belongs to ' Bolshevism ' everywhere." [1]

That statement is clear and unambiguous, and in a fragment found with the same manuscript she writes:

" ' Bolshevism ' is the slogan of practical revolutionary
Socialism, for all working-class efforts to seize power. The
historic service of Bolshevism lies in the opening up of a
social chasm in the midst of *bourgeois* society, and in internationally aggravating class contradictions. In this great
service—as is always the case when judged by great historical
standards—all detail, errors and miscalculations are
swallowed up easily."

It must not be forgotten that she did not conclude this
work on the Russian Revolution. Perhaps it was because

[1] Rosa Luxemburg, " *Die Russiche Revolution*," p. 120.

she had no time, but more likely it was because whilst writing
it she found that her opinion on important points would not
stand the test of reality. In any case, we know that a few
weeks afterwards she corrected her own views in important
details. Adolf Varski, her Polish collaborator, has published
a letter written to him by Rosa Luxemburg approximately
at the end of November in answer to certain doubts he had
expressed concerning the policy of the Bolshevists:

" Our party [in Poland.—P. Fr.] is full of enthusiasm for
Bolshevism, but at the same time it criticises the conclusion
of the Brest-Litovsk Peace, and bolshevist use of the slogan
of ' self-determination '. That is enthusiasm coupled with
criticism, and what more can we ask? I shared all your
reservations and misgivings, but I have abandoned them in
the most important questions, and in others I did not go
quite so far as you do. Terrorism certainly indicates great
weakness, but it is directed against internal enemies who
have placed their hopes on the existence of capitalism outside Russia, and who receive encouragement and support
from it. If a European revolution takes place the counter-
revolutionaries will not only lose this support, but, what is
more important, their courage as well. In short, the
terror in Russia reflects the weakness of the European
proletariat. It is certainly true that the new agrarian
relations which have been created represent the most
dangerous and sensitive point of the whole Russian Revolution, but here too the truth holds good that even the
greatest revolution can bring about only what is historically
ready for fulfilment. This sore point in the Russian
Revolution can be healed only by a European revolution." [1]

Rosa Luxemburg was too far away from the happenings
to be able to estimate every detail of the tangle of cause and
effect which determined the attitude of the Bolshevists and
led to the distortion of the proletarian dictatorship: economic
and cultural backwardness, the dislocation of the State
apparatus and the economic system, counter-revolutionary

[1] Adolf Varski, " *Rosa Luxemburg's Stellung zu den taktischen Problemen der
Revolution* " (" Rosa Luxemburg's Attitude to the Tactical Problems of the
Revolution "), Hamburg, 1922, p. 7. The letter is given by Varski from
memory.

sabotage, the beginning of the civil war, etc. That, however, did not prevent her seeing the dangers which threatened the revolution. Like Lenin and all the prominent bolshevist leaders of the day, she was quite certain that the Russian Revolution was doomed to destruction unless the international proletariat came to its aid by seizing power in other countries—i.e., that " Socialism in one country alone " was impossible. The saving world revolution did not materialise, but at the same time world capitalism was weakened by the war, and revolutionary proletarian action in other countries was strong enough to give the Bolshevists a free hand to win the civil war, time to consolidate their States apparatus, and room to manœuvre in their domestic policy.

This development seemed to discount Rosa Luxemburg's last misgivings with regard to bolshevist policy, but although she may have under-estimated the difficulties, in the long run her ideas have shown themselves to be correct on the whole, and, what is worse, her chief fears have been realised. Some passages of her book read like a prophecy. The continued isolation of the Russian Revolution has had fatal results. The willynilly recognition of the spontaneous peasant revolt and its seizure and distribution of the land have led to severe internal convulsions and to a cruel class struggle between town and country which, despite widespread collectivisation, has not yet entirely ended. The restriction of democracy, which was in the first place a means of self-preservation and a lever which produced enormous achievements, has led to the abolition of democracy altogether, to the narrowing down of dictatorial power into fewer and fewer hands, to the political regimentation of the proletariat, and to the complete paralysis of all mass political initiative. Lenin, too, was quite conscious of these dangers, and he never ceased to counteract them, but the Stalinist régime in the Soviet Union has done what Rosa Luxemburg feared : it has made a virtue of necessity, and in consequence " the vitality of the Soviets themselves " has declined. " Life in every public institution slows down, becomes a caricature of itself, and bureaucracy rises as the only deciding factor." In fact bureaucracy has now developed into a special social layer apart from the rest of society. The ruling group in the Soviet Union has appointed itself the " infallible authority " in the international communist movement; it demands blind obedience and ruthlessly stifles all criticism. At one time Rosa Luxemburg was horrified at the idea that the Bolshevists might ally themselves with German imperialism, and so sacrifice the revolutionary interests of the international proletariat to their own particular interests; to-day the foreign policy of the Soviet Union and its instrument the Communist International have become a factor in international capitalist antagonisms. And, finally, the bloody extermination of the Old Guard of Bolshevism shows a degeneration of the revolution far in excess of Rosa Luxemburg's worst fears.

The actual course of events once again proved the extraordinary keenness of her eye for social development. Her book on the Russian Revolution is the work of a great revolutionary who is not prepared to accept things at their face value. She never sought to evade the stern necessities of history, but to overcome their attendant difficulties by extending the revolutionary front. Like her articles on the Russian Revolution, her book was primarily intended to encourage the German proletariat to take action. Her slogan was not capitulation, but world revolution.

CHAPTER THIRTEEN : THE GERMAN REVOLUTION

1. PRELUDE

THE YEAR 1918 was the worst of all the years Rosa Luxemburg spent in prison. She fought gallantly to keep up her spirits, seized eagerly on every little pleasure that came her way, and sought by hard work to banish thoughts of her loneliness, suffering, and disappointment, but the daily torment of her existence hammered away steadily at her nerves. She fell ill even in Wronke, and she wrote bitterly of the " treatment " the doctor recommended. It reduced itself to the advice given by the vicar of Ufenau to the dying Hutten:

" . . . *Jetzt findet Ruhe hier.*
Horcht nicht hinaus, horcht nicht hinüber mir.
In dieser stillen Bucht erstirbt der Sturm der Zeit.
Vergesset, Hutten, dass ihr Hutten seid ! " [1]

And Hutten could only answer:

" *Dein Rat, mein teurer Freund, ist wundervoll :*
Nicht leben soll ich—wenn ich leben soll." [2]

In Breslau her condition was made worse by complete isolation, a stricter prison régime, and the progressive restriction of her correspondence. Her complaints about the arbitrary treatment accorded her were of no avail, and a commission, appointed to examine preventive arrest cases periodically, to placate public opinion, proved a farce. In March 1918 she wrote to Sonia Liebknecht:

" My complaints have been returned to me rejected together with a very painstaking description of my depravity and incorrigibility. A request for leave has suffered the same fate. Apparently I must wait until we've defeated the whole world."

She could still summon up sufficient courage to meet the chicanery and malice of the authorities with humour, and she could still find strength enough to cheer up Sonia Liebknecht and help her bear her heavy burden. But in 1918 the tone of the few letters she was still permitted to write is strained to breaking-point: " My nerves, my nerves! I can no longer sleep." Suddenly, and without any real reason, she would be tormented by the feeling that something terrible had happened to some one dear to her, and when she heard nothing from Clara Zetkin for a long time, the oppressive feeling became a certainty, particularly as the Zetkin boys were both at the front. In a letter to Luise Kautsky, Rosa Luxemburg wrote:

" I have courage enough to support whatever may happen to me, but I have no longer sufficient courage and strength to help bear the sorrows of others—and certainly not Clara's if anything happens—which ' God forbid '."

[1] " Now find peace here.
No more regard the outside world.
The storm of life abates in this still haven.
Forget then, Hutten, that your name is Hutten ! "
[2] " Your advice, my friend, is wonderful:
I should cease to live that I might live on."

Till then she had always courage and strength enough to help others as well as herself. The happenings outside made a deep impression on her, and her mind was constantly revolving around the terrible possibilities: the victory of German imperialism, and the crushing of the Russian Revolution. Above all, she was depressed by the sullen silence with which the workers, and in particular the German workers, bore everything and continued to do the bloody work of their masters.

But in January 1918, encouraged by the heroic example of the Vienna workers, a new wave of mass strikes swept over Germany as a protest against semi-starvation and the brutal peace of Brest-Litovsk, and in favour of democratic reforms. Many big towns were involved, and in Berlin alone half a million workers were on the streets. Once again the authorities struck out furiously, and once again " the hydra-headed revolution " was decapitated. Military jurisdiction was introduced for political offences committed by civilians, severe sentences were imposed up and down the country, and the prison gates clanged to behind a new batch of Spartakists. In March the authorities managed to arrest the leaders of the military organisation of the Spartakus League, including Leo Jogiches. The leadership now consisted of two or three individuals only, and they had to work under most trying and difficult conditions. Whilst Ludendorff was conducting his desperate offensive on the Western Front, the working class seemed to be in a torpor, and it caused Rosa Luxemburg to write bitterly in the *Sparkatusbriefe* of June 1918:

" The German proletariat failed to bring the chariot of imperialism to a halt, and it is now being dragged behind it helplessly to crush Socialism and democracy all over Europe. The German workers are now wading through blood, over the bodies of Russian, Ukrainian, Finn, and Baltic revolutionary workers, destroying the national existence of Belgians, Poles, Lithuanians, and Roumanians, trampling down France and planting the victorious banner of German imperialism everywhere.

" But each new military victory Germany's cannon fodder helps to win on foreign soil means a new political and social triumph for reaction at home. Every blow delivered at the Red Guards in Finland and South Russia increases the power of the East Elbian Junkers and of Pan-German capitalism. Every Flanders town razed by the German Army means a new position lost to German democracy. Even now, in the midst of war, the German working class is being scourged with whips and scorpions as it thoroughly deserves."

Her gnawing anxiety was that the German Revolution would come too late to save the Russian Revolution. She was quite certain that it would come, but although she watched anxiously, she could still find no evidence of the elementary process which was nevertheless going on in the structure of German society and noiselessly approaching its culmination. Revulsion at the mass slaughter and hatred of the ruling classes responsible for it were there, but as yet they were still unspoken. The resentment at the intensifying régime of semi-starvation was there, accumulating for the final outburst. The ground began to tremble under the feet of the ruling classes. Fear began to manifest itself more openly, panic threatened, and wider and wider gaps began to show in the front of the " bitter-enders ". The Brest-Litovsk peace began to prove a doubtful advantage to German imperialism. Although it urgently needed the troops it had stationed in the East, it was compelled to draw a *cordon sanitaire* around them, because the soldiers who had defeated the remnants of the Russian armies in the East and in the Ukraine had themselves become infected with Bolshevism, and troops transferred from the East to the West took the infection with them. Ludendorff flung youths and half cripples into battle, but in Germany there were already hundreds of thousands of deserters. They were the first-fruits of the progressive demoralisation of German society, and in their turn they furthered the process of demoralisation at home. A mass revolt was brewing. The factories became centres of conspiracy. The radical elements rallied everywhere: propagating revolutionary ideas, but at the same time preventing any premature outbreak. When it came, they wanted it to be a knock-out blow.

On October 1st two important happenings occurred at the extreme poles of German society. Hindenburg and Ludendorff, who had for some time been making frantic appeals to the government, now demanded that immediate peace proposals should be made to the enemy. At the same time a joint conference took place between the Spartakus League and the Left-Wing Radicals, who had their headquarters in Bremen, where their organ *Arbeiter-Politik* appeared. It was the war council of the approaching revolution. A programme of action was adopted culminating in a demand for a united Republic for the whole of Germany, " not as a final aim, but as a test of the democratic pretences of the ruling classes and their agents ". It was also decided to intensify the agitation amongst the troops to the utmost and to begin the formation of workers' and soldiers' councils.

The break-up of the Hohenzollern régime began. Now that the threat had become so real, the authorities were panic-stricken, and contradictory measures were hurried through. An attempt was made to save the old order by reforms. A " parliamentary " government was formed by Prince Max of Baden, and Scheidemann joined it. Save the monarchy and pacify the masses, was its political programme. As victory was now out of the question, the Kaiser left to parliament the task of concluding a peace. The General Staff urged surrender, but at the same time it prepared to make a desperate throw, and tried to incite the masses against the very peace negotiations it was itself demanding. A number of political leaders were released, but at the same time masses of political suspects from the army and the factories were flung into prison. The introduction of democracy into the whole of political life was announced, but at the same time troops the Government thought still reliable were concentrated in Berlin to crush any rising of the people. Freedom of assembly was proclaimed, but police prohibitions made it a farce, and demonstrations were fired upon. Each new measure, each new act of violence, and each new concession completed the process of dislocation.

Rosa Luxemburg now found her imprisonment intolerable, and she shook at the bars and demanded her immediate release. She was in a fever of impatience to be at liberty again; to act, direct, and encourage. On October 18th she wrote to Sonia Liebknecht:

" One thing is quite certain: my mood is such that a

visit from friends under the control of the prison authorities has become quite impossible. I have stood everything patiently for years, and if necessary I could stand it patiently for years more, but under different circumstances. Now that the general move has started, something has snapped in my psychological stoicism. A discussion under supervision, with no possibility of talking about the things which really interest me, has become so intolerable that I would sooner have no visits at all—until we can see each other in freedom. In any case, it can't last much longer. If they release Dittmann and Kurt Eisner, they can't very well keep me much longer in prison, and Karl will soon be free too."

On October 20th an amnesty was issued for convicted political prisoners, and on October 23rd Karl Liebknecht was freed and escorted home in triumph by the Berlin workers. The amnesty did not apply to Rosa Luxemburg, however, as she was not serving a sentence: she was " merely under preventive arrest ", and there she stayed. In fact, the preventive-arrest warrant against her was renewed as usual. Whether the reason was that despite the general collapse the militarists were still more powerful than the Government, or whether the Government thought Liebknecht alone would be quite enough trouble, the fact remains that for another three weeks Rosa Luxemburg was kept cooped up, whilst all around the old order was toppling.

2. NOVEMBER

Events now went forward at a great speed. The fronts collapsed. On October 26th, Ludendorff, who had been the real ruler of Germany, fled abroad with a false passport. On October 28th the German Admiralty suffered an epileptic fit and determined to " save the honour of the navy " by sacrificing the lives of 80,000 men in a " decisive " naval battle in the North Sea. That provoked the final blow.

The navy was even more strongly infected with revolutionary ideas than the army, and as early as 1917 an organised action against the authorities had taken place. Two sailors Reichpietsch and Kobes were executed in connection with it. There were secret revolutionary councils on all vessels, and they kept a mistrustful watch on the officers. The sailors were still ready to go into action to defend Germany against an enemy attack, but they were not prepared to let their lives be sacrificed in a senseless slaughter. When the order " Action Stations " was given, the stokers raked out the fires and prevented the insane plan. On board, the officers had already lost command, but on land they made a last attempt to crush the rising by arresting 600 sailors. The others then revolted in real earnest and joined forces with the workers of Kiel. Within a day or so the movement had developed into a general strike in ships and factories. On November 4th the Governor of Kiel was forced to resign and the Workers' and Sailors' Council made itself master of the town. The Government still believed it was dealing with an isolated mutiny, and it sent the social-democratic leader, Gustav Noske, to restore order. But it was the German Revolution, and it now spread from town to town like fire through stubble.

In the two weeks since his release, Karl Liebknecht had been working feverishly: studying the mood of the workers and soldiers, speaking in one factory after the other, urging the masses on to revolt. He was co-opted into the revolutionary Shop Stewards' organisation, which had existed since the great January strike, and consisted of representatives of the trade unions in the factories. It was the nucleus of a workers' council, and at the same time a revolutionary committee of action. Sessions of this body were held almost daily, and work went ahead swiftly to prepare the final revolt. The police did their utmost to capture its members, and in particular Liebknecht, who was unable to go home, and spent his nights in all sorts of places, sleeping on forms in workers' meeting-places, in furniture pantechnicons, or in the forest of Treptow, with the police always on his heels. He had differences of opinion with the Shop Steward leaders. He wanted the mobilisation of the masses, demonstration of workers on the streets in order to win the soldiers, and intensive propaganda in the factories and barracks. The most daring elements in the Shop Stewards' organisation had conspiratorial ideas; they counted their revolvers and engaged in endless technical preparations. Their slogan was " All or nothing ", and the hesitant joined them. The hour of revolt was fixed—and postponed again and again. In the end the conspirators had just time to place themselves at the head of the workers of Berlin when they finally acted on their own. It was new confirmation of Rosa Luxemburg's theory that revolutions cannot be "made", that revolutions spring from the will of the masses when the situation is ripe, and that all the carefully concocted "preparations" never come to any satisfactory conclusion and often threaten to miss the decisive moment altogether.

On November 9th the hour struck for Berlin, which was already surrounded by revolution in a great semicircle, on the north, west, and south. Hundreds of thousands of workers poured out of the factories. All idea of resistance was abandoned, and even the special detachments of reactionary officers capitulated. Wilhelm II fled over the Dutch frontier. Prince Max announced the abdication of the Kaiser and the renouncement of succession by the Crown Prince. With the assistance of the social-democratic leaders he still hoped to save the crown for some other Hohenzollern, and he handed over the office of Reich's Chancellor to the social democrat and ex-saddler Fritz Ebert, who accepted it with the assurance: " I hate revolution like mortal sin." At the same time Karl Liebknecht proclaimed the Socialist Republic from the balcony of the Imperial Palace to a vast crowd of working men.

Councils were elected in the factories and in the barracks, and an Executive Committee of Workers' and Soldiers' Councils was formed which claimed full power throughout the Reich. All government buildings were occupied by workers. The prisons were stormed and hundreds of political prisoners released, including Leo Jogiches.

Once the revolution was victorious in Berlin it spread automatically to all other big towns: in Breslau the masses forced the opening of the prisons on November 9th, and Rosa Luxemburg was free at last. She went straight from prison to the Cathedral Square, where she addressed great masses of cheering workers. On November 10th she arrived in Berlin, where she was greeted with joy by all her old friends—but with concealed sadness, for they suddenly realised what the years in prison had done to her: she had aged terribly, and her black hair had gone quite white. She was a sick woman, but her eyes shone with the old fire and energy. Although she urgently needed rest and recuperation, there was no rest for her. Two months were left of her life, and they were filled to the

utmost with almost superhuman efforts. Without a thought
for her own health or safety, she strained every effort both
physically and mentally. She gave herself up completely,
with enthusiasm and joy, to " the colourful, fascinating,
tremendous spectacle of revolution ".

Her passionate efforts to urge the masses forward to revolutionary action filled many people with deep misgiving, and
even many of those who admired her profoundly though they
did not agree with her politically now felt that she had lost all
sense of proportion and reality; that she was rushing forward
regardless of all obstacles, that she was uncritically copying
Russian methods without considering the great difference
in the German situation. However, when such objections
are examined, they are found to be based on a failure to
understand revolutionary politics. Not that the policy of the
Spartakus League, or of Rosa Luxemburg herself, was faultless
in those stormy days. Whoever is called upon to take decisions of far-reaching significance in such a chaotic struggle
of mass forces must inevitably make mistakes, even if he has
a genius for grasping the significance of a situation. And
whoever has the courage to take action, and is not content to
let himself be dragged along in the wake of events, will go
forward resolutely, and by his resolution often succeed in
shaping a situation to his will. A revolution advancing
irresistibly to victory will bury the mistakes of the revolutionary
party under the ruins of the society it overthrows, and bring
about in reality what only a moment before seemed like an
illusion of optimistic revolutionaries.

Rosa Luxemburg's fundamental attitude was determined
by the basic law of all revolutions :

" Either it must advance rapidly and with determination,
breaking down all resistance with an iron hand, and
advancing its aims further and further as it proceeds, or it
will soon be flung back beyond its own weaker beginnings
and succumb to the counter-revolution." [1]

But even in days of rapid revolutionary development her
temperament, impetuous though it was, was still curbed
and guided by her reason. The fact that the first revolutionary

[1] Rosa Luxemburg, " *Die Russische Revolution* " (" The Russian Revolution "), p. 78.

K

period nevertheless ended in what later proved to be a decisive defeat of the working class was not so much due to the many errors committed by the revolutionaries as that those errors were inevitable owing to the extraordinary difficulty of the situation.

3. THE GATHERING OF FORCES

The outward form of the German Revolution was so strikingly similar to that of the French February Revolution of 1848 that the question involuntarily arises: how was it possible that a period of development from primarily manufacture economy to modern large-scale industry, fundamentally changing the social composition of the people, did not produce entirely different results, did not result immediately in the indisputable victory of the proletarian revolution? The truth is that the German Revolution took place under conditions which could hardly have been more unfavourable. Like the Russian Revolution of March 1917, it abolished the last remnants of feudalism in the governance of the State, and it gave birth in redoubled measure to all the illusions attendant on modern democracy, and in particular the idea that Socialism can be achieved through parliament. Above all, there was no revolutionary peasantry in Germany in 1918. The German peasant had made great sacrifices and suffered considerably during the war, but he still believed that, materially at least, he was certain of his reward, thanks to the war-loan script carefully stored away in his cupboard, and all he wanted beyond that was the repeal of war-time restrictions. On the other hand, the German capitalist class was incomparably more powerful and more class-conscious than its Russian counterpart. At the same time, the Russian Revolution, which seemed destined to be the strongest bulwark of all revolutionary movements, and was that in fact for a long time, was also a source of dangerous weakness during the decisive period of the German Revolution. It clearly demonstrated the character and aims of the revolution, and the *bourgeoisie* grasped its implications even more quickly than did the proletariat. The capitalist class and its *petit-bourgeois* and feudalist satellites quickly realised what was at stake, and although they were compelled to make political and economic concessions to the working class, they did so with the idea of reversing the situation at a later and more favourable date. At the same time, knowing that its very existence was at stake, the *bourgeoisie* was ruthlessly determined to retain political power and crush its enemies with any means that offered. It therefore rallied round the banner of the orthodox social-democratic leaders: Stinnes came to an understanding with Legien, the leader of the trade unions, and Hindenburg, the representative of the military caste, placed himself at the disposal of Ebert. The leading representative of the East-Elbian Junkers, Herr von Heydebrand und der Lasa, once known as " the uncrowned king of Prussia ", assured President Ebert of his loyalty and sympathy, and the representative of the highest caste of State officialdom, Kapp, later the leader of the abortive Kapp Putsch, did the same.

The confidence of the German capitalist class in Ebert and his friends was thoroughly deserved. From the very beginning Ebert, Scheidemann, Noske, Legien, and the rest were consciously counter-revolutionary both in their views and in their actions. On November 10th Ebert was made head of the Government by the Berlin Workers' and Soldiers' Council ; on the same day he concluded an alliance with the General Staff, with Groener and Hindenburg, with a view to crushing the Berlin workers by force of arms. During the war the influence of the Social Democratic Party on the working class had steadily declined, but it was still a power to be reckoned with, and the revolution again increased its prestige as the party of August Bebel. Many people who had previously been politically indifferent—clerical employees, the *petit-bourgeoisie*, and great numbers of soldiers—all in all a strong contingent, now flocked to the Social Democratic Party, and for a long time their confidence could be abused with impunity.

Even where the example of the Russian Revolution had been most effective, its results were of doubtful value. The Workers' and Soldiers' Councils, natural child of any modern revolution, arose where the masses themselves had taken the initiative, but in large areas of Germany where the change had come about mechanically, merely as the repetition of November 9th in Berlin, the councils were more of a decorative appendage than anything else, and they were usually the result of a compromise between the old party leaders and the new Independent Social Democratic Party, and sometimes even *bourgeois* parties—in short, they were not real organs of mass power. Further, although the lower officials of the Social Democratic Party were sincerely in favour of the revolution, they still looked to their leaders for guidance. The workers in the Independent Social Democratic Party were revolutionary enough, particularly in the big industrial towns, but they were restrained at every turn by their leaders, Haase, Kautsky, Hilferding, and Bernstein, who wanted a revolution without the unavoidable social upheaval any revolution must bring with it, and their party was very similar to the Menshevist Party after the March Revolution in Russia. The Spartakus League was the only organisation in Germany which showed any revolutionary determination and unity.

The working-class movement was thus composed of many groups at various different stages of political development, and, in addition, the major strength of the counter-revolution was within its own ranks. There was another fact of great significance: history gave the revolution no imperative objective. Peace and land were the two great slogans which carried the Russian Revolution to victory, but in Germany peace had already been obtained, and defeated German imperialism was prepared to pay anything for it providing it could retain power at home; and although there was considerable impoverishment amongst the peasantry, land-hunger was not strong enough to goad the rural areas to revolt. The working masses were certainly in favour of socialisation, but the majority of them realised what it meant and how it ought to be carried out only after all chance of doing so had been lost.

However, even in this uncertain situation there was one factor which demanded a decision: the working class was armed. Now, it is a law of history that no class is prepared to let itself be disarmed without a struggle, just as no society can exist but one in which the ruling class has undisputed control of the armed forces. This factor made civil war inevitable.

The most important factors determining the relation of forces in war are well known, and yet it is the practical test which finally determines which side is the stronger. In revolution, however, which is an elementary process of a very different order, intellectual and psychological factors play a much greater rôle: revolution disturbs the basis of society much more deeply than does war, and therefore sudden changes in the understanding and determination of the masses are always likely.

As far as it was possible to recognise the character of the main actors in the drama, the significance of their actions, and the relation of forces in the revolution, Rosa Luxemburg succeeded with great acumen, and what she said and wrote at the time still stands to-day. She grasped the difficulties of the situation with rare intuition, but, far from capitulating to them, she set herself the task of overcoming them. She accepted the dictum of Saint-Just: " *Oser, c'est toute la politique de l'heure actuelle* ", as the law of revolution, but she never lost her head. She wanted no ephemeral success, and her actions immediately on her arrival in Berlin were very level-headed. Followers of the Independent Social Democratic Party had occupied the buildings of three *bourgeois* newspapers and were issuing the newspapers on their own account. A group of Spartakists did the same with the *Lokalanzeiger*, and turned it into the *Rote Fahne*. Rosa Luxemburg had no respect for *bourgeois* law or for the capital behind the *Lokalanzeiger*, but because she saw clearly that her party would not be strong enough to hold the position it had seized if its action were challenged, she insisted on evacuation.

However, both a revolutionary organ and a revolutionary organisation were urgently necessary. The Spartakus League was still rudimentary, and consisted chiefly of innumerable small and almost autonomous groups scattered all over the country. Whilst Liebknecht agitated tirelessly in the factories and barracks, on public squares and in the streets, ably supported by other prominent speakers of the Spartakus League, Paul Levi, Hermann Duncker, Wilhelm Pieck, and others, Leo Jogiches took the task of organisation in hand. The publication of a newspaper was attended with innumerable difficulties, chiefly because the new Government used war-time restrictions on the use of paper as a political weapon against the Left, but on November 18th the first number of the *Rote Fahne* finally appeared, bearing the names of Karl Liebknecht and Rosa Luxemburg. Rosa Luxemburg was the real editor, and with a group of brilliant contributors, including Paul Levi, August Thalheimer, and Paul Lange, at her command, she directed the paper at her own discretion,

but always with tact and circumspection, and secure in the
absolute authority and respect she enjoyed amongst all her
collaborators.   She determined the contents of each issue, and
thus determined the policy of the organisation itself.   She dealt
with all the questions of the day in vigorous and inspired
articles, interpreting their significance and revealing their
consequences.   As though from a great height, her eye ranged
over the whole field of revolutionary action.   She kept a close
watch on the enemies of the revolution, and, like Marat before
her, she revealed a great flair for recognising counter-revolutionary conspiracies even when others would have thought
the evidence insufficient, and later on her judgement was
vindicated again and again when the facts came to light.
At the same time she carefully studied the actions and re-
actions of the masses, critically examined their weaknesses,
welcomed their achievements with enthusiasm, and systematically guided their energies to the great objective: the
seizure of power.   Under her editorship the *Rote Fahne* became
part and parcel of the history of the day.   It proved to be her
last proclamation to the working class, her political testament.

4. THE PROGRAMME OF THE REVOLUTION

Her very first article showed how far her ideas had developed
since the writing of her book on the Russian Revolution.
After a few brief sentences summing up the results of the first
week of the Revolution she enumerates the chief points of a
revolutionary programme:

" The abolition of capitalist rule and the creation of a
socialist order of society—this and nothing else is the historical theme of the German Revolution.   It is a tremendous
task and it cannot be performed overnight with a few
decrees from above, but only by the conscious action of the
toiling masses in town and country, and by the highest
degree of intellectual maturity and idealism on the part
of those masses pursuing their aim through all vicissitudes
until final victory.

" The aim of the revolution determines the way in which
it can be achieved; the task determines the methods necessary to accomplish it.   The guiding principle for all the

actions of a revolutionary government must be: all power in the hands of the masses, in the hands of Workers' and Soldiers' Councils, and all possible precautions to protect the work of the revolution against its ever-present enemies.

" Every step, every action of a revolutionary government should point like a compass in the one direction:

" The extension and re-election of local Workers' and Soldiers' Councils in order that the first impulsive and chaotic gesture which brought them into being may now be replaced by a conscious process of understanding the aims, tasks, and methods of the revolution. . . .

" The speediest possible convening of the Reich's parliament of workers and soldiers in order to constitute the proletarians of all Germany as a class, as a compact political power, and to rally them behind the work of the revolution as its bulwark and driving force.

" The speediest possible organisation—not of the 'peasants' —but of the rural proletarians and small peasants, social strata which as yet have remained outside the Revolution.

" The formation of a proletarian Red Guard for the permanent defence of the revolution, and the training of a workers' militia in order to develop the whole of the proletariat into a revolutionary defence force prepared for instant action.

" The exclusion from all share in the State administration, the judiciary, and the army of the old absolutist military and police organs taken over by the revolution.

" The immediate confiscation of all dynastic wealth and property, and of all large-scale landed property as a first measure to guarantee the feeding of the populace, because hunger is one of the most dangerous allies of the counter-revolution.

" The immediate convening of a world congress of workers to stress the socialist and international character of the revolution, because the future of the German Revolution can be guaranteed only in the International, in the world revolution of the proletariat."

She then compares this revolutionary programme with the actions of the " Revolutionary Government " of Ebert and Haase: the preservation of the old State apparatus, the sanctification of private property and normal capital relations, and the encouragement of counter-revolutionary activities. And in this political indictment the passage occurs:

> " The present government is calling a National Assembly in order to create a *bourgeois* counter-weight to the Workers' and Soldiers' Councils, and thus divert the revolution into the channels of an ordinary *bourgeois* revolution, away from its socialist aims."

Only a little while before she had criticised the bolshevist policy for refusing to permit the existence of parliament side by side with Soviets, but she now put forward clear and definite alternatives: either parliament or the Workers' and Soldiers' Councils. This is clearly a revision of her pre-liminary criticism of the Russian Revolution, but it is not a mere copying of the Russian example. Experience in Germany had caused her to recognise the necessity of what had taken place in Russia. A prophecy made by Friedrich Engels in a letter to August Bebel on December 11th, 1884, had come true:

> " In any case, our only opponent on the day of the crisis and on the day afterwards will be the whole reaction grouped around the standard of pure democracy."

Everybody in Germany who was opposed to the intro-duction of Socialism and opposed to working-class rule, from the extreme Right to many of the leaders of the Independent Social Democratic Party, was in favour of the National Assembly. The fiercest opponents of the general franchise, the people who even during the national holocaust had been unwilling to surrender one iota of their class privi-leges, were now full of enthusiasm for absolute democracy and equal rights for all. And those who only a few weeks before had been imperial " Marxists ", who had done their best to the very end to save the monarchy, and who were now working to establish a bloody *bourgeois* dictatorship, came out in favour of absolute democracy: not the democracy of all great revo-lutionaries from Robespierre to Babeuf and Blanqui, and from Marx to Lenin—i.e., a real democracy of the masses—but the banal pseudo-democracy of *bourgeois* parliamentarism. Thus the alternatives, National Assembly and Workers' Councils, became the two opposite poles of German society, and between these two lay the decision: back to capitalism or forward to Socialism. Rosa Luxemburg insisted on the fundamental importance of this issue, and on November 20th she launched a vigorous attack on the leaders of the Independent Social Democratic Party, who were in favour of a National Assembly, but who wished to have the elections postponed in the hope of avoiding civil war:

> "The traditions of Lamartine, Garnier Pagès, and Ledru-Rollin, the *petit-bourgeois* illusionists and babblers of 1848, are still with us it seems, but without brilliance or talent, and without the attraction of novelty. We have them in a dull and pedantic German edition in our Kautskys, Hilferdings, and Haases. . . .
>
> "The ' civil war ' they are so anxiously trying to exorcise is unavoidable. Civil war is only another name for class war, and the idea of Socialism without a class struggle, Socialism by a majority decision of parliament, is a ridiculous, *petit-bourgeois* illusion. . . .
>
> "The question of the National Assembly is not a matter of tactics; it is not a matter of greater ' convenience '. It is a matter of principle, a question of the socialist character of the revolution. . . .
>
> "Whoever pleads for a National Assembly is consciously or unconsciously depressing the revolution to the historical level of a *bourgeois* revolution: he is a camouflaged agent of the *bourgeoisie* or an unconscious representative of the *petit-bourgeoisie*. . . .
>
> "The alternatives before us to-day are not democracy and dictatorship. They are *bourgeois* democracy and socialist democracy. The dictatorship of the proletariat is democracy in a socialist sense. The dictatorship of the proletariat does not mean bombs, *Putsches*, riots, and ' anarchy ', as the agents of capitalist profit deliberately pretend; it means the use of political power for the introduction of Socialism and for the expropriation of the capitalist class in the interests and by the will of the revolutionary majority of the proletariat—i.e., in the spirit of socialist democracy.

" Without the conscious will and the conscious action of
the majority of the proletariat there can be no Socialism,
and in order to strengthen this conscious will and action, a
class instrument is necessary: the Reich's parliament of the
proletarians in town and country."

National Assembly or Workers' and Soldiers' Councils?
That was now the central question. The establishment of
Workers' and Soldiers' Councils was the main plank of the
Spartakus programme published by Rosa Luxemburg in the
Rote Fahne on December 14th. The World War had put
society before: " the continuation of capitalism with new
wars and a final descent into bloody chaos or the abolition of
capitalist exploitation ". Socialism was the only salvation of
humanity, and Socialism could be brought about only by the
action of the working masses:

" Therefore the proletarian masses must replace the sur-
viving instruments of *bourgeois* class dominance, the federal
councils, the parliaments and Diets, the municipal councils,
etc., from the leading organs of the State down to the
smallest municipality, with their own class instruments:
Workers' and Soldiers' Councils; they must occupy all
public posts, superintend all public activity, and measure
all the needs of the State by their own class interests and
socialist tasks. The State can be imbued with a socialist
spirit only in constant and vital co-operation between the
masses of the people and their class instruments, the
Workers' and Soldiers' Councils. . . .
" The proletarian masses must develop from mere
machines in the process of production into thinking, free,
and independent controllers of this process. They must
develop a feeling of responsibility as active members of a
commonwealth in sole possession of all social wealth.
They must be industrious without the crack of the whip,
develop their utmost capacities without the slave-driver, be
disciplined without the capitalist yoke, and establish order
without dominance. The highest idealism in the interests
of all, the strictest self-discipline, and the most active civic
sense on the part of the masses represent the moral basis of
socialist society, just as stupidity, egoism, and corruption
represent the moral basis of capitalist society."

A wave of incitement and calumny poured over the Spartakus League. Its leaders and its members were represented as beasts in human form, anxious to drown society in blood and establish a reign of terror. The bloody crimes which the Government itself was feverishly preparing were all put down to the account of Spartakus, and newspapers, leaflets, and placards trumpeted out its alleged crimes and atrocities. Rosa Luxemburg answered:

" In all *bourgeois* revolutions bloodshed, terrorism, and political murder have always been weapons in the hands of rising classes, but the proletarian revolution needs no terrorism to attain its ends, and its supporters abominate murder. It needs none of these weapons because it fights against institutions, not against individuals. Because it does not enter the struggle with naïve illusions, it needs no bloody terror to revenge its disappointments. The proletarian revolution is not the desperate attempt of a minority to shape the world by violence according to its own ideals. It is the action of the overwhelming majority of the working people called upon to fulfil a historic mission and to make historical necessity into historical reality."

This proclamation of the aims and methods of proletarian revolution came from the heart, and behind it one can sense the pain Rosa Luxemburg felt at the use of terror in the Russian Revolution, though she recognised its necessity as an extreme measure of defence in dire circumstances. At the same time it was an appeal to the German workers to arm themselves morally against those excesses which are never completely avoidable in desperate struggles, but which must be counteracted as far as possible by a consciousness of deep responsibility. This attitude had nothing in common with the theories of Tolstoi or Gandhi, and she was well aware that desperate diseases often require desperate remedies: " It is madness to believe that capitalists will ever submit to the verdict of a socialist parliamentary majority and abandon their property, their profits, and their privilege of exploiting their fellow-men." And there were already more than enough indications that the imperialist capitalist class, as the last great representative of social exploitation, would outdo all its predecessors in baseness, cynicism, and brutality, that it would sooner see the whole world turned into a heap of smoking ruins rather than renounce its claim to exploit humanity. There was no hesitation at all in her mind :

" All this resistance must be broken step by step with an iron hand and with ruthless energy. *Bourgeois* counter-revolutionary violence must be met with the proletarian revolutionary violence. The attacks, intrigues, and conspiracies of the *bourgeoisie* must be foiled by the unwavering determination, watchfulness, and constant activity of the proletarian masses. The threatening counter-revolutionary danger must be met by arming the people and disarming the ruling classes. *Bourgeois* parliamentary obstruction must be met by the active organisation of the masses of workers and soldiers. . . .

" The struggle for Socialism is the most tremendous civil war the world has ever seen, and the proletarian revolution must provide itself with all the equipment necessary to win ; it must learn to use it, to fight with it and to be victorious.

" The dictatorship of the proletariat is the equipment of the masses of the working people with political power to carry out the tasks of the revolution, and it is therefore truly democratic. Not the pseudo-democracy in which worker sits cheek by jowl with capitalist, and impoverished farm labourer with rich junker to debate solemnly on their vital interests, but real democracy in which millions of proletarians take State power into their own hands and use it, like the God Thor his hammer, to crush the ruling classes—that is the only democracy which is not a deception and a sham."

After proclaiming the general principles of revolutionary action, the Spartakus Programme enumerates the tasks to be performed in order to conquer and consolidate power, prepare for a socialist economic order, increase living standards, and raise the general level of mass culture. It declares itself to be the most conscious section of the working class, aiming to guide the class as a whole in the performance of its historical task, representing Socialism and the interests of the world revolution in all national questions at every stage of the revolution. It refused to share power with enemies of the revolution, or to take up the reins of government before the appointed time merely because they were slack in other hands. The programme is thus a determined rejection of any policy of adventurism or *putschism* :

> " The Spartakus League will never take power except in accordance with the clearly expressed will of the great majority of the proletarian masses of Germany consciously supporting its ideas, aims, and methods."

Two weeks later Rosa Luxemburg presented this programme to the inaugural Congress of the Communist Party of Germany. She declared it to be the resuscitation of the fundamental principles of the " Communist Manifesto ", and it is true that the same ideas concerning the character of the revolutionary struggle, the same aims, the same methods, and the same spirit are present in the birth certificate of modern scientific Socialism and in this last programmatic document drawn up by Rosa Luxemburg. This great similarity was caused by a corresponding similarity of the respective political situations in which the documents were drawn up. In February 1848 Germany was on the eve of a *bourgeois* revolution, which Marx regarded as the immediate predecessor of a proletarian revolution. In December 1918 the last remnants of feudalism were brushed to one side and the *bourgeois* revolution was completed. *Bourgeoisie* and proletariat now faced each other for the final struggle. After seventy years of tremendous social development, the curve of revolution ran parallel once again to the days of the March Revolution, though in a much wider circle and on a much greater scale. However, the programme of the Spartakus League was not a mere copy of the " Communist Manifesto ", but a summary of the political situation in Germany, so that the two documents offer a further example of the complete harmony of ideas between Karl Marx and Rosa Luxemburg, and at the same time her independence in the application of his methods.

5. The Counter-Revolution Attacks

When Rosa Luxemburg published the programme of the Spartakus League revolution and counter-revolution were already at grips in Germany. The enemies of the revolution had worked circumspectly and cunningly. On November 10th

Ebert concluded the alliance with General Army Headquarters, whose preliminary aim was to defeat the Berlin
workers. On November 30th Reich's Commissar Winnig, a
former trade-union leader, raised an army for the struggle
against Bolshevist Russia, and a great number of so-called
Free Corps were founded, allegedly intended for use against
Poland. Ten *élite* divisions marched into Berlin, but they
quickly melted away in the fire of the revolution, and the social-
democratic commandant of Berlin, Wels, then founded the
Republic Soldiers' League. It was financed directly by
capitalist groups, and totalled about 15,000 men. The
military forces on the side of the revolution were weak. The
Berlin Police President, Emil Eichhorn, a member of the
Independent Social Democratic Party, had formed a security
police force out of trade-unionists. The so-called People's
Marine Division, totalling about 3,000 men, was stationed
in the old Imperial Palace. It was a politically unreliable
body, and for some time it was under the command of Wilhelm
II's old friend, Count Wolff Metternich. There was also a
small force of Spartakists organised in the Red Soldiers'
League. However, in addition, many thousands of workers
were now armed, and prepared to defend the revolution.

On December 6th the counter-revolution ventured its first
open action. In Hamburg and the Rhineland counter-
revolutionary conspiracies were discovered. In Berlin a
group of soldiers " loyal to the government " proclaimed
Ebert President of the Republic and demanded that he should
take complete power. Another group arrested the Executive
Committee of the Workers' and Soldiers' Councils, and a
third group occupied the offices of the *Rote Fahne*. In the
north of Berlin a demonstration organised by the Red Soldiers'
League with the knowledge and permission of the authorities
was fired on under the pretext that a Spartakist *Putsch* was
planned. Eighteen demonstrators were killed and thirty
wounded. An investigation instituted by the Police President
revealed the fact that all these happenings had a common
origin, and all signs indicated that the guilty parties sat in the
Berlin Commandant's office, in the War Ministry, and in the
Foreign Office. The happenings shook the prestige of the
Government, and, following an appeal by the Spartakus
League, hundreds of thousands of workers demonstrated on

the streets of Berlin against the machinations of the counter-revolution. However, no direct measures were taken to protect the revolution.

The campaign of incitement against Spartakus was now intensified to the pitch of hysteria. Spartakist *Putsches* were announced every day, "Bolshevism" and "Spartakus" became the bogies of frightened *bourgeois* everywhere. "Bolshevism nationalises women!" Every crime up and down the country was attributed to Spartakus. Karl Liebknecht, Rosa Luxemburg, and their followers were presented as a horde of murderous and sadistic beasts, and the Anti-Bolshevist League, liberally supplied with Government money, invented new monstrosities every day and sent them out into the world on sensational posters which appeared on walls and hoardings everywhere. Spies and groups of *agents-provocateurs* were organised, an atmosphere of murder and pogrom was deliberately fomented, and the killing of the Spartakist leaders was openly advocated in public meetings and in the Press. Without interference by the social-democratic authorities the *Heimatdienst*, the corrupt tool of the old imperial Government, issued huge placards:

> "Workers! Citizens!
> Our Fatherland is threatened with destruction. Save it! It is no longer threatened from without, but from within. Spartakus threatens it. Kill their leaders! Kill Liebknecht! When they are dead you will have peace, work and bread.
>
> Soldiers from the Front."

On December 7th Karl Liebknecht was seized in the offices of the *Rote Fahne*, but before he could be carried off, the hurriedly-alarmed police arrived and freed him. It was later discovered that the plan had been to kidnap and murder him. The social democrat Wels organised a body of mercenaries whose single instruction was to "hound the leaders of the Spartakus League and prevent their organisational work". There was worse still intended behind this formula, and the Spartakist leaders now lived in constant danger. Overwhelmed with work, Rosa Luxemburg had visited her home in the quiet suburb of Südende only very rarely, and now it became quite impossible. Her enemies were constantly on the watch for her there, and the whole district was under the dictatorship of the local Vigilant Committee.[1] Every night she stayed at a different hotel under a false name, and left early in the morning to escape capture, so that she seldom had sufficient sleep. The editorial offices of the *Rote Fahne* were not safe, and they were repeatedly threatened by misled and incited groups of soldiers.

She kept a cool head and a clear intellect in every danger, in the rapid whirl of events, and in the hurly-burly of the editorial offices, which were constantly visited by large numbers of workers and soldiers seeking advice, and by all sorts of doubtful characters. She resolutely thrust aside " the minor inconveniences " of such a life; her body had no right to be tired and exhausted or hungry because she had no time to eat properly; it had to obey the dictates of her will. And when in those critical days work was interrupted again and again, and the editorial programme had to be re-cast frequently as the result of fresh news and further discussions and decisions, her nerves were not allowed to give way under the strain. Her will-power succeeded in calling on unsuspected physical reserves, and the "fascinating spectacle of revolution" sustained her mind.

Despite all the efforts, lies, conspiracies, incitement, provocations, and bloody violence of the reaction, the revolution won new ground every day. Troops coming back from the front, under the influence of an unscrupulous campaign of incitement, and often furious with anger at " Spartakus, the cause of all the trouble ", very rapidly developed into supporters of the revolution. And the workers began to use their own weapon, the strike, more and more frequently. A vast wave of strikes swept over the country from Upper Silesia to Rhineland-Westphalia. New forms of strike organisation and strike leadership developed, and the elementary force of these strikes, in which hundreds of thousands took part, caused panic in the camp of " law and order ". The so-called socialist Government prepared to crush the strikes by military force, and even the most radical member of the Government, Emil Barth, complained furiously that the glorious revolution was degenerating into a mere wage movement.

---

[1] *Bürgerrat*, the *bourgeois*, middle-class counterpiece to the Workers' and Soldiers' Councils.

Well-meaning historians have reproached the German working class for failing to show sufficient idealism in the days of revolution, and for thinking only of its own miserable existence, instead of the great tasks of the revolution. But what a lack of historical understanding! After long years of semi-starvation, it was inevitable that the working class should utilise its new-won power to improve its own material conditions. In any case, the strikes were not mere wage movements: they were part and parcel of the revolution. The prize at stake in all these movements, not only historically and objectively, but openly proclaimed by the strikers themselves, was power in the factories and a socialist reorganisation of production. Rosa Luxemburg therefore welcome them with enthusiasm, and the lessons of 1905 had taught her the rôle played by economic struggles in times of social transition. In her work " The Mass Strike, the Party and the Trade Unions " she had prophesied:

" A revolutionary period would alter the character of the trade-union struggle in Germany too, and intensify it to such an extent that the present-day guerilla struggle carried on by the trade unions would appear as child's play. And on the other hand, the political struggle would receive new impetus and fresh forces from the elementary economic strike wave. Action and reaction between the economic and the political struggles—so to speak the regulating mechanism of revolutionary proletarian action—would result naturally from the given conditions in Germany as well as elsewhere." [1]

This daring prophecy was hardly listened to in Germany at the time, but during the revolution it was even outdone by reality, because the conscious will of the proletariat was expressed in this elementary strike-wave, which aimed not only at immediate economic improvements, but at Socialism. In an article published in the *Rote Fahne* on November 27th, 1918, she wrote:

" Instead of waiting for the benevolent decrees of the government or the decisions of the wonderful National Assembly, the masses are instinctively adopting the only

[1] Rosa Luxemburg, " Collected Works " (German), Vol. IV., p. 452.

real means of getting Socialism: the struggle against
capitalism. . . . The strike movement is a proof that the
political revolution has penetrated to the roots of the social
order. The revolution is turning to its own natural basis,
it is brushing aside the cardboard scenery of ministerial
changes and ministerial decrees, which do not affect the
social relationship between capital and labour at all, and
stepping before the footlights in person.

"In the present revolution strikes are not mere trade-
union conflicts about unimportant matters, about mere
wage questions; they are the natural answer of the masses
to the tremendous upheaval brought about in capital relations by the collapse of German imperialism and by the
short political revolution of the workers and soldiers. . . .
They open up a period of direct action on the part of the
broadest masses, and the socialisation decrees of the government and the measures announced by other bodies are no
more than attendant music."

She was full of optimism, and there was no doubt that
the masses were moving rapidly to the Left. However, this
movement was elementary; it was taking place as the direct
consequence of current events, and not all its political consequences were realised by the masses. Action and reaction
between political and economic struggles does not function
with the precision of cog-wheels, and in particular the composition of the Workers' and Soldiers' Councils lagged behind
the increasing radicalisation of the masses. This was a
matter of very great importance, because in the first period
of the revolution the Workers' and Soldiers' Councils were
in a position to exercise public functions as a matter of revolutionary right if they were so minded, or to renounce their
power in favour of the old governing and administrative
institutions. Throughout the country the official social democrats were doing their utmost to persuade the Councils to
abandon their powers, and at the same time the social-
democratic leaders were working feverishly to rebuild the old
State apparatus. This greatly facilitated the work and organisation of the counter-revolution.

The great contradiction between the spirit of the masses and
the political aims of the old parties expressed itself at the first

Congress of the Workers' and Soldiers' Councils in Berlin from December 16th to 20th, 1918. The delegates were not elected directly, but appointed by the local Councils. It represented the attitude of the masses in the first days of the revolution, but that was all, and it lacked even the great-hearted illusions of those first days. It represented the past, not the present; the backward small and middle-sized towns rather than the big industrial areas. In political character it was rather an Upper House than a People's Parliament. There were 489 delegates present, of whom 288 were Social Democrats, 80 Independent Social Democrats, and only 10 Spartakists. Social reality outside the Congress doors was very different.

When the Congress met, its character was still in doubt, but everywhere great hopes were placed on it. Rosa Luxemburg demanded in the *Rote Fahne* that it should dismiss the Ebert–Scheidemann Cabinet, which had developed into a counter-revolutionary centre; disarm all units which did not unconditionally recognise the authority of the Workers' and Soldiers' Councils; disarm the reactionary units formed by the Government; form a Red Guard; reject the National Assembly as an attempt to divert the revolution; and invest the Workers' and Soldiers' Councils with all power. The Spartakus League called a demonstration of Berlin workers in support of these demands, and hundreds of thousands of workers went on to the streets in the biggest demonstration Berlin had ever seen. A deputation laid the demands of the Spartakus League before the Congress, and they led to the adoption of a number of platonic and ambiguous resolutions such as one for " immediate measures (unspecified) for the disarming of the counter-revolution ", but for the rest the managers of the Congress did their utmost to isolate it from the masses. After the adoption of these vague and benevolent phrases a well-prepared blow was launched at the revolution : a resolution was adopted declaring, " This Reich's Congress of Workers' and Soldiers' Councils throughout Germany, representing full political power, hereby transfers all legislative and executive power to the Council of People's Commissars until such time as the National Assembly may make other arrangements."

The elections for the National Assembly were fixed for January 19th, 1919. With this the Workers' and Soldiers'

Councils had committed political suicide and appointed the *bourgeoisie* their heir.

Rosa Luxemburg at once recognised the far-reaching consequences of this decision:

> " It was not due only to the general inadequacy of the first stage of the revolution, but to the particular difficulties attending this proletarian revolution, and the peculiarities of its historical situation. In all former revolutions the combatants faced each other with visor up : class against class, programme against programme, banner against banner. In the present revolution the defenders of the old order no longer do battle under the insignia of the ruling classes, but under the banner of the ' Social Democratic Party '. If the cardinal question of the revolution was clearly and openly, capitalism or Socialism, the vast masses of the people would not hesitate for one moment." [1]

Despite this reverse, she still remained optimistic, because the soldiers were rapidly abandoning the livery of imperialism, donning their overalls, and re-establishing their connections with the social basis in which their class-consciousness was rooted. In addition, questions of great moment were arising : unemployment, the economic struggle between capital and labour, and the bankruptcy of the State finances. As a result class differentiation would inevitably grow clearer and sharper, and revolutionary tension increase. Time was working for the revolution. Passionately desirous of forcing a decision as she was, bitterly as she hated the renegades who had gone over to the enemy, her mind and will still mastered her impatience, and she set two tasks to her party and the working class : the spread of enlightenment concerning the aims and character of the revolution and the machinations of its enemies; and the defence, consolidation, and gradual extension of all revolutionary positions. No premature attacks, no struggling for aims not yet accepted by the overwhelming mass of the working class, and no *Putsches* ! A month before she had revealed the secret background of the lying campaign against the alleged *putschist* plans of the Spartakus League:

[1] In the *Rote Fahne*, December 21st, 1918.

" But there is someone else who needs terrorism, chaos and anarchy to-day, and that is the *bourgeoisie* and all its parasitic hangers-on who are now trembling for the safety of their property, their privileges, their profits, and their rule. These are the people who are trying to saddle the socialist proletariat with the responsibility for chaos and *Putsches*, whilst themselves preparing to let loose chaos and anarchy at the critical moment in order to throttle the proletarian revolution and rebuild the class dictatorship of capitalism on the ruins. . . . From our historical vantage point we can smile coolly. We can see through their game, we know the actors, we know their managers and we know their rôles." [1]

The organisers of the counter-revolution—Ebert, Scheidemann, and the Generals—also knew that time was working in favour of the revolution, and that their moral success at the Congress of Workers' and Soldiers' Councils would soon be lost unless they quickly succeeded in destroying the power of the revolution. They chose their first objective. After the counter-revolutionary *Putsch* of December 6th the People's Marine Division deposed its commander, Count Metternich, and in his place elected an ordinary A.B. named Radtke. With this the Division became dangerous. It was quartered in the heart of Berlin—in the old Imperial Palace—and it dominated the ministerial quarters. At the same time the Division had announced that in the event of the Government breaking up it would support the Independent Social Democratic Party. The majority of the men were by no means Spartakists, but they were sincerely in favour of the revolution. The next step after the Congress, therefore, was to pick a quarrel with them, and a campaign of slander was directed this time at the People's Marine Division, instead of exclusively at Spartakus. Later on the untruth of the innumerable assertions made was frankly admitted. Provocative demands which meant the dissolution of the Division were put, and rejected. Fire was opened on a demonstration of sailors, who then seized the social-democratic Berlin Commandant, Wels, as a hostage. That was the signal for action. The sailors had not expected fighting, and they had made no pre-

[1] *Rote Fahne*, November 24th, 1918.

parations to defend themselves. Normal sentry duty was in
force, but there were no more than a hundred men actually
on the spot when the attack was launched. However, they
rejected the ultimatum to surrender, which was accompanied
by hypocritical promises, and on Christmas Day artillery fire
was opened. Although the bombardment continued for
several hours, the sailors refused to be impressed. Eichhorn's
police and groups of armed workers came to their assistance,
and men and women approached the attackers, mixed with
them, hindered their free movement, and finally persuaded
them to lay down arms. By evening the fighting was over and
negotiations had begun. Concessions were made to the
sailors, and Wels, who had been kept in a place of safety
during the bombardment, was compelled to resign.

This was a clear victory for the revolution, and the gulf
between revolution and counter-revolution had widened. If
there had ever been any real chance of class conciliation, the
attack on the sailors had destroyed it. It was clear after
Berlin's " Bloody Christmas " that the decisive battle must
soon come.

6. The Founding of the German Communist Party

The Spartakus League was a loose organisation of a few
thousand members only. Its core was the old Left Wing of
Social Democracy, a Marxist *élite* schooled in Rosa Luxemburg's tactical ideas. The majority of the Socialist Youth
joined forces with the League, which then recruited additional
supporters amongst the many people who had been driven to
the Left Wing of the working-class movement by their opposition to the war. During the war years all these elements had
run risks and incurred dangers quite new to the working-class
movement in Western Europe. They were all enthusiastic
adherents of the revolution, though many of them still had
very romantic ideas about it. The enormous difficulties of
illegal work during the war years had prevented any rigidly
disciplined and centralised organisation, and when the revolution came the League was really a loose federation of local
groups and no more. It had such groups in almost all
towns, but it was not a strong political party. The Independent Social Democratic Party was formed as a breakaway
from the old party at Easter 1917, and the Spartakus League

joined it as an affiliated body, maintaining its own organisation, discipline, and political programme, and taking advantage of the existence of this larger organisation to propagate
its own ideas, though in reality only very few of the Spartakus
groups were sufficiently alive to the great chances affiliation
offered them.

Apart from the Spartakus League there was a group of Left-
Wing radicals with its centre in Bremen, and with branches in
North Germany, Saxony, and the Rhineland. It issued a legal
organ, the *Arbeiterpolitik*, and was in general agreement with
the Spartakus League on fundamental principles, but from the
beginning it was more closely associated with the Bolshevists.
Chance factors connected with the organisation of both groups
—differences originating in the Russian and Polish movements
—and minor disagreements on tactical matters had prevented
organisational amalgamation. In the end all that still
separated the two groups was the affiliation of the Spartakus
League to the Independent Social Democratic Party, with
which the Left-Wing Radicals disagreed.

The Left Wing of the German working-class movement was
thus not organisationally prepared for the great tasks of the
revolutionary period, and before long amalgamation and the
formation of a centrally-organised political party became
urgently necessary as the only means of giving the spontaneous
revolutionary movement throughout the country a strong
organisational backbone and a common marching route. In
addition, it was of primary importance to give the supporters
of the Independent Social Democratic Party some revolutionary
clarity. The leaders of the I.S.D.P. were members of the
Government, together with Noske and Scheidemann, and they
bore a joint responsibility for all the official acts of the Government, though it is very unlikely that they knew anything
definite about the counter-revolutionary machinations of the
Ebert clique. However, a growing opposition to their
participation in the Government developed. The opposition
was not very clear about its own political attitude, and it was
completely unorganised, but it was quite firm in its rejection
of the policy of the party leaders. Since the counter-
revolutionary *Putsches* of December at least, this opposition
represented the majority of the party in the most important
centres: Berlin, Saxony, and the Rhineland.

The Spartakus League did its best to win over this instinctively revolutionary wing of the I.S.D.P., and it demanded the immediate convening of a party congress. After listening to a speech by Rosa Luxemburg, a general meeting of the party in Berlin almost unanimously adopted this demand, and other parts of the country followed its example. However, the party leaders opposed the calling of a congress with an obstinacy they had never shown to the reactionary proposals of the Right-Wing socialists. They feared, with very good reason, that a party congress would result in their defeat and probably in their deposition.

In the meantime the struggle between revolution and counter-revolution was steadily approaching its climax, and the Spartakus League therefore called a national conference on its own at the end of the year. The first act of this conference was the founding of the " Communist Party of Germany (Spartakus League) ". The Left-Wing Radicals held a simultaneous conference and decided to join the new party. The most important political question was whether the new party should take part in the National Assembly elections or not. Rosa Luxemburg wrote strongly in the *Rote Fahne* in favour of doing so :

" We are now in the midst of revolution, and the National Assembly is a counter-revolutionary fortress erected against the revolutionary proletariat. Our task is to take this fortress by storm and raze it to the ground. In order to mobilise the masses against the National Assembly and lead them in a decisive struggle against it, we must utilise the elections and the platform of the National Assembly itself. . . . Our aim in participating in the National Assembly must be to expose and roundly denounce all the tricks and machinations of this fine assembly, to reveal its counter-revolutionary activities step by step to the masses, and appeal to them to intervene and force a decision."

The other leaders of the Spartakus League were in complete agreement with Rosa Luxemburg, though it went against Liebknecht's grain, but the great majority of the delegates to the conference, and the great majority of the members behind them, were unable to understand the contradiction between a rejection of the National Assembly on principle and yet participation in the National Assembly elections. The Russian example was too close for them to see the details; they saw only the final period of victory, and not the many previous months of careful and often complicated manœuvring which led up to the November victory. This majority was so certain of the victory of the German Revolution—it seemed almost within grasp—that participation in parliamentary elections appeared as a highly doubtful circumlocution—or even worse. In vain Rosa Luxemburg warned the delegates against under-estimating the difficulties ahead, against counting on a quick and easy victory, and against neglecting any means at all of winning adherents. The inaugural Congress of the German Communist Party rejected the proposal to participate in the National Assembly elections by 62 to 23 votes. Leo Jogiches was deeply shocked at this result, and took it as a sign that the decision to form a Communist Party had been premature; but Rosa Luxemburg shrugged her shoulders resignedly, declaring that a new-born babe always squalled first. In a letter to Clara Zetkin, who was also deeply perturbed by the decision of the Congress, she expressed her firm conviction that the new party would find the right path before long despite all its errors, because it embraced the revolutionary core of the German proletariat.

The tension which developed at the Congress between the sober wisdom of the leaders and the revolutionary impatience of the younger elements was lessened immediately Rosa Luxemburg addressed the Congress on the party programme. The delegates had anxiously observed what a great effort of will was necessary before her exhausted body could triumph over the effects of long imprisonment, ceaseless excitement, nervous tension, and serious illness, but no sooner had she begun to speak than inspiration worked wonders and she was suddenly her old self again. All her physical weakness fell away from her, all her energy returned, and, for the last time, her passionate temperament and brilliant oratory held her audience spellbound: convincing, gripping, stirring, and inspiring. It was an unforgettable experience for all who were present.

Her speech was full of confidence in the final victory and vigorous in its demand for revolutionary action, but at the same time it curbed excessive expectations, showed the real situation with extraordinary clarity, and assisted the party to retain its elasticity. She saw a long road ahead, a road with many twists and turns, as she had prophesied in the Spartakus Programme: the proletarian revolution could advance by stages only, step by step along a road of bitter and often heart-rending experience, through defeat after defeat, to final maturity and complete victory:

"We must no longer harbour the illusions of the first phase of revolution, the idea of November 9th that the over-throw of one capitalist government and its replacement by another was sufficient to ensure the victory of the socialist revolution. Victory can be won only if the Ebert–Scheide-mann government is overthrown by a socialist, revolutionary struggle of the proletariat. There are still one or two errors which the German Revolution has not yet completely abandoned, errors which unfortunately show very clearly that we are not yet in a position to win victory by over-throwing the government. The revolution of November 9th was chiefly a political revolution, whereas the real revolution must be chiefly an economic one. Further, the revolution of November 9th was mostly a matter of the towns, whilst the rural areas were, and still are, almost untouched. . . . If we are serious in our desire for a socialist transformation of society we must pay attention to the rural as well as to the industrial areas, and in the rural areas we have un-fortunately hardly begun our work. . . .

"History is not making things as easy for us as it did for *bourgeois* revolutions; then it was sufficient to overthrow the central government and replace the old rulers by a few dozen new men. But we must work from below to the top, and that is in exact accordance with the mass character of our revolution and its aims, which involve the fundamental nature of our present social order. . . . Below, where the individual employer faces his individual wage-slaves, where all the organs of political class power directly face the objects of this class power, the masses, we must work step by step to wrench power from the hands of the ruling class and take it into our own.

"As I describe it the process probably appears longer and more difficult than you feel inclined to believe at the moment, but it is a very good thing that we should realise as clearly as possible the difficulties and complications of our revolution. I shall not venture to prophesy how long the whole process will take, but what does that matter so long as our lives are long enough to bring it to its end? "

Chapter Fourteen : THE LAMP LIES SHATTERED

1. The January Fighting

Rosa Luxemburg delivered this speech on January 1st, 1919; its peroration was an exhortation to revolutionary socialists to judge the situation realistically, and to make up their minds to some solid pick-and-spade work before social conditions would be ripe for the decisive struggle. A few days later street-fighting broke out in Berlin and led to the defeat of the working class. The event went into history as the Spartakus Rising, and the defeat opened the door to the counter-revolution. What brought about this sudden change in the situation? Was it the result of the unfortunate decision to boycott the National Assembly? Did that decision inevitably lead to an attempt to prevent the elections by force? Nothing of the sort: none of the delegates who voted against participation ever considered such a possibility, and the leadership of the new party certainly had no intention of abandoning the tactical policy laid down by Rosa Luxemburg in agreement with all her collaborators. But perhaps the Russian Embassy jockeyed Spartakus into a desperate adventure to relieve pressure on the Bolshevists? More than one history-book subsequently made this suggestion. There was no Russian Embassy at the time, however, because the Government of Prince Max of Baden had expelled the Ambassador and his suite on November 4th as the result of a frame-up (a forerunner of the " Zinoviev Letter ") organised by Philipp Scheidemann. Karl Radek was the only " Russian " of any importance in Berlin at the time, and a letter written by him to the Central Committee of the new party during the actual fighting proves clearly that he had nothing to do with it. In any case, the idea that veteran revolutionary leaders like Rosa Luxemburg and Leo Jogiches would let themselves be thrust into an adventure by " advisers " is an absurdity. Another explanation is that Rosa Luxemburg and her friends suddenly, and for no apparent reason, lost their heads and suddenly launched a *Putsch* for which no preparations of any kind had been made. There are otherwise quite reasonable people who feel they must, even unwillingly, believe something of the sort, because unless the real truth is accepted there is no alternative but to believe something incredible.

The real truth is that there was no Spartakist rising at all. Convincing proof of this can be obtained from a perusal of the leading articles in the *Rote Fahne*, which were always an accurate reflection of the party policy. The leading articles which appeared during the critical days were: January 1st, " Behind the Scenes of the Counter-Revolution ", dealing with the official documents relating to the war against Russia; January 2nd, " Slave-Traders ", dealing with the same subject; January 3rd, " Our First Party Congress ", dealing with the Congress proceedings; January 4th, " The Prospects of the Revolution in Italy "; January 5th, " Gangsters of Mining Capital ", dealing with the economic struggle in the Ruhr district; and January 6th, " Unemployment ". These articles prove clearly that the leaders of the Communist Party were reckoning with a gradual revolutionary process, and certainly not with immediate armed struggles on the streets of Berlin.

The truth is that the January fighting was carefully prepared and cunningly launched by the leaders of the counter-revolution. At the time the iniquity was probably without parallel in history, but the advent of Fascism has since made the world very familiar with such methods. Let the facts speak:

In October 1925 a political libel action was heard before the Munich court—the so-called " *Dolchstoss* " [1] process—and under oath General Groener described Reich President Ebert's conspiracy with the General Staff: " On December 29th Ebert ordered Noske to lead the troops against Spartakus. The volunteer corps assembled on that day and

[1] *Dolchstoss*: "stab-in-the-back". The theory held in patriotic circles to explain away Germany's defeat in the World War.—TR.

everything was ready for the opening of hostilities." The decision to launch the decisive action was therefore taken on the day the inaugural Congress of the Communist Party opened. The preparations, of course, went farther back. For weeks previously volunteer corps had been mobilised under the pretext of defending the frontiers against the Poles. On December 27th their concentration around Berlin began. It was impossible to conceal these preparations entirely, and Ebert obtained the consent of the Independent Social-Democratic Party members of his Cabinet by misrepresentation. As they would never have been willing to accept responsibility for the opening of civil war, it became necessary to exclude them from the Government altogether. On the same day they were called upon to agree to the reinstatement of the old Hohenzollern generals and to the raising of an army for war against Poland and Russia. War against Russia was already being waged in the Baltic provinces under the leadership of the Social Democrat, Winnig. The demand led to the break-up of the Cabinet, and at the end of the year the Independents resigned, and a Right-Wing social-democratic government, consisting of Ebert, Scheidemann, Landsberg, Wissel, and Noske, was formed. Noske then took command of the troops with the notorious and prophetic observation: " Someone must be the bloodhound."

In his memoirs General Maercker declares: " In the first days of January a meeting at which Noske was present, took place at General-Staff Headquarters with the leaders of the Volunteer Corps, and the details of the march into Berlin were discussed and settled." On January 4th Ebert and Noske inspected the troops assembled outside Berlin. They were not regular army troops, but six Volunteer Corps consisting of trained soldiers picked for their reliability from the ranks of the old army and having a very high percentage of officers. In order to conceal their strength they were known comprehensively as the Lüttwitz Detachment. They were well armed and equipped, and their weapons included flame-throwers.

In order to prepare public opinion for what was coming, a new campaign of incitement against Spartakus began. It opened on December 24th and increased in strength daily, ably led by the social-democratic *Vorwärts*. The victims of the Christmas Day attack on the People's Marine Division were buried on December 29th, and hundreds of thousands of workers followed the coffins to the cemetery. The official Social Democratic Party chose just this day for a demonstration, and the leaflets it issued read:

> "Liebknecht and Rosa Luxemburg are shamelessly besmirching the honour of the revolution and endangering its achievements. The masses must no longer inactively watch these physical forcists and their supporters hampering the work of the republican authorities, inciting the people to civil war, and stifling the right of free speech with their dirty paws. They have nothing but lies, slander and violence for all who stand in their path, and in their monstrous insolence they act as though they were masters of Berlin. . . ."

At the demonstration organised by the Social Democratic Party the Vigilant Committee distributed leaflets containing further, hardly-veiled, incitement to murder Karl Liebknecht:

> "The Christmas provocations of Spartakus will lead the people into the abyss. . . . The brutal violence of this band of criminals can be met only by counter-violence. . . . Do you want peace? Then see to it, every man of you, that the violence of Spartakus is ended. . . . Do you want liberty? Then do away with the armed loafers who follow Liebknecht. . . ."

A few days later the Anti-Bolshevist League publicly put a price of 10,000 marks on the head of Karl Radek. Tremendous sums were poured out by government and private-capitalist sources to bolster up this reckless campaign of murderous incitement.

On January 1st the *Politisch-Parlamentarischen Nachrichten*,[1] issued by the social democrats Heilmann and Hofrichter, opened up a campaign of slander against the radical Police President of Berlin, Emil Eichhorn. Eichhorn was a man of the highest character and personal rectitude, and known as such to everyone, including those who slandered him, but this did not prevent them from deliberately bringing a false charge of appropriating public moneys against him. At the same time the men who were already concentrating counter-

[1] "Political and Parliamentary Correspondence."

revolutionary troops around Berlin to crush the workers charged him with preparing to launch civil war, although they knew very well that he had not sufficient arms under his control to equip his own small police force. On January 3rd he was called to the Ministry of the Interior, overwhelmed with false charges, and requested to resign. He demanded that the charges against him should be put into writing, and promised to answer them all within twenty-four hours. To his face this very reasonable request was granted, but the Government dared not place such a document before the general public, and the next day he was deposed. The social democrat Eugen Ernst, later to be a supporter of the Kapp Putsch, was appointed in his stead. Eichhorn refused to submit, and insisted that the charges against him should be drawn up and presented formally. In addition, he had not been appointed by the Minister of the Interior, but by the Berlin Executive of the Workers' and Soldiers' Council as a revolutionary measure, and he refused to hand over his position to the counter-revolution.

When the deposition order arrived, the Berlin Committee of the Independent Social Democratic Party was in joint session with the Revolutionary Shop Stewards, and a resolution supporting Eichhorn was adopted. With a view to avoiding a direct conflict, Eichhorn announced that he would be prepared to accept the decision of the Berlin Executive, in which the Right-Wing social democrats had a majority, but the Government rejected even this offer; it wanted the conflict as an excuse for launching its long-prepared military action. The Executive Committee of the Independent Social Democratic Party and the Revolutionary Shop Stewards then called for a demonstration on January 5th. The Communist Party joined in, and hundreds of thousands of workers took part in tremendous processions which marched to the Police Presidium and demanded that Eichhorn should retain his post, declaring themselves prepared to defend him.

Under the impression created by this enormous demonstration, the Berlin Executive of the Independent Social Democratic Party and the Revolutionary Shop Stewards met again, together with two representatives of the Communist Party, Karl Liebknecht and Wilhelm Pieck. They believed that they had the support of the Berlin garrison, and in addition military assistance had been promised from Spandau and Frankfort-on-the-Oder. The session therefore decided to resist the deposition of Eichhorn and to overthrow the Ebert–Scheidemann Government. A " Revolutionary Committee " was elected, led by Georg Ledebour, Karl Liebknecht, and Paul Scholze.

It may be doubted, with good reason, whether this decision was correct, and whether the men who took it were capable of leading such a great undertaking to victory, but, in any case, whilst the discussion was still proceeding things were happening on the streets which made an armed conflict inevitable. On December 25th groups of revolutionary workers had spontaneously occupied the editorial offices of the *Vorwärts* as a reprisal for the unprovoked attack on the People's Marine Division. Their action was the result of their indignation at the attitude of a paper which was really the property of the Berlin workers, but which had been seized by the Central Committee of the Social Democratic Party during the war, with the support of the imperial authorities. The building was evacuated at Rosa Luxemburg's insistence. At the end of the great demonstration before the Police Presidium a suggestion arose from the masses to seize the *Vorwärts* again. The slogan caught on, and a group of revolutionary workers then occupied the *Vorwärts* offices and the whole building of the Central Committee of the Social Democratic Party in the Linden Strasse. The same evening all other important newspaper and printing-offices were seized, and the next day the Reich's Stationery Office and its printing-works.

There is no doubt that these actions coincided with the spirit of the masses, but this time they were not so spontaneous as at first appeared. The slogan was given out by the enemy, and later on the Committee of Investigation appointed by the Prussian Diet decided, on the evidence before it, that the occupations were carried out under the leadership of *agents-provocateurs* in the pay of the Berlin Commandant's Office, and that groups of revolutionary workers fell into the trap prepared for them.

2. SPARTAKUS AND THE JANUARY FIGHTING

The initiative was thus in the hands of the counter-revolution, but nevertheless the workers held some fairly good cards. They had a considerable quantity of arms and they were ready to use them. Determined action would in all probability have brought out the Berlin regiments on the side of the revolution, though they had declared themselves neutral and remained in their barracks. A carefully prepared and vigorously conducted military action would probably have proved too much for the counter-revolution. In short, victory for the workers in Berlin was by no means impossible, but in the event of victory terrible dangers threatened from the general backwardness of the movement outside Berlin. In the upshot, however, the defeat of the workers was sealed by the complete failure of their leadership. The "Revolutionary Committee" which had so valiantly proclaimed armed resistance and the overthrow of the Government showed itself completely incapable of leadership. It issued an appeal for a new demonstration on January 6th, distributed a certain number of rifles, and made a feeble attempt to seize the War Ministry. That was all. It did not bother its head about the armed workers in the newspaper offices; it neither took over command itself nor gave any instructions as to what they should do, but left them in useless occupation of points of no strategic significance. The only measure of any military value on the side of the revolution throughout the whole fighting was taken by the workers themselves at their own initiative when they occupied the railway stations. In the meantime the precious "Revolutionary Committee" remained in constant session, talking, talking, talking—until finally it seized on negotiations with the enemy as a means of extricating itself from a position in which it was too incapable to do anything else. The result was confusion and demoralisation in the ranks of the armed workers.

And the Communist Party? Liebknecht and Pieck had voted for the action, and there is no doubt that Liebknecht's great prestige did much to bring about the decision. Liebknecht was a man of impetuous action; he was no careful strategist accustomed to weigh up every detail of a situation, and his enthusiasm and indignation carried him away. He and Pieck acted on their own initiative in voting for the action, and they did so without the knowledge of their party, whose leadership was vigorously opposed to staking the whole existence of the revolution in such a way. Rosa Luxemburg

I.

overwhelmed Liebknecht with reproaches for his arbitrary action, pointing out with indignation and astonishment that he had thrown all the tactical principles of the Spartakus Programme overboard. She was not opposed on principle to armed action, but if it came she wanted its defensive character to be clear beyond all doubt. The young Communist Party enjoyed a great amount of sympathy amongst the working masses of Berlin, but it was not the undisputed leader of the working class, and it was not in a position to undertake the enormous task of organising and leading the final struggle for power. And if it had won power it would probably have proved too weak to hold it. In these circumstances, therefore, Rosa Luxemburg was in favour of determined resistance to the counter-revolutionary attack, but under slogans which would not frighten off the vacillating sections of the workers and soldiers, but actually bring them into the struggle. Throughout the fighting, therefore, the *Rote Fahne* demanded : the disarming of the counter-revolution, the arming of the workers, the unification of all troops loyal to the revolution, and new elections for the Workers' and Soldiers' Councils. The aim of the latter demand was to defeat the Ebert–Scheidemann clique in the decisive centre of the revolution, and make the councils into real centres of action. At the same time once the struggle had begun, the *Rote Fahne* urged its prosecution with all possible energy and determination, and day after day Rosa Luxemburg tried to get the leaders of the movement to act. On January 7th she wrote :

" Are the leaders up to the mark? Are the Revolutionary Shop Stewards and the radical elements in the Independent Social Democratic Party abreast of the increasing mass initiative? The masses have followed the appeal to action with impetuous energy. . . . They are waiting for further instructions and actions from their leaders.

" What have these leaders done or decided in the meantime? Nothing! Perhaps they are discussing their tasks very thoroughly, but the time has now come to act.

" The Ebert–Scheidemann clique are not wasting their time in endless discussions. Behind the scenes they are preparing their action with the usual energy and cunning of counter-revolutionaries ; they are loading their weapons for the final surprise attack to destroy the revolution.

"There is no time to be lost. Energetic measures must be taken at once. The vacillating elements amongst the troops can be won for the cause of the proletariat only by vigorous and determined action on the part of the revolutionary bodies.

"Act, and act with courage and energy, that is now the one duty of the Revolutionary Shop Stewards and of all honest socialist leaders. Disarm the counter-revolution, arm the masses, occupy all important positions. Act quickly. The revolution demands it."

Rosa Luxemburg regarded the negotiations between the "Revolutionary Committee" and the leaders of the counter-revolution as a trap, and although she had not been consulted when the movement was launched, she now demanded that talk should cease and give place to determined action. She was absolutely right: the counter-revolution was exploiting the negotiations merely in order to demoralise its enemies. When it was ready it broke all its promises, ignored the truce to which it had agreed, and launched its attack with the utmost ruthlessness.

The best account of Rosa Luxemburg's attitude during the fighting is given by Clara Zetkin in her book "*Um Rosa Luxemburgs Stellung zur russischen Revolution,*" [1] and she reports on the basis of a letter from Leo Jogiches:

"As heartening and hopeful as they were, Rosa Luxemburg did not look at the events from a parochial standpoint, but from the standpoint of the movement as a whole, including the attitude of the broad masses throughout Germany. In consequence her demand for the overthrow of the Ebert–Scheidemann government was a propaganda slogan to rally the revolutionary proletariat rather than a tangible object of revolutionary action. Under given conditions, confined chiefly to Berlin, such an action could in the best case become no more than a 'Berlin Commune', and probably on a smaller historical scale. Her only immediate aim was therefore the vigorous repulse of all counter-revolutionary attacks, i.e., in given conditions the reinstatement of Eichhorn, the withdrawal of the counter-revolutionary troops called to Berlin to crush the workers,

[1] "Rosa Luxemburg's Attitude to the Russian Revolution."

the arming of the workers, and the transfer of all executive military power to the revolutionary political representatives of the proletariat. But at least these demands were to be won by action and not by negotiation.

" The young Communist Party led by Rosa Luxemburg was therefore faced with a very difficult task involving many conflicts. It could not accept the object of the movement— the overthrow of the government—as its own, but at the same time it could not let itself be separated from the masses who had joined in the movement. Despite the difference of opinion the party had to remain with the masses in order to strengthen them in their struggle against the counter-revolution, and further the process of revolutionary maturity by making the circumstances and significance of their action abundantly clear to them. The Communist Party therefore had to show its own face, and make its own position crystal clear, but without breaking the revolutionary solidarity it owed to the fighting workers. Its rôle in the action had to be at once negative and critical on the one hand, and positive and encouraging on the other."

There was another factor which supported this argument for Rosa Luxemburg. She had pointed out again and again that in times of revolutionary tension the psychological attitude of the masses made tremendous and rapid progress : " The hours of the revolution count for months in history and their days for years."

In the meantime the action was spreading throughout the country. In the Rhineland counter-revolutionary troops were defeated in a pitched battle, and in Düsseldorf and in Bremen the local Workers' and Soldiers' Councils took power. A struggle conducted with determination and energy in Berlin would have compelled the enemy to make big concessions, and have won new ground for the revolution. For all these reasons Rosa Luxemburg, and with her the leadership of the Communist Party, were unable to accept the proposal of Karl Radek that the party should call on the workers to break off the struggle and beat a retreat. In addition, in January 1919 the young Communist Party was by no means as well organised, disciplined, and consolidated as the Bolshevist Party in July 1917 when it carried out a dangerous but successful retreat from a similarly precarious situation. The German Communist Party was not strong enough then to take over the undisputed leadership either in advance or retreat.

All these considerations justify the general policy pursued by the party under Rosa Luxemburg's leadership in those critical weeks. However, there still remains a residue which causes real misgiving. The party tactics consisted in defending the revolution, but the defence should have been conducted actively and not passively; it should have consisted of mobilising every possible resource of the revolutionary proletariat for an offensive to compel the enemy to retreat both politically and militarily. And when it became only too clear that this mobilisation of the revolutionary masses was impossible, and that a military offensive was also impossible, then surely energetic pressure should have been put on the "Revolutionary Committee" in the interests of thousands of workers occupying strategically very unfavourable positions and in order to arrange for their retreat to safety?

Rosa Luxemburg criticised the "Revolutionary Committee" in the *Rote Fahne*, and that was her natural rôle, but the Communist Party was actively engaged in the struggle, and its representatives were in the leadership. It bore the joint responsibility together with the other bodies engaged. It is impossible to discover now what influence the Central Committee of the Communist Party exercised on the leadership of the movement, or even if it exercised any at all, and we know nothing of any other opinions which may have been expressed at the meetings of the Central Committee apart from those of Rosa Luxemburg. We also know nothing of any party decisions or what was done to carry them out if any were taken.

Throughout the fighting Karl Liebknecht was with the workers; hungry, without sufficient sleep, and in constant danger, he went from position to position, giving the workers advice and moral support. However, he was acting the whole time almost out of touch with the party leadership, and there is no documentary evidence of any kind concerning the opinions, intentions, and measures of the Central Committee of the Communist Party during the fighting, beyond the letter of Leo Jogiches quoted by Clara Zetkin.

According to the statements of those who worked with Rosa Luxemburg in the critical days, a great alteration took place in her. During the first tense months of the revolution she had remained calm and confident, and given confidence to everyone around her. She had always found time to help others, to cheer them up and encourage them with a smile and an appraising glance, or perhaps criticise them with an ironical remark, meant and taken in good part so that the sting was lost in a feeling of personal warmth. For the movement as a whole and for the smaller circle of her immediate and devoted collaborators Rosa Luxemburg was a living flame, a source of strength for all.

In the January days, however, those who were in touch with her felt that she, too, was torn by internal conflicts. She became taciturn and reserved. Her indomitable spirit had always commanded her body, and she had risen easily above her physical infirmities. But now it seemed that the point had come when even her will could no longer triumph. The tremendous pace at which she had been living seemed to have completed the destructive work of the war years in prison; she became subject to sudden lapses into unconsciousness, and they happened almost every day. Advice to take rest, to place herself in the hands of a doctor, was rejected as almost treachery in the given situation, and if she noticed anyone about to approach the subject a glance was sufficient to make him pause. A last great struggle was proceeding between her iron will and her failing body, and what her will-power still achieved amounts almost to a miracle. Daily her articles appeared in the *Rote Fahne*, and betrayed nothing of her terrible struggle to keep going. She still held the reins of editorship firmly in her hands, and her articles were as strikingly penned and as intellectually vigorous as ever. But they were temporary successes of sheer will-power and bought at a great price.

3. The Man-hunt Begins

In the night of January 8th machine-gun fire was opened on the building in the Wilhelm Strasse which housed the editorial offices of the *Rote Fahne*. This was followed by a half-hearted attempt to take the house by storm, but the gallant attackers suddenly lost courage and beat a hasty retreat because it was " generally known " that the Sparta-kists had turned the house into a fortress. As a matter of fact there was one woman in the editorial offices at the time. Fortunately, she was not hit. There were never arms in the building and never any guard, and at any time a group of armed men could have arrested everybody in the building. However, the warning was heeded, and on January 9th the offices were evacuated. A patrol of government troops was already before the door. As usual, Rosa Luxemburg cared nothing for personal danger. One look at the men and she decided that only unemployment and ignorance could have driven them into the camp of the counter-revolution, and she immediately began to show them how they were letting themselves be misused against their own real interests. It was only with difficulty that she was extricated from the dangerous situation which developed. Soon after that Hugo Eberlein found her in the street in the midst of a violent argument on the right and wrongs of the situation, and again there was difficulty in persuading her to come away. She was contemptuous of danger, and, in fact, she was rather inclined to seek it from an exaggerated feeling of responsibility, from an idea that she should take every risk that an ordinary member of the movement might have to take, though the risks attendant on her own rôle in the movement were in reality far greater.

For a few days she lived in the house of a doctor near Hallesches Tor, though the place was in the fighting area. Both she and Leo Jogiches, experienced conspiratorial workers though they were, ignored all precautions as though danger did not exist. They met other leaders and representatives of the fighting groups in restaurants, cafés, etc., and always in and around the comparatively small area in which the chief fighting was going on. They seemed not to realise that a net was being flung around them. In the evening of January 10th the Town Commandant carried out a series of raids with a view to seizing leaders of the Communist Party and the Independent Social Democratic Party. Georg Ledebour and Ernst Meyer were arrested in their homes and treated in a way that indicated clearly that their lives were in danger.

Ledebour's arrest was unexpected, because he had been one of the negotiators with the Government, and the negotiations were to be continued the next morning. He appealed to the Government against his arrest, but they refused to release him. The reason was clear enough: the Ebert clique had used the negotiations to their own advantage, as Rosa Luxemburg had prophesied, and now there was a danger that the other side might agree to evacuation, and this had to be prevented if the counter-revolution was to secure a definite military victory. This was proved subsequently before a court of inquiry by the evidence of Major von Stephani, who was in command of the counter-revolutionary forces. According to his own statement he was given instructions to take the *Vorwärts* building on January 9th, but he considered the undertaking too risky without previous artillery preparation, and proposed that negotiations should be opened up with the revolutionary garrison to secure its evacuation. However, the man who had brought him his orders (it was Brutus Molkenbuhr, the son of a prominent member of the Central Committee of the Social Democratic Party) insisted that the *Vorwärts* should be taken by force of arms. Major von Stephani seems to have had misgivings, because it was not until the morning of January 11th that the attack began, after artillery and mortar fire which did considerable damage and caused severe losses to the garrison. As the first attempt to storm the building failed, the bombardment was resumed. It continued for two hours and finally rendered the position untenable. The garrison then sent a deputation headed by the worker-poet Werner Möller and the author Wolfgang Fernbach to negotiate with the besiegers. One of the deputation was sent back with a demand for unconditional surrender. After consideration the 300 workers in the *Vorwärts* building decided to submit in order to save further useless bloodshed, and they did so, but in the meantime the remaining members of the deputation, including its two leaders, had been slaughtered in cold blood.

The White Terror had begun.

The head office of the Communist Party in the Friedrich Strasse were then seized (they were undefended) and demolished. Leo Jogiches and Hugo Eberlein were arrested, but Eberlein managed to escape, and Jogiches had just time to tell him to advise the leadership of the party to leave Berlin for Frankfort-on-Main, where it could work in safety. An incident which happened at about the same time made his advice seem very good indeed: a woman comrade, sent out to discover what was happening in the *Rote Fahne* building, was seized as Rosa Luxemburg by the mercenaries and subjected to terrible treatment before she finally managed to escape from them. It left no doubt as to Rosa Luxemburg's fate if she were caught. She was urged to follow the advice of Jogiches and leave Berlin, but she refused, declaring that she and Liebknecht must remain in Berlin to prevent the defeat of the workers causing demoralisation.[1]

On January 11th, in the evening, a meeting took place in Rosa Luxemburg's refuge at Hallesches Tor, and Liebknecht was also present. It was decided that the place was no longer safe, and Rosa Luxemburg and Karl Liebknecht were then quartered on a working-class family in Neukölln, where it was fairly safe, because the counter-revolutionary forces hardly showed their faces in that solidly working-class district. However, on January 13th they left the place, probably owing to a false alarm, and friends in Wilmersdorf, a middle-class suburb in the south-west of Berlin, gave them shelter. It was in this refuge that their last articles were written. Rosa Luxemburg's " Order Rules in Berlin " analysed the weaknesses of the movement which had just been defeated. However, it was done with care and circumspection, because in the hour of defeat she was anxious to prevent any panic, and to give back the revolutionary workers their confidence in their final victory. She was in no doubt about the implications of the defeat, and she recognised far more clearly than anyone else how serious it was, but it did not shake her firm belief in the final victory of the revolution. As for herself, she knew the fate awaiting her should she fall into the hands of the counter-revolution and its mercenaries, but she had little thought of her own safety or of the dangers which threatened her. Her thoughts were all concentrated on the future. But in Karl Liebknecht's article a premonition of personal disaster coupled itself with firm belief in ultimate victory:

" Spartakus is fire and spirit. Spartakus is heart and

[1] The attitude of Karl Liebknecht and Rosa Luxemburg has occasionally been compared with Lenin's attitude during the July days of 1917, when after carefully weighing up the situation, he decided to save himself by flight. However, we now know from Krupskaya's memoirs that both Lenin and Zinoviev were prepared to give themselves up for trial, and that they finally fled only at the insistence of bolshevist workers.

soul. Spartakus is revolutionary will and revolutionary action. Despite all!"

4. THE MURDERS

When Karl Liebknecht and Rosa Luxemburg arrived in Wilmersdorf the net closed around them. Innumerable paid spies in the service of various counter-revolutionary bodies were ferreting after them everywhere. The Anti-Bolshevist League, founded by Russian aristocrats and amply supplied with funds from various sources, led the murder campaign. It had a network of paid agents all over Germany, and it set prices on the heads of Karl Liebknecht, Rosa Luxemburg, and Karl Radek. It was one of their agents, von Tyszka, also in the pay of the Berlin Town Commandant, who had attempted to seize Karl Liebknecht on December 7th. And it was von Tyszka and a Lieutenant Gürgen who arrested Ernst Meyer and Georg Ledebour on the instructions of the Town Commandant. The Vigilant Committee of Berlin also had its agents throughout the town, and branches in the various middle-class suburbs, including Wilmersdorf. A further organisation of spies and *agents-provocateurs* was directed from the Eden Hotel, the temporary headquarters of the Household Cavalry Division. And then there was the spy organisation of the so-called Reichstag Regiment founded by the Social Democratic Party, known officially as " Auxiliary Organisation of the Social Democratic Party, Section XIV ". The activities of this institution were probed at a later date in connection with libel proceedings, and the findings of the court showed that in the names of Philipp Scheidemann and Georg Sklarz (afterwards publicly exposed as a corrupt speculator) a price of 100,000 marks was set on the heads of Karl Liebknecht and Rosa Luxemburg. Hessel, the leader of Section XIV, Sonnenfeld, the paymaster of the regiment, and Krasnik, an officer, all declared under oath that Fritz Henk, the son-in-law of Philipp Scheidemann, had expressly confirmed to them the existence of the price on the heads of the two revolutionary leaders, and informed them that the money would be paid out the moment it was earned. A number of other members of the regiment went into the witness-box and confirmed the previous evidence on oath, declaring that although the order for the murder of Liebknecht and Luxemburg had never been put into writing, its existence was common knowledge in the regiment, as also was the fact that there was a reward of 100,000 marks waiting for whoever brought in the two, dead or alive.

Both *bourgeois* and social-democratic organisations did their utmost to hound down the two leaders of the revolutionary proletariat, co-operating with each other in eager rivalry. Their liaison-officer had his desk in the Berlin Town Commandant's Office.

The atmosphere for murder had to be prepared too, and the anti-Spartakus campaign, which had been going on since the very first days of the revolution, sounding a discordant note in the general official atmosphere of fraternisation, now developed into a hysterical frenzy. The armed mercenaries of the counter-revolution were savagely slaughtering their prisoners, and the Press sang hymns in praise of the "Deliverers", and described with gusto the blood-and-brain-bespattered walls against which batches of workers were being mown down. The unscrupulous and reckless campaign of incitement in the Press turned the middle and lower-middle classes into a bloodthirsty mob eager to drive men and women before the rifles of execution commandos on the slightest suspicion, and amongst the revolutionary workers who died in this way were many harmless and perfectly innocent people. The crusade culminated in the shout for the blood of Liebknecht and Luxemburg to crown the bloody saturnalia. The social-democratic *Vorwärts* took the palm for shamelessness with a poem by Artur Zickler published on January 13th and ending with the verse:

> " *Vielhundert Tote in einer Reih'*—
> *Proletarier !*
> *Karl, Rosa, Radek und Kumpanei*—
> *Es ist keiner dabei, es ist keiner dabei !*
> *Proletarier !* " [1]

And it was the *Vorwärts* which had the honour of announcing in advance of all other papers on Thursday, January 16th, that

> " Many hundred corpses in a row—
> Proletarians !
> Karl, Rosa, Radek and Co.,—
> Not one lies there, not one lies there !
> Proletarians ! "

Liebknecht had been " shot whilst attempting to escape " and Luxemburg " killed by the people ".

Almost every detail of the crime is known exactly. Leo Jogiches worked relentlessly to discover the whole truth and publish it in the *Rote Fahne*. He collaborated closely with social-democratic representatives of the Executive Committee of the Workers' and Soldiers' Council who were officially appointed to assist the Public Prosecutor Jorns in his investigations. Although they were finally compelled to withdraw from the proceedings as a formal protest against the deliberate and cynical attempts of Jorns to suppress as much evidence as possible, their preliminary co-operation was very useful to Jogiches. Further details came out in various subsequent libel trials—for instance, Scheidemann *v.* Prinz and others, which was heard in December 1920. The whole affair was also thoroughly thrashed out by the special committee of investigation appointed by the Prussian Diet, whose proceedings and findings are published in the official documents of the Diet. And the finishing touches were put to the brutal picture during the unsuccessful action for libel brought by Jorns against Bornstein, the editor of the *Tagebuch* in 1929–30.

On January 15th, at about nine o'clock in the evening, Karl Liebknecht, Rosa Luxemburg, and Wilhelm Pieck were arrested at No. 53, Mannheimer Strasse in Wilmersdorf by a group of soldiers. At first both Liebknecht and Luxemburg gave false names, thinking that perhaps the raid was accidental. However, they appear to have been denounced by a spy who had wormed his way into Liebknecht's confidence. Karl Liebknecht was first taken to the headquarters of the Vigilant Committee, and from there to the headquarters of the Household Cavalry Division in the Eden Hotel. Rosa Luxemburg and Wilhelm Pieck were taken there later.

When the first news of the arrests reached the Eden Hotel arrangements were made by Captain Pabst for the killing of both Karl Liebknecht and Rosa Luxemburg. The moment Liebknecht was brought in he was struck twice over the head with rifle-butts. He subsequently asked to be bandaged, but this was refused. Rosa Luxemburg, who was brought in later, was received with wild shouts and a torrent of brutal abuse. Whilst Pieck was held under guard in the corridor, Karl Liebknecht and Rosa Luxemburg were led into Captain Pabst's room for " questioning ". Shortly afterwards Liebknecht was taken away from the hotel. On leaving the building he was again struck on the head with a rifle-butt and then dragged into a car by Captain Horst von Pflugk-Hartung and his brother Captain Heinz von Pflugk-Hartung, Lieutenants Liepmann, von Rittgen, Stiege, and Schulz, and a trooper named Friedrich. In the Tiergarten he was dragged half-unconscious from the car and murdered a little distance away. The first shot was fired by Captain Horst von Pflugk-Hartung. The corpse was then taken back to the car and driven to the nearest mortuary, where it was delivered up as that of " an unknown man found dead in the Tiergarten ".

Shortly afterwards Rosa Luxemburg was led from the Hotel Eden by Lieutenant Vogel. Before the door a trooper named Runge was waiting with orders from Lieutenant Vogel and Captain Horst von Pflugk-Hartung to strike her to the ground with the butt of his carbine. He smashed her skull with two blows and she was then lifted half-dead into a waiting car, and accompanied by Lieutenant Vogel and a number of other officers. One of them struck her on the head with the butt of his revolver, and Lieutenant Vogel killed her with a shot in the head at point-blank range. The car stopped at the Liechtenstein Bridge over the Landwehr Canal, and her corpse was then flung from the bridge into the water, from which it was not recovered until the following May.

5. EPILOGUE

" As though lashed on by invisible beings, the horses of the Sun-God career forward with the frail chariot of our destiny; and nothing remains for us but to hold the reins with calm courage. . . . If I am to fall then a clap of thunder, the blast of the wind, or even a false step would hurl me into the depths—and there I would lie with thousands of others. I have never scorned to cast the bloody dice for small gain with good comrades on the battlefield, and should I haggle now when the stake is all a free man holds dear in life ? " (Goethe, " Egmont ").

There is something of Rosa Luxemburg's philosophy in these lines. She knew her personal stake in the game, for many had set it before her and lost. She knew that the tremendous step forward for which she was working could not be taken without the willing sacrifice of thousands, and the sacrifice of her life was the fulfilment of a destiny freely embraced. When she wrote to Sonia Liebknecht: " I hope to die at my post: on the street or in prison ", she meant it, and the idea held no terrors for her.

No one can say what effect her influence would have had on the history of the past twenty years. Had she lived, the history of the German working class might have been different. But as she could hardly have survived to see the victory of her cause, her death—met bravely at the hands of the enemy in a time of struggle—seems a fitting and proper end to the life of one who never ceased to fight for the things she had at heart. It raises her end above its attendant bestiality. Her death became a symbol. Acting under orders, an oaf, degenerate by nature and brutalised in war, smashed the vessel of genius. Blind Hödur, the ignorance and slavishness of the masses in the service of capitalist barbarism, struck down the hope of proletarian freedom.

The news of the murders broke the heart of Franz Mehring, and he died on January 29th. Old and frail, he could no longer stand a shock like that. From the moment the news was broken to him his death was certain. Leo Jogiches, who had in the meantime recovered his freedom, was hard hit by the terrible news, and seemed to have become an old man in a day. He immediately began a Press campaign against the crime and the men behind the scenes. He published the accounts of eye-witnesses and a photo of the drinking-bout at which the murderers celebrated their crime. It sealed his own death warrant. On March 10th, 1919, he was arrested, taken to the Police Headquarters at Alexander Platz, and there murdered in cold blood by a detective named Tamschik. During the same period thousands of revolutionary workers laid down their lives in the cause of Spartakus, killed in action or murdered as prisoners in the subsequent White terror.

The counter-revolution celebrated an orgy over their graves, believing that the social revolution was defeated for ever. A howl of delight went up, and the blindfolded whore in the service of the *bourgeoisie* came forward to justify the crimes. The Public Prosecutor Jorns did his utmost to pervert the law and hide all traces of the murderers, but the *Rote Fahne* was still alive, and it roused the conscience of the people with detail after detail of the crimes Jorns was striving to conceal, until in the end the authorities were compelled to arrest some of the murderers. The official investigation became a debauch of perjury and suppression, but when finally the farce unrolled before the court, the truth became visible despite the network of officially encouraged and shameless lying, intimidation, corruption, and bribery. The official military inquiry acquitted all the aristocratic murderers. Lieutenant Liepmann was sentenced to a short term of house arrest. Lieutenant Vogel received two years imprisonment for a misdemeanour as officer of the guard, and for disposing illegally of a corpse. Trooper Runge was sentenced to two years imprisonment for attempted manslaughter. Lieutenant Vogel was supplied with a false passport and a motor-car by his superiors and taken over the frontier to await an amnesty. The detective Tamschik who had murdered Leo Jogiches, then murdered Dorrenbach, the leader of the sailors, and was later promoted to Police Lieutenant by the social-democratic Minister Severing " in recognition of his services ".

The January fighting was followed by a crusade of Noske's White Guards from town to town throughout the country, and the *bourgeois* republic was saved. The victory of the counter-revolution in January 1919 led directly and logically to the victory of Hitler in January 1933. Under Hitler the murderers are in high office to-day, including Captain Pabst, who organised the murders. The Public Prosecutor Jorns, exposed and convicted as a perverter of justice, is now President of Hitler's " People's Court ", and a worthy representative of fascist Justice.

Many of the old Spartakus fighters have since been murdered or buried alive in concentration camps. The possessions of Rosa Luxemburg were plundered by the armed mercenaries of the counter-revolution, and irreplaceable manuscripts destroyed. In 1933 her works were publicly burned, together with almost everything else of cultural value in German literature. The monument raised above her grave to her and to those who fell with her in the January fighting by the workers of Berlin has been razed to the ground.

But worse than this desecration of her last resting-place was the desecration of her memory committed by those who should have been the first to preserve her political heritage. Whilst pursuing, for reasons of prestige, a dishonest cult with her name and that of Karl Liebknecht they waged a fierce and unscrupulous campaign against something they called "Luxemburgism", created by perverting her ideas and misrepresenting her political work. They disparaged her rôle in the working-class movement, outlawed her followers, many of whom had founded the party with her; and placed obstacle after obstacle in the way of any publication of her works. And finally, many of her close collaborators, and in particular her Polish comrades in arms, lost their lives in the Lubianka and other prisons as victims of Stalin's campaign of extermination against the Old Guard of the revolution.

The icy breath of a long period of reaction has frozen the fields of independent thought.

When Rosa Luxemburg's mishandled body sank below the dark waters of the Landwehr Canal, the German proletariat at first refused to believe in her death. It seemed impossible that such enthusiasm, genius, and will-power could have been blotted out by a rifle-butt in the hands of a moron, and rumours, eagerly believed, went round the working-class quarters that she had escaped, that she was in hiding until she could once again place herself at the head of the revolutionary movement.

The rumours were false, and yet a grain of truth was in them. Her physical body will never again take its place in the struggle for social revolution, but no bonfire and no dictatorial order can destroy her ideas. They live on in the minds of her adherents and in the masses of the proletariat. Those forces which strive to turn back the course of history will go down in the end, no matter how much they may seem to succeed for a time. The seed has been sown, and it will bear fruit in the future. Who knows the names of those who triumphed in the Thermidor? But Babeuf's ideas fructified the revolutionary movement of the French proletariat and assisted it to new life thirty years after his execution. To-day the names of Liebknecht and Luxemburg are an inspiration to all who love liberty, and a promise for the future of mankind.

The victorious advance of modern barbarism will reach its limits, and then the movement to social progress and human liberty will set in afresh. The victors in the final battle for human emancipation will spring from the seed Rosa Luxemburg sowed.